# The
# Ginger Child

Also by Patrick Flanery:

*Absolution*
*Fallen Land*
*I Am No One*
*Night for Day*

# The Ginger Child

## On Family, Loss and Adoption

PATRICK FLANERY

Atlantic Books
London

First published in Great Britain in 2019 by Atlantic Books,
an imprint of Atlantic Books Ltd.
This paperback edition first published in Great Britain in 2020
by Atlantic Books.

10 9 8 7 6 5 4 3 2 1

A CIP catalogue record for this book is available from the British Library.

Every effort has been made to trace or contact all copyright holders. The
publishers will be pleased to make good any omissions or rectify any
mistakes brought to their attention at the earliest opportunity.

*Interior: Monkeyboy* © Kate Gottgens, on p. 136 is reproduced
with kind permission of the artist

Paperback ISBN 978 1 78649 726 0

E-book ISBN 978 1 78649 725 3

Printed in Great Britain

Atlantic Books
An Imprint of Atlantic Books Ltd
Ormond House
26–27 Boswell Street
London
WC1N 3JZ

www.atlantic-books.co.uk

# CONTENTS

ginger, *n.* and *adj.*[1]

A. *n.*

    1. a.

        The rhizome of the plant *Zingiber officinale*, which has a distinctive aroma and hot spicy taste, and is used in cooking and as a medicinal agent.

B. *adj.*

    1.

        c.

        Of a person: having reddish-yellow or (light) orange-brown hair, and typically characterized by pale skin and freckles. Hence more generally: red-haired.

    3.

        [Short for ginger beer. Cockney rhyming slang for queer.] … (frequently derogatory and offensive). Homosexual.

*

ginger, *adj.*[2] (and *adv.*)

Origin: Formed within English, by back-formation. Etymon: gingerly *adv.*
…
Cautious, careful; gentle… Also: easily hurt or broken; sensitive, fragile.

*Oxford English Dictionary*, Third Edition, 2017

# MOTHERS

Today, many days, I play a private game, imagining hypothetical mothers. Not my own mother, who I know well. Not mothers who would bear a child, abandon it, relinquish it, or have it taken away, a child we would then adopt, but mothers who would bear a child for us, altruistically.

I look through profiles of friends and acquaintances on social media, think of possibilities, past promises.

When I see your picture with your husband and children, I remember how you and I pledged to have a child together if we were both still single at thirty-seven. I wonder if you ever think of that now.

At the time, when we were in our twenties, did you want me to say, 'let's have a child *now*, let's not wait'? Although that was what I felt, I could not muster the courage to say it for fear you would laugh at me in your charming, heart-breaking way.

A couple of years ago, when we saw each other for the first time in more than a decade, it felt to me that not even five minutes had passed. Although we both now have husbands and you have children and another pregnancy would be a risk not worth taking just for the sake of a friend's desire to have his own child, I cannot help imagining what might have been.

Today, of course, the idea tips us over into the fantastic. But I still think about it, what you having a child for me and my husband, what raising that child, what the closer bond created between us, would do to all of us, for the good.

But I do not expect.

You understand, I hope.


I see your picture, with your two children, your wife, and think about the processes you went through, different anonymous donors, speculating about which traits your children may have inherited from those unknowable men, the way the two girls are so wildly different in appearance and character, both of them dark-haired while you are blonde, as if your genes had left no visible trace on either of them. I think about your generous assertion, after giving birth to the first child, that if you were younger you'd happily get pregnant for us but you could not conceive of a second pregnancy, the first was so difficult and you were getting old, your body could not take the further damage, the risk was so great. And then, a few years later, you decided to try again, for yourself and your wife, and were successful.


I look at you building a career, negotiating the frustrations of distant family and complexities of sibling relationships, doing it all with such an elegant determination to get things right, while worrying whether you will have the life you want in the end.

Does it ever occur to you that we could reach a mutually beneficial agreement that would give you some*thing* in exchange for the some*one* we so desire? Such wondering about your own wondering leaves me feeling poorer and meaner, uglier, because it should not be about money, any of this, but only about love.

You will undoubtedly have your own child or children, and why want the complication of another child, even a child not biologically yours but with that connection nonetheless, of having carried her or him in your body for nine months, a child who would appear before your own children as the first child, the child you relinquished because he or she was not yours to keep.

How would you explain that, if we did it?

And would it be so difficult to explain, in the end?

Would it require no more than saying, I had *that* child for *them* because I could? But she is not my child in the way that you are my children, you might say to your sons, your daughters, if that day ever came.

I pass you on the street as you are talking on your phone, saying, 'No, Kev, honestly, I *got* it. Don't you understand I'm serious when I say I don't want a kid?' What would happen if I waited for you, a stranger, to finish your conversation and then asked in the politest, least threatening way I could muster, 'But would you have a kid for us? I'd pay you. I'd pay you however much you want, even if I don't have it, even if the law won't let me, I'll give you whatever you think you need to make it worth your while, I'll rob banks to pay you,' and I know, in that thinking, how deep my desperation has become.

It feels as if I spend whole days out in the world, on trains and trams and undergrounds, sniffing out fertility and sympathy and if not willingness then openness and radical politics and the selflessness such an act would require, to do this without paying scores of thousands of dollars to lawyers and clinics.

And yet I still imagine, you know, robbing a bank if that's what it takes.

(Not that I would.)

I meet you for the first time in fourteen years and although you are now, like me, in your early forties, you are single and unlikely ever to have a child of your own. Sitting across from you over coffee I think, why would it not be possible? I think this and at the same time I know: this will not happen.

3

Yet my brain oscillates between the wondering and the knowing, and when it does not oscillate, holding one in dominance over the other, it holds both the wondering and the knowing (this cannot be) at the same time, concurrent, living the cognitive dissonance of desire and despair.

I look at you, and you, and you, and you, having one child, two, three, more, sharing photos of them online, expecting us, your friends, to click and like and love and comment with amusement and joy and commiseration when things get difficult, and I think, does it ever occur to you that you have been given a gift you might have shared? By which I mean not the children, obviously, but the exceptional ease with which you and your partners have them.

And this thinking goes on, stretches over years, loops through the lives of all these possible candidates, friends and acquaintances, strangers, colleagues, and the horror of it is that I cannot bring myself to ask the question, to face the disappointment when each and every one of you would, I am certain, say no.

Some of you will read this and see yourself, or not see yourself, and some of you not among the yous will see yourself anyway. And I suspect that some of you, whether you are among the yous I mean or not, will feel anger, irritation, but perhaps also sympathy or compassion, and I know that you might feel things I cannot begin to predict or imagine, that your own capacity for cognitive dissonance, for the wondering and the knowing to settle alongside each other concurrently in your own minds, may outstrip my capacity to imagine what you feel.

And I am sorry if that happens: I am sorry it is happening to you, and also: I am sorry, but that is just what happens, because I desire what you might provide, have provided, still (some of you) may yet provide, no matter how impossible that provision feels or seems to you and me and everyone around us.

*

4

I suggest to my husband that we send out an email, blind-copying everyone we would potentially consider, explaining what we are doing, what we are seeking, how we expect no reply, if the answer is no we do not want to hear it articulated, silence would be preferable so that when we see you again we can carry on with our relationships as if nothing had ever been said.

But if the answer is yes, then, you know, please write.

It is too great a thing to ask, he says. We cannot ask.

Over time, as months and years pass, I begin to wonder why we could not make ourselves more bohemian. We know performance artists and writers and queer scholars and activists. We are proximate to a milieu that I'm convinced could help facilitate our parenthood, bring forth a constellation of people who might be a community of parents to the child for whom I long.

But perhaps our petit-bourgeois childhoods, our attachment to things, our sense of our own marginality here as immigrants, however privileged we are compared to some, militates against us embarking on a form of family-making that would demand from us and everyone involved a sense of radical fluidity and flexibility. Stable, stuck in our ways, habit-lovers, we are neither radically fluid nor flexible. Surely the bohemian family of multiple parents and multiple homes, in which my own choices about parenting would always have to accommodate the choices and feelings of others in this notional constellation, would drive me mad.

As if the desire itself has not already.

I catch a clip of that film from the 1990s about the murderous rich boy lovers. One turns to the other, man to man, sneering, *if you could get pregnant you would, wouldn't you?*

Of course I would.

# BIRTH

Y ou and I are standing on the stump of a tree in your front yard, on the parkway, that strip of lawn between sidewalk and street. Your house is a few doors down from mine. We have just exchanged vows, though I am only two years old, you a year older, and now we each unroll a baby from our matching raglan shirts and hold these plastic infants up for our mothers' approval and laughter.

This has been your idea, the marriage and instant reproduction, you coaching me through the language of vows, providing your dolls as our children. How traditionalist of you to think marriage should precede reproduction, how precocious to understand babies emerge from the lower abdomen.

But how radical, too, that you should suggest I, a boy, might give birth just the same as you.

Forty years later, I find you online, click through the family photos you've made publicly available, your three children, flesh and blood, not plastic, three children who look uncannily like my memory of you, the five of you now living in the same city as your parents and your sister and her husband and their three children, all of you so close.

What might have happened if your family had not moved away? We would never have been lovers, because that would have been, for me, an impossibility, for you an exercise in futility and frustration.

But perhaps we could have been the sort of friends who remain close throughout their lives, rather than people who drift from such closeness into total strangerhood, so that I wonder now: do you remember me, and our first family? Does someone, you or your mother, still have those children we carried?

# QUESTIONS

B ut would you take a ginger child?

We are sitting in a café in the midst of a London park on a bright autumn day. Mary, the brunette social worker who has asked this question, is in her fifties. It is November 2012.

My husband and I glance at each other, bewildered.

We would take a ginger child, a black child, an African, an Asian, an Australian, a South Pacific Islander, a Caribbean, a Latin American, a Native North American, an Eastern European. We would take a mixed-race child, a Christian, Jewish, Muslim, Buddhist, Hindu or Atheist child.

In this moment, we are open to a child from anywhere, of any race, religion or national origin.

I am American, white, of German, English and Irish ancestry (as far as I know). My husband, Andrew, is South African, white, of Dutch, French and English ancestry (as far as he knows). Given the long history of my family on the North American continent, and of my husband's family on the African continent, we assume our genetic makeup may be more varied than genealogy and family lore suggest.

This, and the fact of our coming from racially and ethnically heterogeneous countries, makes us believe in our capacity to parent a child of any background or identity or race. And after setting aside the idea of making a family through surrogacy, choosing instead to pursue adoption, we are willing to consider any relatively healthy child.

Yes, of course, we say, we cannot understand why red hair is so often reviled in Britain. We would absolutely take a red-haired child.

Mary is relieved.

We have a ginger child now, very sweet boy, two years old, but no one wants him, she says.

Because he has red hair? I ask, again bewildered.

Parents think ginger children will be badly behaved, she says.

Fears of the Celtic. Fears of the fiery. Misplaced fears. Nothing but rank prejudice. We would take the ginger boy now, this instant, except we are only at the beginning of the process. We have not been vetted or approved as adopters.

What are the red lines? Mary asks. What wouldn't you be able to cope with?

Serious physical or mental disability, I say.

Autism, Andrew says. Sexual abuse.

What about neglect? Mary asks. Or physical abuse?

We both hesitate, but yes, we could handle a child who has been neglected or physically abused, although in this moment I am not thinking about what the long-term effects of abuse and neglect might be, the degrees of severity, the way neglect itself is also a form of abuse, since abuse means, first, a chronic corruption of 'practice or custom', according to my dictionary, and what is neglect but a failure of practice to care?

Physical disability seems clear-cut. I know that I could not look after a child with reduced mobility, who struggled to move through the world. I imagine a paraplegic, a quadriplegic, a child confined to a wheelchair, and know I am not up to meeting such needs.

I know we could not handle a child with a serious chronic disease, such as HIV. I know I could not handle a deaf or blind child. This is not a judgement against children who fit any of those categories, but an honest acknowledgement of my own and my husband's limitations as potential parents. We would find it too difficult.

9

Why would we find it too difficult?

The first answer, one to which I will return over the coming years, is that the red lines of capacity and incapacity have been drawn by Andrew's and my individual traumas, but also by my desire, problematic as I know it is, for us to turn ourselves into that camera-ready middle-class same-sex couple with a toddling baby crawling across the lawn we don't have in front of the house we don't own.

I know that desire is selfish, perhaps even unethical, and I wonder if our reservations, all those red lines, disqualify us from being parents at all. Couples with biological children have no guarantee that things will go well, and here in the first meeting about adoption we find ourselves ticking boxes, saying no to one category of complication or disorder or life experience and yes to another.

This form of calculus arises from being made to think about what it means to construct a family without the biological capacity to reproduce. Surely people who conceive biological children are never made to consider what they will or will not be able to handle before ever laying eyes on the child, unless an ultrasound or amniocentesis reveals complications before birth, or unless you know that you or your partner is likely to pass on a particular illness. Which is not to say that such couples don't consider it, but they are usually not forced to do so.

If you are not asked questions about your own capacity as a parent before being allowed anywhere within sight of a child who might one day be yours, it is possible you never consider what you might or might not be capable of handling.

Imagine a doctor asking a couple struggling to conceive: how would you manage if your daughter ends up with autism? How will you cope if your boy develops ADHD? What is your network of support? How many close friends live near you? How much do you trust them? How many family members live within an hour of you? Who can you call for help in the middle of the night? What kind of leave does your employer offer? What are your financial resources? If you lose your job, will you have the means to meet the needs of your child?

If people were asked these questions, the birth rate would plummet.

Maybe it should.

Being made to think about what you *might* be capable of handling is enough to shatter every rosy vision of babies crawling over grass in suburban gardens under a clear bright sky. It kills the joy of imagining a family before a solid hope that what you want will even be possible has the chance to take root.

What about serious mental disability? Mary asks. Could you handle that?

Mary's voice is crisp, cajoling. She has a script. She asks everyone the same questions. Given our answers already, I wonder how she could ask this.

My coffee has gone cold. Young women with babies and toddlers have packed the café since we sat down. A boy is shouting for a muffin. A girl cries.

Mary's choice of venue, where she meets all prospective adopters, feels like a test. Can we manage to discuss these most intimate questions about parenting and face up to our own childlessness in the presence of so much natural reproduction? Wouldn't it be more humane to conduct this interview in private?

The truth is, her question about mental disability throws me into murkier territory.

We want a child under the age of eighteen months, preferably as young as possible. How, at that age, can one be certain what disabilities might be at play? We do not require a genius, but we do want someone who will grow to independence. We want to be parents, not lifelong caregivers, and in this way, there is something selfish in our desire to adopt, although the entire British social care system almost never acknowledges this. Adopters must hew to a narrative of altruism: we put ourselves forward to do the job that the state is unable to do. Which is not to say that Andrew and I are unmotivated in part by an altruistic impulse. When we got together a decade earlier, we knew that making a family would not be straightforward. I knew this when I asked him, very early in our dating life, rounding the corner from Broad Street to Turl Street one wet autumn night in Oxford, whether he wanted children. Having decided that I loved him enough to want us to stay together forever, having decided that if children were not part of his vision for his own life then this was not going to work, I had to know. And the truth is, I was not imagining adoption. I was already thinking of alternatives. But perhaps adoption is the parenting role male couples like us are meant by nature to fulfil.

In light of Mary's question, I ask myself what constitutes mental disability. Is mental illness a disability? Even if it technically is, would I construe it as such?

I could handle a depressed or traumatized child, even one with PTSD, but I could not handle a psychotic one, assuming psychosis would even be apparent in one so young. I know that I cannot spend the balance of my life looking after someone who is seriously mentally ill. I could parent a child with OCD, but not one with autism, unless it was at the very mildest end of the spectrum. I could manage one with ADHD, but not with bipolar disorder.

Epilepsy? No.

Developmental disability? No.

Schizophrenia? No.

Down syndrome, Fragile X? No, neither.

Any serious genetic condition affecting mental ability? No.

Life-threatening nut allergies? Yes.

Why one and not the other? Part of every decision comes down to perception, which itself is determined by social constructions of what each variety of disability or disease or disorder appears to mean. The balance of the decision is produced by being forced, in a café full of mothers and children, to consider one's own character on the fly, with no chance for reflection.

I know that I am temperamentally disinclined to bend my life towards the management and care of a person with certain kinds of problems. Some problems appear manageable, others do not. And in most cases I am conscious that these perceptions are not necessarily stable or permanent, but highly context specific. This comes in part from living in a country I have adopted, but which has not, I feel, adopted me. I will always be an outsider here, and as someone who is other in multiple ways, I cannot imagine struggling to raise a child with serious medical problems. So I can imagine that if we lived in South Africa, for instance, I might well be prepared to take on an HIV-positive child, but not in Britain. Never in Britain.

Sitting in this café with the grinding roar of a coffee machine and the burble of babies and chatter of mothers and crying of toddlers and sing-songing offers of cake as balm for those children's anxiousness or sadness or momentary grief, I wonder if all my reservations, each one in turn, should disqualify me from being a parent in the first place. I think of all the people I have heard on television or radio over the years describing the struggles of raising children with exceptional needs, the way so many of them resort to the formulation, 'we weren't coping' or 'we couldn't cope'. What do those biological parents do when they realize that their own child's needs have outmatched their capacity to meet them?

How quickly Andrew and I find the algebra of accommodation comes into play: from imagining an ideal child, an infant willingly given up by its birth parents, a child in 'perfect' physical and mental health without reduced capacities, a smiling baby who has been loved and attended to every second of its life – never left to cry itself to sleep, never wanting for food or affection, diaper always promptly changed, read to and cuddled and kissed, hearing songs and going to sleep staring at a mobile hanging above its crib, lovingly bathed and laughed with, soothed and reassured, taken for walks to the park and trips to museums, held up to paintings and works of art to look closely at the details, treated in all the ways my mother treated me as a child – we are forced to consider every possible complication we might face, and the compromises we will inevitably need to make.

This rationalizing happens in the span of a moment in a café crowded with mothers and children.

I have to remind myself how we got here. We were willing to do this because we know other couples who have adopted successfully. Only a few months ago, a friend and her husband adopted a two-year-old girl. A few years earlier, acquaintances in Manchester adopted two boys. I look at their pictures on social media. The boys are healthy. Everyone is smiling. Whatever difficulties they may experience are not presented for an online audience. This is in contrast to some people we know with biological children who sarcastically gripe about the horrors of parenthood ('kids are the worst'), and others who seem not to be enjoying any of what they're doing, moaning every time there's a snow day or school vacation, who have no idea how to fill the hours alone with their children and appear to resent the responsibility of looking after the gift – in some cases many gifts – they have given themselves.

You should not be so ungrateful, not even in jest, I want to tell them.

Mary spends an hour asking us questions and half an hour making proclamations:

It is not important that we are a same-sex couple.

(We didn't ask whether it was. British law allows for same-sex adoption.)

It is not a problem that I write novels.

(I didn't think it would be. Why would it? Is writing novels regarded as undesirable in some quarters?)

Although, she has to admit, she wonders what kind of novels I write. She had another novelist who was approved as an adopter, and he wrote gay porn, she titters. As if she thinks all novelists who happen to be men in same-sex relationships must write porn.

No, I don't write gay porn, I tell her, or any other kind of porn.

Mary tells us that all the children available – nearly all – have been forcibly taken from their parents because of abuse or neglect. In Britain, there is no culture of young mothers giving up unwanted pregnancies. It happens, but only very rarely.

Somehow, this is news to me. And the idea of being presented with a child taken from its birth parents is chilling. How is this approach to forming a family any less ethically compromised than surrogacy?

Although Mary has told us nothing we do not already know, there is a quality in her tone, a patronizing, shaming edge, a desire to shock and put off any prospective adopters still clinging to rose-tinted visions of parenthood, that irritates the hell out of me.

As we walk back to the car, I tell Andrew I cannot do this.

We have to find another way.

# TERRY

Terry is four and I am six. Our mothers met each other volunteering. Terry has recently been adopted. He has an older brother, Todd, also adopted. Terry has dark red hair that falls to the nape of his neck. While Todd, adopted from a South Korean orphanage, is calm and sweet-natured, Terry, adopted from the state foster care system, is totally out of control.

Because their parents have to be out of town for a night, Terry and Todd stay with us.

For Christmas that year, I received an electric train set. The circular track is bracketed to a large square panel sealed in green plastic. The train – an engine and half a dozen cars – goes round and round with mesmerizing speed and elegance.

Every week my mother takes me to the Union Pacific corporate headquarters in downtown Omaha to see the exquisitely detailed model trains in the lobby, engines mounted on plinths with buttons which, when pushed, make the wheels turn. We took the train to California and back when I was four, and although the crew forgot to refill the water tanks in Denver and there was nothing but fruit juice and booze until we reached Arizona and the train smelled of vomit and on the way home I lost the stuffed horse with velveteen hooves that my aunt gave me for Christmas, trains remain the most thrilling machinery I can imagine.

I love my train set more than my cardboard brick building blocks and *Star Wars* action figures, more than all my puppets or stuffed animals. The electric train is the pinnacle of my possessions and waking up to find its huge green track propped behind the tree was the greatest Christmas surprise ever.

Perhaps because I am an only child growing up on a street where everyone else is much older, my playdates with other children, boys in particular, often end badly. I hate sharing as much as I long for friends.

Terry insists on playing with the train. Though I hesitate, my mother says I should let him have a turn. We sit on the floor of my playroom in the basement of our house, a playroom that was the bedroom of the previous owners' teenage daughter, and which is carpeted with mustard-yellow wall-to-wall shag pile beneath a suspended ceiling of acoustic tiles. Disco seventies chic.

Terry runs wildly around the room. He throws my toys. Somehow, he breaks the train within moments of starting to play with it. Or at least he breaks some element of the electronic mechanism by forcing the train along the tracks.

Bewilderingly, my parents never have it fixed and for years the track and train cars gather dust in a corner of the basement utility room, until eventually, once my attachment to them has attenuated, we sell them at a garage sale with the disclaimer that the set needs repair.

The train is beside the point. My encounter with Terry is the first time I am conscious of meeting someone who is adopted. My mother has explained what this means. She explains, too, that Terry behaves the way he does because he is adopted.

And the association sticks:

An adopted child, I am already conditioned to believe, is a child out of all control.

# NUCLEAR

When I phone my mother to tell her that Andrew and I have decided not to pursue adoption, I am surprised at how relieved she sounds.

You know, she says, I was about to adopt a child from South Korea when you came along.

No, I never knew this.

Oh, sure, it was all in the works. I'd been in touch with the agency, we went through the interviews, it was going ahead.

She had miscarried and, instead of trying again immediately, she thought she and my father should adopt.

I never knew about the miscarriage either. How is it that I have reached my late thirties without knowing either of these things? Or did I know them at one point, perhaps a decade or more ago, and found the information so unsettling I repressed it?

I feel a sudden sense of loss for the sibling I never knew, a feeling more like melancholy than sadness or grief, and which leaves me wondering who that other person might have been, or if I myself might have been that other person, arrived earlier, in a different form, a different sex. I try to imagine what it would have been like to have an older brother or sister, whether it would have made growing up with my father easier or more difficult. Or, what would it have been like to have a Korean older sibling? How might that person have shifted our family? Would it have saved us from ourselves, from the triad that was so disastrous for each of us? Might my father and Korean big sister have bonded in ways that would have made my childhood even worse than it was? Would she have resented my arrival and usurpation of her place and taken out her frustrations on me? Or would the Korean child have been enough? Would that girl's or boy's arrival have condemned me to nonexistence?

Surrogacy is a good choice, my mother says. It means you won't have all the complications, all the other people involved. It can just be the two of you and your child. Your own child.

My parents decided early on in their marriage that they would not have children, instead devoting themselves to teaching and journalism and activism. It was the early 1960s. They lived first in California's San Joaquin Valley, my mother teaching in schools where the children of Mexican farmworkers sat alongside the children of families who had migrated west during the years of the Dust Bowl.

Later my parents moved to Los Angeles, then to Chicago, then Baltimore, each move prompted by my father's graduate studies or jobs. He wrote his doctoral dissertation on the press coverage of the 1968 protests in Chicago during the Democratic Convention and following Martin Luther King, Jr.'s assassination. My parents were often participating in those protests themselves, being tear-gassed and going to bear witness to the murder of Black Panthers Fred Hampton and Mark Clark, and finding their community organizing group in Evanston infiltrated by the FBI (or so they suspected).

My mother was teaching in Lincolnwood, Illinois, fighting alongside other teachers for equal pay and the right to wear slacks instead of skirts. They won the battle of fashion but not of finance. At some point in her early thirties, my mother tells me, as my father became ever more consumed by his work, first as a doctoral student and then as a reporter at the *Baltimore Sun*, she realized if she did not have a child she would spend the rest of her life alone.

As she commuted to work on her master's degree, she had time to think about this on walks from the train station through Baltimore's Inner Harbor, keys poking out between her fingers because they lived in a neighbourhood where women had been attacked and murdered, as happened in the alley behind their building on the first night they moved there from Chicago. My parents mistook the screams for a cat fight and only discovered the truth in the morning.

After Nixon's resignation, they moved back to California because my father, who was being groomed to become the *Baltimore Sun*'s Washington correspondent, felt compelled to return to the San Joaquin Valley, where my mother had lived since the age of seven, where she did not want to live again, where my father had taken a teaching job without first asking how she felt about it, where they bought a bungalow in Fresno on the affordable end of Van Ness Avenue, known locally as Christmas Tree Lane, where, in due course, I spent most of the first two years of my life, crawling and toddling around a garden that my mother later told me reminded her of Munchkinland and that seemed, from the vantage of my Omaha childhood with its apocalyptic thunderstorms and tornados, its inhuman winters and oppressive summers, like a lost wonderland from which I had been unjustly removed.

I have not asked whether the pregnancy that ended in miscarriage was planned, whether she convinced my father to start trying, or if it was a surprise to him, or a surprise to them both. I have never asked my mother if she was on the pill, or what kinds of birth control she used. If they were about to adopt a child from South Korea, my father must have agreed to this at least. And when I was conceived, had she convinced him to try again, or was it an accident, even a planned one?

I never have the courage to ask these questions.

In a way, I don't need the answers.

# GENETICS

Put off by our meeting with Mary to discuss adoption, I start investigating surrogacy. Andrew is less convinced. He worries about the cost, especially since we don't own property, and he worries about the ethics of paying a woman to produce a child, but I begin fantasizing about being present in the hospital room for the birth of our baby. This fantasy is so bewitching I become convinced I would spend everything we've saved to have a child, would be content to stay in our small rented flat if it could just be the three of us together without the complications of birth parents and birth siblings and birth grandparents and aunts and uncles and cousins and the constant intervention and monitoring of the state.

When I talk about our plans with a gay friend in New York, he makes a snide comment about all the gay couples he knows breeding 'trophy babies'. I don't even try to explain that there is nothing 'trophy' about my desire for a child of my own. I want a baby with whom I share more than a legal relationship, a child who has the legacy of my family in his or her genes. Like so much else I have been feeling lately, I recognize the selfishness of these desires.

But I have no siblings and only tenuous relationships with my extended family. When I grow old, it will just be me and my husband and his family, his three adult nieces and whatever families they may have, his various far-flung cousins, but I will otherwise be entirely alone in the world, without any close biological connections. I have only two first cousins, one of whom has children, and I have had no contact with this extended family in nearly two decades, nor do I foresee that situation changing since they have had nothing whatsoever to say to me since I came out. Apart from my aunt, no one in the extended family bothered to acknowledge the announcements I sent when Andrew and I had our civil union in 2005. It feels as though I have been lopped off the family tree.

Part of what makes life bearable as we age is a sense of direct biological connection to other people. If the biological bond was not so important, why else would adopted children so often seek out their birth parents and vice versa? For the children, part of the drive to know the people who made them must be about seeing who they are likely to become as they age, as well as wanting to know why those parents were unable to keep them in the first place. For the birth parents, it must be about knowing that some part of themselves will persist when they are gone, as well as wanting to explain why they had to make those painful choices or explain why the choice was not theirs to make.

I can't help wanting biological connection despite knowing that the planet does not need another child, perhaps now least of all.

I can't help it despite knowing that I might bring into the world a child who will have a horrendously difficult life, for whom the planet will become a radically unstable and unliveable place, where climatic and other forms of devastation seem destined to be the norm.

The impulse is not logical. It is hardwired, biological, even for a man like me.

We find ourselves at a colleague's fiftieth birthday party where we meet a professor of human genetics. I tell her about our confusion over whether to pursue adoption or surrogacy, and explain how much about my own life seems to militate against my reproducing: the fact that I was nearly a full month late being born and that my mother nearly died from complications following the delivery, the fact that I turned out more attracted to men than to women.

These must be signs from the universe that I should not reproduce.

And yet, I say, I feel this powerful compulsion to have my own biological children.

The professor looks at me and smiles.

If that's the case, then you have to listen to it, she says. The other factors are beside the point.

But surrogacy is expensive, and difficult, and what about all the ethical problems, I say.

She smiles again.

You'll just have to find a way.

Now, when I write to ask her if I have remembered the conversation correctly, she responds suggesting that perhaps she was speaking to me then as a parent instead of a scientist. In any case, she says, the desire to have children is not a matter of logic. Some people feel the urge, others don't, and the feeling can change as time passes. The drive to have children is primal, beyond rationality.

When I show my mother an earlier version of this chapter, she is quick to make a correction. She does not want me to think I was responsible for her nearly dying. The complications following my birth were medical in origin rather than biological or physiological. I should not blame myself for the trauma she suffered.

Does that correction, I wonder, make me feel less certain of the universe standing between me and reproduction?

It's a question I still cannot answer.

# SURROGATES

British law not only discourages surrogacy, it makes it all but structurally impossible. While surrogacy itself is legal, it is illegal to enter into a contract for surrogacy, illegal to advertise that you are a couple looking for a surrogate, illegal to advertise your willingness to be a surrogate, and illegal to pay a surrogate anything but reasonable costs. At birth, the surrogate mother is the legal parent to the child, even if she has no genetic connection. If she is married, her husband is the legal father. The intended parents, who *do* have a genetic connection (either a donor father using a third party's donor egg, or an embryo from two opposite-sex parents that the intended mother cannot carry), have no rights whatsoever under the law. The intended parents must trust that the surrogate will keep her word and give up the baby to them at birth, and they must convince a court to issue a parental order. There have been cases of surrogates in Britain refusing to give up the children they have carried, and protracted legal battles by intended parents to secure parental orders.[1]

Despite these extraordinary risks, Andrew and I decide to explore this option. Because of the legal restrictions, there are no commercial surrogacy agencies as there are in the US, but instead registered charities that operate as introduction services for surrogates and would-be parents. The one that we settle on, which has the most positive online reviews at the time, runs regular introduction meetings. I read the website, heartened by stories of successful introductions, of couples and surrogates getting to know one another, of undergoing IVF treatment, of the failures and successes and hopes and happy results. It all suddenly seems possible. The only significant barrier we can see is negotiating our capacity to take such a risk, to have our hearts broken and find that the baby we would be expecting, genetically either mine or Andrew's, was not going to be ours to raise, or that we would have to fight the surrogate in the courts to win the child who should by logic be ours.

But as I scan these stories I am half-conscious of another barrier: our difficulty in navigating British social relations. Introduction mixers, the charity's website explains, happen at various locations, but usually pubs. Andrew and I have never felt comfortable in pubs, and neither of us has ever been able to explain to ourselves or to anyone else why we should feel so alienated by one of the most important arenas of social interaction in Britain. It is not only a question of sexuality – we feel no more at home in gay pubs or gay-friendly pubs. Perhaps this is a function of having grown up in puritanical societies, or being raised by older parents, or of not coming from a culture where drinking is the keystone of social interaction, but it is also about a sense I have of the British pub as a zone of latent violence where I always feel vulnerable.

Nonetheless, we decide we have to get past this. We wait for the charity to announce its next London mixer, preparing ourselves to appear more at ease than we actually will be.

When the announcement comes, the event has been scheduled at a chain pub in a remote part of London, just inside the M25, in a semi-rural area. Whether we drive or go by public transport, it will take hours to get there. More to the point, the location makes the event feel sordid. In the pictures online, the pub looks run-down, the kind of place where prostitutes and johns might meet, or where people would get drunk before lurking in nearby bushes, hoping for a quick fuck with a stranger. Choosing it for a mixer at which the most profound relationship of trust and mutual understanding has to be kindled suggests to us – Andrew in particular – that the surrogacy charity itself views the entire enterprise as if it has to be hidden from the public, out on the margins of the city. As if it were shameful or only barely legal. And perhaps it is both of those things.

We get cold feet. We decide not to go.

Over the coming years, friends – always women, usually older than us – will ask, 'Don't you know someone who could have a baby for you?' No, we say. Our friends who might do this are either too old, or would probably be unwilling. I know I should not resent those friends who explicitly said at one time or another 'I'd have a child for you but the first pregnancy was so difficult' only then to have another child of their own. They owe nothing to me, not even that throwaway comment.

But neither the impulse to parent nor the emotions it triggers are logical.

And if these older women, our close friends and mentors, wise and ethical and progressive all, wonder about the possibility of a friend having a child for us, is it really so unthinkable a suggestion?

I discover that a New York acquaintance in a same-sex relationship has convinced his sister to have a child for him as a traditional surrogate, using her own egg and my friend's partner's sperm. From the beginning, it goes badly. The sister decides she cannot manage the joint custody they informally agreed upon and the daughter she gives birth to now lives with her, only seeing her father and uncle for visits.

Meanwhile, friends in Paris, a male same-sex couple who both work in finance, have a son in the US through a surrogate. When we see them, they joke that instead of a Ferrari they now have a boy in a crib. The whole process cost them nearly two hundred thousand dollars.

Andrew and I do not have that kind of money, although my father could afford to pay for us to have a surrogate, even just get us most of the way there. When I raise this as a possibility, he suggests instead that he might come to live with us in London. And then, he says, I could help.

I tell him the British government has made such immigration impossible, but I see that he appreciates the situation with acute clarity: what I am asking for is a huge gift, as great a gift as the private undergraduate education he and my mother paid for. What he asks of me in return is a huge gift: my care of him as he ages, in the moment when I want to focus my attention on a child.

For many reasons, it is an exchange I cannot make.

I look again at other surrogacy options. The US is prohibitively expensive. In India, it is ethically out of the question, and in any case the laws soon shift to make it impossible for same-sex couples to travel there for surrogacy without lying and breaking the law. I think once more about the British surrogacy charities, their mixers and introduction parties, the air of shame and marginality that attaches to them. My heart sinks.

None of it looks possible.

And so, again, we find ourselves back at the beginning.

# HUGO

H ugo is four, he is five, he is six. Over the course of three years I see him several times with his adoptive parents in Cape Town. They are both corporate lawyers who could afford surrogacy but have made the decision instead to adopt one of South Africa's legion of orphans. The first time we meet Hugo we are having dinner with the family at their home in Constantia, around the corner from the botanical gardens. Their house is on a quiet street, the property surrounded by high walls. They employ a domestic worker who has a daughter Hugo's age, whose English name is Patience. The children are playing together when we arrive, and our friend, the father, decides we need to go to the mall to buy groceries for dinner.

Andrew gets into the front passenger seat and I sit in the back with Hugo and Patience. The contrast between the two children is striking. Although Hugo, who was adopted at eighteen months, has not had to worry about food or security and has had highly attentive parenting, he is almost uncontrollable. He flops around in the back seat, he gets in my face, has no sense of personal space. Patience, who may well have had to worry about whether there would be enough food some days, and whose home life lacks the comforts and securities of Hugo's, chatters away, asking me questions. If I were to choose which child to spend a day with, it would be Patience.

At the mall, Hugo cannot walk a straight line. He breaks from our friend's hand when he tries to hold it, he crouches, he leaps, he runs this way and that, a pinball pinging off obstacles, smashed forward by internal levers.

Back at the house, Patience and her mother leave to make the long journey home to Khayelitsha by minibus taxi. Alone with our friends and Hugo, I am again conscious of the boy's wriggling, fidgeting, his aggressive play with the dogs, the number of times his mother has to call him out on his behaviour. At dinner, Hugo cannot sit still. He seems more frenetic than most five-year-olds. His father gives him a huge bowl of ice cream and I think, what a long night they have before them, all that sugar coursing through the boy's veins.

A year later I see them again when they come to a book launch I have at a Cape Town bookstore. Hugo and his parents are already there when I arrive, and Hugo is at the cash register with the owner. He is using the scanner to ring up a sale.

Do you know Hugo? I ask the owner.

No... but he's very *confident*, the woman says, her face tightening with alarm.

I suggest to Hugo that he go find his parents, which he does, running pell-mell through the small space, locating our friends at the refreshments table.

Throughout my conversation with another author in front of an attentive audience, Hugo flings himself on the ground or speaks loudly and has to be silenced by his mother. Normal behaviour for a six-year-old, perhaps, or at least within the range of normal behaviour, and yet there are other children of the same age present, birth children of other friends, who sit quietly through the event.

Knowing that we have been thinking of trying to have children, our friends urge us, as they have in the past, to adopt from South Africa. I tell them that the government has recently made this much more difficult for people not resident in the country, and in any case, we're not an opposite-sex couple, not like you. Does that make a difference, they ask? Yes, it appears to, I tell them. I've read stories that indicate same-sex couples adopting in South Africa are typically offered only those children who cannot be placed anywhere else, who have serious disabilities or health problems.

We would never get a child as healthy as Hugo, I tell them, not from here.

Years pass, and the next time I see Hugo it is clear he is beginning to settle into his life. Less clingy than I remember, he is also less frenzied, does well in school, and has a rich array of interests and hobbies. He is an excellent swimmer, and he switches between English and Afrikaans and Xhosa with ease and fluency.

Whatever our friends are doing, I can see that their parenting has had a remarkable effect, and this begins gradually to shift my sense of what is possible.

# STAGES

Surrogacy in America is too expensive, surrogacy in India is legally and ethically impossible, surrogacy in Britain requires too great a leap of faith and too much negotiation of cultural habits that continue to bewilder or alienate us, and adopting from abroad would be more complicated and fraught with risk, we suspect, than adopting in Britain.

And so, a year after meeting with Mary the social worker, we decide to file papers starting the adoption approval process. The government has launched a drive to recruit more adopters because there is a shortage, and we are caught up in that campaign. We will be vetted by social workers, and if we are approved, they will help us find a match.

It all sounds so simple.

The approval process has two stages. Stage 1 requires us each to fill out a fifty-page questionnaire and attend four days of workshops run by the council's adoption team, as well as meetings with the social worker who has been assigned to our case.

When Eleanor, who is Sri Lankan by birth, comes to our flat at the end of September 2013, she is nothing like what Andrew or I have been fearing. She is young, intelligent, working on a master's degree, considering pursuing a doctorate. She slips into the conversation that her sister, a writer who lives in Melbourne, has a female partner, and she does this so deftly we instantly feel at ease.

We talk about our backgrounds, our sense of ourselves as migrants, three migrants at the same table. We talk about writing and education and psychology. She asks us our advice about doctoral studies. If this is the person who will be vetting us over the next eight months, I cannot foresee any problems.

Except that Eleanor is pregnant.

Is this a test in the way that meeting with Mary at the beginning of the process, more than a year earlier, might also have been a test? Do they deploy pregnant social workers to prospective adopters as a means of gauging how able we are to handle the reality of being confronted with people who have biological children, whose route to parenthood is so much simpler than our own? Is it cruel to dispatch a visibly pregnant woman to interview would-be adopters, or is it a logical choice, a way of seeing how serious and well adjusted we might already be, or, conversely, to see how liable to being triggered by such a vision we might equally – even concomitantly – be.

Our affective response to Eleanor's pregnancy is not the problem. But her inability to stay with us through the whole process is.

Eleanor is our social worker only for this first stage, for the initial home visit, and for a follow-up visit in her office to submit our details for a background check. After those two meetings we will never see her again, except in passing. But if she is representative of the kind of social workers we'll encounter, then this will all go smoothly. We try to trust in that.

Near the end of October, we attend the first two-day workshop, led by social workers Caroline and Claudia. The venue is in a part of London we have never visited. We take a train, walk twenty minutes, take another train, walk twenty minutes, trying to find our way through a maze of social housing estates.

The workshop is held in a room on the top floor of a multi-use building. Chairs are arranged in a circle. Among the prospective adopters, there is a single woman and five other couples: a young couple planning to adopt the child of a family member, an older couple planning something similar, two other same-sex male couples, an opposite-sex couple roughly our age. The people we get along with best are the latter couple, Luc and Chloe. Luc, who is Belgian, works as a lawyer, and Chloe, who is British, administers a charity. Our ease with one another is less a matter of class than of education. We speak the same language in a way that the other couples do not.

As an ice-breaker, we are asked to pair up with another couple and we gravitate to Luc and Chloe. Strangely, the exercise requires that we tell the other person two true things about ourselves and one lie, and the other person has to guess what is true and what is false. In a process that requires what feels like total disclosure of the most intimate details of one's life, couple-hood, thinking, attitudes and ideology, it seems perverse to demand that we begin with a lie. I pair up with Chloe, who easily sees through mine: I tell her I was on the high school swim team. She notes that if that were true, my shoulders would probably still be more developed than they are. I, on the other hand, do not see through hers.

If there is a point the social workers are trying to make about the transparency of one's lies or the impossibility of knowing whether lies will be legible as such, then it is not made clearly, nor do they suggest that this might have been their intention. What the exercise does is leave me unmoored, but also on guard, because we are being asked to reveal so much about ourselves to strangers. I begin to wonder whether it is a test of our capacity to be vulnerable, to set ourselves on a new path in life that will require ongoing and radical forms of vulnerability.

Caroline and Claudia have organized a varied programme. There are guest speakers, including an adoptive mother who tells us she has not had a week go by without seeing a social worker since adopting two brothers fifteen years ago. The boys have been especially chal-lenging and the mother looks exhausted. She is thin, shrivelled, and says she has not slept regularly for years. She gives the impression of someone barely holding it together.

Another guest speaker, a woman whose children were taken into foster care and subsequently adopted, has managed to get her life back on track. With her new partner she has another child, who is thriving. She talks about the difficulty of that early separation from her children, and the further difficulty of trying to explain to them in subsequent contact how it is that her new child is allowed to live with her while they are not.

I begin to think about the possibility of adopting a child whom the courts might require to have direct contact with one or both of its birth parents, or with biological siblings who might be in foster care or placed with other adoptive families or who even might live with the birth parents or other relatives, and suddenly the entire proposition seems wildly complex and freighted with greater uncertainty than I had allowed myself to imagine.

What would it mean to have to negotiate not just our own relationship with a child we might adopt, but also our relationship with that child's extended biological family who could prove hostile to us in ways that would always be unpredictable? My mind is given to imagining worst-case scenarios. I start to envision encounters with knife-wielding biological fathers, being stalked by screaming biological mothers, navigating weddings and funerals and birthdays with people who might hate the sight of us for the rest of our lives. An orphan would be better. Where are all the orphans? Where are the sweet-natured Annies and Oliver Twists?

There is lunch, there are tea breaks, the sandwiches are adequate, and we sit in our plastic chairs, either perched with plates on our laps, or pulled up to tables. We try to make small talk with the other participants, but every interaction feels forced.

*

The most positive voice in the programme of speakers is a man who adopted a brother and sister several years earlier. The siblings are now flourishing and, at the ages of seven and eight, show no sign of any long-term ill effects from their difficult early beginnings. He says the happiest day in the whole experience was when the adoptions were finalized in court and he could say goodbye, permanently, to the social workers. Even now he is impatient with them, with their vocabularies of grief and trauma and loss, and it strikes me that in fact he has not said goodbye permanently, he is still in the orbit of the social care system, drawn back to report, to present himself as a success story.

Happiness and normalcy, however those might be construed, however subjective and potentially problematic, are always possible, he insists, especially once you get away from the social workers.

The following day, Caroline, who is my age, sidles over to me during a tea break and says that she has looked up my books but won't, she assures me, read them before she's written her report on Andrew's and my participation in the workshops. I want to say, you mean we're being assessed even while we're sitting here and answering your inane questions and participating in role-playing activities that have as little to do with real parenting as pruning roses might? No one told us we were being assessed already. And then I want to say, why should my books have anything to do with my ability to parent? Do you turn up to other prospective adopters' places of work and linger outside the window just to see *where* they work, but promise not to go inside in case you might notice something that would prejudice you against them? It seems a bizarre thing to say, bizarre that first Mary and now Caroline, these two senior social workers, would somehow feel it acceptable even to suggest the possibility that my creative work might impinge upon my capacity to parent an adopted child, even if they were both scrupulous about not reading the books until after all was said and done, however it might be done.

I want to say, go ahead, read the books, and you will see that they are attuned to the experiences of people affected by trauma. But I also know that the dark mood and even darker events described in my first two books might be enough to prejudice such people as Mary and Caroline against me. If he can imagine that, well, what might he be capable of doing? Imagination and action, fantasy and capacity, seem blurred in their questions. And why is creativity itself so suspect? Would they say the same thing to a heterosexual woman novelist? Or a straight male visual artist? Or a composer? An actor? A theatre director?

At some point in the course of these days, the medical officer in the adoption team comes to speak to the group. Although frequently bored or irritated by the other activities and presentations, I have been able to see their value, admiring both the honesty and quality of the information presented even when the tone has shifted into a wheedling downbeat wooliness that seems to occlude truth rather than reveal it.

The medical officer is different.

She perches on the edge of a table and takes us through an interminable series of slides and short films. Blunt and yet weirdly ironic about the consequences of physical and sexual abuse, she even resorts to gallows humour about the physiological effects of different forms of substance abuse.

Her demeanour tells us that she has seen everything and regards it as her role to kill our last illusions that we will ever be matched with a child one could hope to call 'normal'. They will all of them, every last one, be seriously fucked up, even if, by some miracle, we get a child at birth, which is never going to happen. The trauma of separation from the birth mother does irreparable harm, she says, and for all the others, well, there's a reason they're up for adoption. They haven't been given up freely by their parents. They've been taken because they've been badly treated, and that bad treatment has lifelong consequences to the brain and body and mind.

Even the system itself, I realize, is determined to construct adopted children as out of control, almost as destined to fail.

This would be bad enough but I also notice two other things that trouble me. The medical officer does not conceive of the children having come from anyone but a mother. Birth fathers do not exist in her schema in any way whatsoever, and there is no suggestion that a child might grieve or be traumatized by the loss of one. At the same time, there is an assumption only of an adoptive mother, and not a single reference to an adoptive father, let alone two fathers.

At the end of the workshop, I complain to Caroline. What does such a presentation say to the male couple who cannot locate themselves in the narrative being offered? What does that do to our sense of how the system sees or understands us, assuming it understands us in the first place?

For the first time she looks tense. Her chin trembles. She chews her lip and nods but does not have an answer.

I'll feed that back, she says.

# YOU

You are born. About this time there is so little I will ever know. I know it is a spring birth, as if you, too, are one of May's flowers. I know that you are your parents' fifth child. Beyond that, I know almost nothing, and must pick through the details I eventually learn to sketch a picture of what might have been. Only the people who were there will know for certain, only they can potentially tell your story as it actually happened.

If I were to fill in the blanks in my knowledge, I might imagine that for the first hours of your life you are utterly adored. I want to believe your arrival is full of joy and contentment.

This is what I would wish. The rest is a matter of conjecture, of perhaps.

Perhaps your mother giggles and sticks out her tongue at you, blowing raspberries. Perhaps she gives you a traditional name not because she has a taste for tradition, but because it is the name of an actor she fancies.

Perhaps your father is there to hold you not long after your birth. Perhaps he is affectionate, kisses you, cuddles you, finds himself brought to tears by the sight of you, as I would have been in his place, if you had been mine.

Perhaps the three of you take a taxi home – or your grandmother, your mother's mother, comes to give you a lift while your grandfather looks after your four brothers and sisters.

Perhaps, for the first time since your birth, you cry in the car because you are hungry and your mother tells you to shush. Perhaps that is the first time she shouts at you, if she shouts at you, as I hope that she did not. I have no way of knowing.

Perhaps your father tells her to feed you and your mother says she just has and your father tells her to feed you again and this time she does, and you settle, and the crying comes to an end.

Perhaps, when you get home, your mother announces she's going to bed and places you on a blanket on the floor of the living room, so that your siblings can toddle over to see what you are. Perhaps they lean over your supine form, poking you, sticking out their tongues, blowing raspberries themselves as a television roars in the background.

Perhaps.

# WORRY

Between the two workshops in October and December, we go for medical check-ups that constitute no more than answering a few questions, giving a urine sample, being weighed and measured. I have lost ten pounds since I last weighed myself, as if the preoccupation of thinking about adoption has sped up my metabolism.

No blood test? I ask the doctor.

No blood test, she says, and signs the form.

It feels like a strange moment of the system trusting us, whether it intends to or not.

Our background checks come back clear, and we begin completing our fifty-page workbooks. On the first page it asks us to draw a spider with legs representing our expectations and worries.

Only eight legs?

Only eight expectations and worries? How many of each?

Could it be an anatomically incorrect spider?

I have so many worries, so few expectations.

I cannot think in this way, so I re-format the page, killing the spider and producing instead a table of responses. I wonder what the social workers will make of this refusal to bend myself to their form. Is the spider a test of our capacity to complete juvenile worksheets and colouring books? Are the best prospective adopters inclined to decorate their pages with glitter and sequins and feathers? I start to fear that the system might expect a male couple in particular to perform a fabulousness that Andrew and I cannot muster.

I have only one expectation, of a rigorous but fair process. Only one leg, if I had stuck with the spider, and so many more to represent worries.

It still has not been made clear how many home visits we can expect, of what duration they will be, or what will be covered over the course of these visits. (And in the end, it is never made clear how many home visits we should expect, how frequently they will occur, or how long each one will last. Everything is vague.)

But these are minor concerns, little posterior legs on the spider of expectation and worry, when compared to the large, elongated anterior legs, thick with hair, upon which are articulated my concerns that the social care system views the entire process of adoption through the lens of trauma, refusing to countenance the possibility that one might be motivated by the simple desire to create a family.

As if that were ever a simple desire, and yet is that not how all human cultures inevitably treat it unless you happen to be single or a same-sex couple?

The thinking rather appears to be that the most suitable adopter is one embarking on the process for entirely selfless reasons, and doing so as surrogate for the state, with the implicit suggestion that if we are lucky enough to adopt a child, that child will never really be ours, not entirely. Until it is an adult, it will be liable to reclamation by the state (if the state judges us inept). At least, this is the impression I have formed: that being already in the eye of the state, these children will continue to be watched until they are adults. Even if this is not actually or not always the case, there is no denying that once the child has reached adulthood, it will have the freedom to turn its back on us and return to the arms of its birth parents, shunning us as the inept stand-ins for the better parenting it imagines it might have had.

I say *it* rather than *he* or *she*, because I am trying, still, to imagine a child in the abstract, without gender or personality.

And while it is true that altruism is a significant part of Andrew's and my reasoning behind the impulse to adopt, it is no less important than the selfish desire to create a family.

The other large twitching leg of worry is about prejudice, and my experiences over the next three years will do little if anything to dissipate this feeling. I worry about encountering people in the system who are biased against same-sex couples adopting. This concern is based not only on my experiences of homophobia from at least the age of ten onwards, but on having read various blogs by same-sex adoptive couples in Britain – male couples in particular – who have experienced undisguised bias and prejudice from social workers across the country.

In writing my responses, I adopt a tone that is both formal and, I hope, elementary. I try to be clear, to sound authoritative. But reading it once I have finished makes me uncomfortable. I write of the absence of joy in the process but can see no joy in my own formulations, no articulation of the guarded hopefulness I feel, only the guardedness itself, and the impulse to criticize a system that is only just getting to know me.

The next page offers questions that Andrew and I must answer together, questions that wonder what we are worried about – always this foregrounding of worry, anxiety, concern – and what we have to offer. I wonder why the form requires us to start with the negative (with worry) rather than the positive (with what we can offer).

Since honesty seems a requirement, we are honest.

We are worried about contact with the birth family over the long term and how this might affect a child's bond with us. We worry about how the birth family might view us as same-sex parents, and how my modest public profile might complicate contact with siblings, birth parents, extended family, and our desire to have some semblance of a private life.

We worry about being equipped to meet the emotional and

psychological needs of a child who has suffered any form of abuse or neglect. (I wonder, is this particular worry not sufficient to stop us in our tracks? Any child we might adopt in Britain *will* have suffered abuse or neglect, almost without question. This is what we've been told.)

In terms of what we can offer, we claim to be empathetic and committed to each other, which we both believe is true. We mention our experiences of looking after children, our love of reading, art, music, cooking, travel, all things we would share with a child. We assert our commitment to equality and a sense of global consciousness informed by our childhoods in the United States and South Africa. We describe the stable home we would provide, the network of friends and family who would support us, and the unconditional love we would offer.

The workbook asks us to draw a picture of a 'twisting path' representing our journey to this point, including bridges but also obstructions, including 'boulders, chasms and landslides'. We are asked to rank a list of reasons for adopting from most acceptable (altruism being the obvious intended response) to the least acceptable (this end of the spectrum is all about adopting to strengthen a relationship or fill a gap or prove one's worth to a notional wider community).

They also want to know why our own parents had children, and this is the first question that gives me real pause. I know that my father did not want children, a fact my mother shared with me when I was only twelve. My mother made the decision, and either my father changed his mind or he went along with it because he was afraid of being alone. In Andrew's case, he was unexpected, a late-in-life baby, but no less wanted for that. We are asked to rehearse what we most look forward to in parenting. We make noises about offering the kind of love and nurture we ourselves experienced, although I think about wanting to be a different sort of father to the one I had – in fact, not to be a *father* at all, but instead a parent, without the baggage of *fatherhood*. This is something I do not write and never mention to anyone other than Andrew. Some things, I decide, are none of the social workers' business.

The first major section of the workbook ends, again, with worry. What five things worry us most about being a parent? We have no difficulty coming up with a list:

1. The long-term welfare and wellbeing of a child in an unpredictable world.
2. The experience of a child with same-sex parents in a society that is not uniformly accepting of such relationships, or indeed of same-sex couples raising children.
3. The quality of a child's education in a system driven by standardization.
4. The influence of a child's peer groups once she or he goes to school.
5. Being able fully to meet the emotional, psychological, educational and social needs of a child with a very different background to our own.

Is it the case that being a parent means finding ways of managing worry without losing one's mind, or feeling overwhelmed or helpless or torn apart by despair?

Looking at this list of worries, I wonder why anyone would have a child, let alone adopt one, and I begin to understand the thinking of a friend who describes herself as an antinatalist, opposed to reproduction because the planet cannot sustain it. I have never pushed her on this belief, but wonder whether she means only intentional reproduction or *all* reproduction. Does she mean merely the reproduction of people like us, who want to have children for, presumably, largely selfish reasons? Does she think that the high-minded should make way for those who would never consider such a position, or who are disempowered from making their own reproductive choices? Or does she think that everyone should be sterilized and the planet left to survive what remains of our species for the next century, making way for another species' rise to dominance? Is she on the side of the antinatalist philosophers who believe we have no right to bring a person into a world of suffering, because we cannot guarantee their happiness, and what little happiness might exist in any given life cannot outweigh all the pain, sadness and grief?

Despite my own misgivings about reproduction, the arguments of antinatalists irritate me because they seem to fail to see how privileged their position is. There is the privilege of being able and free to reproduce in the first place (though there are undoubtedly those who cannot reproduce who hew to the antinatalist line). There is the privilege of living in a society or inhabiting a position in one's society where the choice is yours to make ('I could reproduce, but I will not, for ethical or philosophical reasons'). The privilege of not feeling the need to parent. The privilege of believing that you will never need the support of children as you age. The privilege of believing that you will miss nothing emotionally or psychologically or socially by not having children – nothing, at least, that you cannot bear.

Undoubtedly, the antinatalist philosophers would argue that I fail fundamentally to understand their position, and that my arguments against them fail, equally fundamentally, to convince on philosophical grounds, but I am not a philosopher and not interested in winning on those terms. Winning, in fact, is not the point, but contesting is, and I think especially so because the philosophy of antinatalism seems so absolutist in its aims, so determined to insist on its correctness.

There is a group of queer theorists whose own thinking often seems in concert with certain strands of antinatalism. Lee Edelman, whose *No Future: Queer Theory and the Death Drive*, a work of sophisticated cultural criticism indebted to the thinking of psychoanalyst Jacques Lacan, also criticizes gay men – like American writer Dan Savage – who embrace parenthood through adoption. Edelman charges Savage with advancing a 'message... of compulsory reproduction', which he describes as being on a continuum with anti-choice movements: 'choose life, for life and the baby and meaning hang together in the balance, confronting the lethal counterweight of narcissism, AIDS, and death'. This position, Edelman says, is tantamount to a 'fascism of the baby's face, which encourages parents, whether gay or straight, to join in a rousing chorus of "Tomorrow Belongs to Me"' (the song sung by the blonde and blue-eyed Hitlerjugend in the film of the musical *Cabaret*).[2]

Intellectually I can understand the arguments of someone like Edelman, who makes compelling points about the supremacy of the Child in American culture, about the ways in which the American right so often uses the figure of the Child as a cudgel to beat women in particular, but queer communities too, denying us the full exercise and enjoyment of our human rights – in the case of women to make their own reproductive choices; in the case of queer people, simply to be and live freely. Nonetheless, such radical position-taking and polemic seems to turn the energies of a fight for equality back onto those of us in the queer community who experience, who live daily with, a yearning to parent. Might that impulse not be radical in its own way?

It is unthinkable to me that I should disavow my desire to have a child because theorists like Edelman see it as 'psychically invested in preserving the familiar familial narrativity of reproductive futurism' rather than embracing 'what is queerest about us, queerest within us'. As if the desire to live one's same-sex attraction *and also* to be a parent were not itself a radically queer act. At this stage in my life, I am unwilling to 'insist that the future stop here', with me – in other words, to mark myself as the end point of my own hereditary line, to call a halt and say I will be the last of my people.[3]

Perhaps my investment in the possibility of parenthood lies in my own childhood. Perhaps I grew up in too normative an environment. Perhaps what was positive in my own upbringing was powerful enough to inculcate that investment in a narrative of reproductive futurism, even in the face of hatred and excoriation from the religious right and bewilderment and disdain from some within the left queer community. I cannot find it in myself to apologize for the urgent hope that parenthood might yet be part of the life I've been given.

## HOTEL

In *Hotel*, the fifth season of Ryan Murphy and Brad Falchuk's series *American Horror Story*, Lady Gaga stars as Elizabeth, The Countess, a neo-noir femme fatale vampire who abducts children she believes are suffering from neglect and turns them into vampires. Although the mechanics of this transformation are largely typical of vampire mythology, in this case requiring no more than feeding the victim-convert a few drops of one's own infected blood, and while there is an element of the supernatural (Elizabeth is notionally immortal but she and her spawn are rather more susceptible to being killed than vampires in other folkloric traditions), her consorts are a parade of queer characters or out queer actors in straight roles, and her vampirism is described as a virus. (Recall that one of the earliest meanings of 'virus' is semen, either human or animal, as well as venom, as from snakes or spiders.) Elizabeth is actively bisexual, and her vampirism – or the way she inhabits and mobilizes the viral infection that produces vampiric effects – is a hallmark of a queerness that is strenuously both maternal and reginal; she is at once hero-protector and villain-predator reigning over the season and its characters.

Although female, given her predilection for queer male lovers (bisexuals Rudolph Valentino and Tristan Duffy, both played by Finn Wittrock, and gay designer Will Drake, played by Cheyenne Jackson), Elizabeth can also be read as a coded drag queen. Reproducibility seems impossible, at least initially, and the death drive is here literalized and instrumentalized but also transformed and perverted so that it becomes generative of future (immortal) queer generations empowered to reproduce in the same way.

As Elizabeth abducts and 'adopts' the children of opposite-sex couples, turning these children into vampires who sleep in glass coffins and never grow up, *Hotel* offers a queer adoption fantasy gone rogue and rendered grotesque. She spoils the vampire children with video games and candy, gives them free run of the hotel, and allows them to feed on – to murder – unwitting hotel guests.

The stunted psychology and zombie-like affect of Elizabeth's vampire children suggests, however, that transformation before adulthood produces arrested psychological, emotional and intellectual results – but only when the act of infection/conversion is performed by the queer Countess herself. Why should her child vampires alone be zombie-like but her adult conversions not? And why, when other children are turned into vampires by heterosexual carriers of the virus, does their affect remain... unaffected?

The rationale for Elizabeth's particular approach to queer family making lies, implicitly, in the monstrousness of her sole biological 'child', Bartholomew, who is more sinew and tooth and force of fury than human, lacking the ability to grow beyond his tiny stunted form, but nonetheless capable of killing with as much ferocity as a creature many times his size.[4] As if aware that her capacity for biological motherhood is limited to the creation of hideous and violent monstrosities, Elizabeth subsequently, or consequently, converts the human into the monstrous on her own terms, in her own image, creating a family of *beautiful* little monsters, every one of them as ghostly white blonde as she is, but as Bartholomew, crucially, is not.[5] We might understand this dynamic through Freud, who described parental love as 'so moving and at bottom so childish' that it is 'nothing but the parents' narcissism born again'.[6] Faced with a child as physically repulsive as Bartholomew is, Elizabeth's narcissism is forced to find its fulfilment through the adoption and conversion of children who mirror her (childish) vision of her own beautiful self at the same time that her emotional investment remains entirely with Bartholomew, the converted children operating as mere props for her ego.

Through its troubling conflation of the energies of abduction, adoption and conversion, the series implies that a queer family can only be produced or reproduced through violence, that its *result* is violence, that it will be happy with nothing less than abducting and converting beautiful children who remain stunted zombies, or preying upon children to satisfy either an unfulfilled narcissistic impulse or even a psychotic bloodlust. This is a vision of queer family forged in death, which delivers nothing but a legacy of the same. Such a pessimistic and cynical narrative of queer adoption might even be read as implicitly reinforcing conservative religious narratives of queer recruiting and predation. Or, more generously, the series could be read as attempting to turn itself into a funhouse mirror for such nightmare narratives, revealing the monstrousness but also the absurdity of reactionary paranoia about queer parenting.

Attempts by a pair of heterosexual biological parents – Alex and John Lowe (Chloë Sevigny and Wes Bentley) – to reclaim their vampirized young child, Holden (Lennon Henry), end in disaster. In an early episode, Sevigny's character, a paediatrician, admits that she never really wanted children, framing herself as the not-good-enough biological parent, although she recalls that Holden's birth triggered her maternal impulse. In flashbacks to a period prior to his abduction and transformation, Holden appears 'normal', without the zombie affect of his vampiric state. His younger sister, Scarlett (Shree Crooks), is the first in the family to see Holden after his disappearance, and lest we think we might be misreading the young actor's performance, Scarlett reports to her incredulous parents that, although it is definitely her brother, Holden is 'different' and without 'normal feelings'.

Not yet realizing what Holden has become, however, Alex goes to the hotel and brings her son home. The boy's expression is blank, his temperature far below normal, and when Alex leaves him alone for a moment he kills and feeds on the family dog. After he asks for his 'other mommy', Alex returns him to the hotel where she accuses Elizabeth of stealing her son. The Countess insists on the contrary that she has saved him – as she saves all of her children – from neglect and 'a tragic wasted life'. What, one wonders, does she see as their value in the life she gives them (or to which she condemns them)? They certainly have utility as trophy ornaments, as apparatuses of her blood filtration system, and as the equivalent of the household dog or cat that eliminates unwelcome vermin (some of it human). But there is little if any indication that Elizabeth actually loves these children, or that her supposed affection for them is anything other than affectation.

Faced with this enraged biological mother, Elizabeth offers to convert her so that she can remain with her son forever, in exchange for which Alex must also look after the other vampire children (so rendering herself utilitarian), under threat of Holden's own death should she fail in her duties. In this way the birth mother is incorporated into the adoptive queer family, but only as an auxiliary whose service is required to sustain the 'life' of her biological child. Alex consents – what other choice does she have? – but her subsequent conversion is not only a matter of becoming a vampire. She also crosses over into the realm of the queer. The conversion rite begins with her kissing Elizabeth before drinking from a wound slashed in The Countess's exposed breast. This bargain, and its violent terms, both neutralizes the mother's ongoing claim upon her biological child, and eliminates any future possibility of her reproducing in a way that consolidates the power of The Countess.[7]

Alex, however, proves an untrustworthy host for her queer virus, intentionally infecting one of her child patients, Max (Anton Lee Starkman), in order to save him from dying of measles through the negligence of his anti-vaxxer mother (Mädchen Amick). This suggests, once more, the failure of heterosexual parents to care adequately for their offspring, but also the failure of the hetero Alex Lowe to know how to wield the queer power she has been granted.

Left to do what he will, Max kills and feeds on his parents, then infects his classmates and kills all of the teachers in his school, feeding on them as well. Significantly, the affect of *these* vampire children is not flattened in the same way as that of Elizabeth's four child converts. It is as if being out in the world keeps them 'normal', or as if their infection by the heterosexual Alex allows them to *remain* 'normal'.[8] It is exclusively Elizabeth's child converts who exhibit such flatness, as if the abduction/adoption itself produces the flattening, although it could equally be explained by Elizabeth's failure to demonstrate genuine love for her abductee-converts, or by the fact that she is manifestly queer. The series, however, offers none of these possible rationales – it offers no rationale whatsoever. Curiously, when John and Alex decide later to take Holden home, retrieving him from the hotel playroom, his affect is less blank, more natural than it has previously appeared, as if the reassertion of the hetero birth parents' rights over him reawakens his own sense of life and liveliness.

The series complicates all of these reproductive and alienating energies with a flashback in which Elizabeth, already a vampire, visits an illegal abortionist in the 1920s, seeking to terminate the pregnancy that produces Bartholomew. In the midst of the botched abortion, Elizabeth's monstrous offspring attacks and kills the doctor's nurse. The fact of his being 'born' in this way suggests that Bartholomew himself is Elizabeth's punishment for seeking an abortion, reinforcing what often reads as the series' curiously reactionary message, notwithstanding its queer ethos over multiple seasons and its co-creation by Ryan Murphy (who is gay, married, and has children through surrogacy, an experience dramatized and fictionalized in his short-lived series *The New Normal*).[9]

Despite these queer credentials, in *Hotel* the *heterosexual* biological family is presented as the acme of genuine love, even when such families are depicted as profoundly and insolubly fraught. Vampire Donovan (Matt Bomer) is so viciously cruel to his (non-vampire) mother Iris (Kathy Bates) that she decides to take her own life, only for Donovan to 'rescue' her at the last moment by dripping some of his infected blood into his mother's mouth, so transforming her, too, into a vampire. This act of salvation has been prompted by transgender Liz Taylor (Denis O'Hare) reminding Donovan that no one will ever love him more than his mother – horrible though Iris undoubtedly is. Later in the season, Liz's estranged adult son Douglas (Josh Braaten) visits the hotel bar and acknowledges Liz as his father (as was), asserting his willingness to have her in his life once more. The emotional force of this reconciliation and Douglas's acceptance is enough to keep Liz herself from committing suicide over the death of her lover. If there is any queerness in these two biological families, it is only evident in Donovan's infecting of his mother with the virus as a way of bringing her back to 'life', and in Liz Taylor's own identity as a pre-operative transwoman.

So, while this season of *American Horror Story* at once posits queer family as a constellation of elective and radical possibility, one formed (in its vampiric variety) through abduction, conversion, adoption, it also insists that such queer families can only be built on the ruins of a loving biological heterosexual family (however imperfect). Moreover, the loving bonds of that biological family always have the power to transcend its legal dissolution, reaching from its ruins and into the queer family to stake its claim – even in some cases to *reclaim* those members who have been taken from it.

More alarmingly, *Hotel* suggests time and again that the queer family is devoid of genuine love. We do not see Elizabeth or her multiple consorts attending *lovingly* to any of the vampire children. She is, if anything, even more neglectful than the biological parents she reviles, merely fashioning a materialist cage in which the children can play for all eternity and filter her blood supply as they sit mesmerized by video games. The acquisition of children, the creation of family, is framed as an intrinsically utilitarian act: the child helps to maintain one's own life and wellbeing, but in its abducted/converted/adopted iterations it is never the object of altruistic care or unconditional love, nor is it framed as the fulfilment of a legacy that will transcend the adoptive parent's own life. The utilitarian is also, ultimately, the imminently disposable and replaceable. Elizabeth does not hesitate to threaten Holden's life in pursuit of her desires, and the most attention or affection she shows any child is to Bartholomew, her own biological offspring.

It is certainly possible to read *Hotel* as a tongue-in-cheek retort to those conservatives who see nothing but horror in the idea of queer couples raising children, but it can just as easily be read, and much more disturbingly so, as a pointed critique of queer couples who adopt or have children through surrogacy, as if those of us moved by such an impulse are the real monsters, that our desire to parent children neglected by their biological (straight) parents is a hubristic one belying the undoubtedly common occurrence (at least in some affluent circles of queer life) of adopted children being placed in the care of nannies whose own lives are marked by radical precarity, people who are regarded too often by their employers (those queer adoptive parents) as disposable and replaceable.

If even the queer creators behind *Hotel* present – however inadvertently – such a confused narrative of queer family, what hope is there that straight society will ever wholly accept men like my husband and me as parents? It may only be a soap opera from hell, tongue firmly in cheek, but a series like *American Horror Story* still offers narratives that people consume and internalize in ways impossible to police, whatever the intentions and identities of their makers. The creators of *Hotel* are not suggesting their story is anything other than fantasy, and yet fantasy lives in the world, even in the moment of disavowing its reality.

I know that I do not wish – neither does Andrew – to form a family through violence, nor do we want zombie-like copies of ourselves, nor to convert a straight child to a queer one. And yet I also recognize that there *is* in our thinking about the kinds of children we feel we can and cannot parent a tacit acknowledgement that we are looking for a child who will fit into our lives, who can be raised to share and reflect our progressive – even our queer – values. This may not be an impulse to convert, but it is a desire to nurture someone who will share our ethics and morals, even if she or he ultimately arrives at a different system of belief to our own.

# QUEER

At the beginning of this adoption approval process – which feels already, in the midst of completing the Stage 1 workbook, like a process in the legal sense, a mounting and marshalling of evidence in our defence as reasonable, as good, as *good enough* – I did not imagine that the system would require so much self-definition from us, or such extensive self-narration.

We are asked to write a timeline from our own birth to the present, noting in every year a significant memory, an important event, the moving from one home to another, education, jobs, births and deaths in our families, 'other significant deaths and losses', happiness, sadness, loss.

Even in an attempt at balance, the questions and directions always slide into negative affects, so that it feels as though what the social workers want most is to understand how we have suffered, and how resilient we may or may not be.

We complete our timelines and I try, despite the directions, to be upbeat, but reading mine over, I am aware that the life I describe – and the life Andrew describes in his own timeline – is nothing like the usual run of English lives that our social workers are likely to have encountered. Our foreignness marks us in ways that render us increasingly illegible.

After the timeline, the workbook poses a further series of

questions. The first asks me to think of a time when I felt different or isolated and how this felt. As I read it, I laugh out loud.

This is absurd, I say to Andrew.

We just have to get through it, he says.

I compose my answer:

As a man who identifies as queer… I have grown up and continue to live in a world in which I am constantly made to feel my difference even when I do not myself feel as though I am intrinsically different to anyone else. I have been lucky, however, in not experiencing rejection by friends or close family members… I felt quite isolated for much of my child-hood because, apart from my sexuality, I was an unusual child who lived largely in his own mind.

The next question asks me to think of any times in my life when I have had to grapple with 'difficult, painful or worrying experiences'. Again, I laugh, but that laughter is a symptom of the genuine unease I feel. How can these social workers imagine that one does not feel experiences of this kind in such number that it would be ludicrous to try to enumerate them? I answer:

For the sensitive person life is a constant process of negotiat-ing difficulty, pain and worry. To name particular experiences I would not know where to begin, or indeed where to stop. These are not problems, however, but part of the way one tries to live an ethical life. I am lucky in having had parents who raised me to face the difficult, the painful and the worry-ing in as frank a manner as possible, to recognize the complexity of a given situation, and to seek ways to under-stand how best to negotiate the problem at hand. They have helped me, friends have helped me, and my husband always helps me.

The next question wonders when, if ever, I might have had to 'manage change'. I begin to understand that the social workers' assumption – or perhaps fear – is that they will be faced with prospective adopters who have lived such unreflective and stable, unchanging lives that they have no capacity for empathy. I answer:

> Again, life is a constant process of managing change. Much of my childhood and adolescence was not marked by significant change (I spent sixteen years in the same house; changing schools was the most significant change per se). Since leaving Omaha my life has been marked by a series of major changes: moving to New York, to Oxford, to London. Changing *cultures* is one of the most significant changes one could possibly face. Understanding how to live in Britain has not always been easy, and indeed I feel it is an ongoing process that may continue for the rest of my life. Life for me is living through the negotiation of changes both large and small.

The questions continue in this vein, one after another, never rising above the insultingly reductive. And then, at last, I arrive at a page that demands I define my identity in terms of 'gender, language, ethnicity, disability, class, culture, sexuality, spirituality'.

By this point, I am having a perverse kind of fun. I answer:

> I have to begin from a place that resists set categories because I believe identity is fluid. Nonetheless, within the paradigms of this assessment, I am male, English-speaking, second-language French speaking. I am white American, of English, Irish, Scots-Irish and German ancestry. I am a dual American and British citizen who regards himself as American as well as British (but not English).
>
> I have no significant physical disabilities and no mental disabilities. I was raised in a typical middle-class American

home by intellectual and highly politically engaged parents. We were comfortably well off but not rich.

I identify as queer (although for the purposes of this process you might wish simply to identify me as 'gay' even though this is not a label I myself choose, for political reasons).

I was raised in a nominally Christian household (my father was Unitarian, my mother agnostic, though he grew up Congregationalist and she grew up Presbyterian), attending church occasionally, and particularly around the major holidays. I now identify as agnostic, but culturally Christian.

Andrew reads my responses and wonders whether I'm asking for trouble in describing myself as 'queer' instead of 'gay'. But the problem is I don't think of myself as 'gay' even though I am a man whose primary physical attractions are to men, a man who is married to a man who also prefers the term 'queer'. When I was in the process of figuring out who I was, one of the great barriers to self-acceptance was an inability to see myself as 'gay'.

How do I come out when I don't really understand what I am? I once asked my friend Ben, who was among the first people I came out to, telling him then that I *was* gay because I could find no other language to describe what I felt myself to be. I cannot find a category that fits, I told him. Bisexual somehow did not, since I was, at most, bi-affective, or bi-affectionate, but largely homo-sexual.

It was not until 2005, when I began teaching literary theory at the University of Sheffield and had to engage with queer theory seriously for the first time, that I found a language for understanding myself. Even then, the idea of settling on a fixed category ran counter to my sense that I would prefer not to be labelled at all, but rather to be described as a man married to a man, or as one half of a same-sex union. I would not want a straight person to call me queer or to ask if I was queer, but nor would I want, necessarily, for them to describe me as gay. I know that for some people – self-identifying gay people in particular – this may read as a mark of internalized homophobia, but when, as a child, I was becoming conscious of my own attractions and sexuality and the limited range of available identities, 'gay' suggested a rigid category and set of associated behaviours that I could not find a way of fitting inside. I was attracted to boys, but I was other things as well. From a very young age, I was gender-nonconforming. When I was two years old, an elderly neighbour could not understand that I was male. My hair was too long (in fact, long and wispy and white blonde, like those vampire children in *American Horror Story: Hotel*), my affect too feminine, and this neighbour used female pronouns to describe me for years. Another neighbour, an elderly woman who walked past our house every day, made a habit of referring to me condescendingly as 'such a big boy', and I felt no less uncomfortable with this. I was not big, and some part of me was also, I felt certain, not a boy, or not a boy in the way that other boys in my neighbourhood were boys. I recently found photographs from slightly later, from the ages of four, five, six, when my flamboyance and ambiguity strike me as so visible that it's a wonder nobody ever, well, wondered (although of course many undoubtedly did). At the age of five, I am dressed as a butterfly for Halloween, but I love the strap-on wings so much that I wear them throughout the year as a costume for playing outside in the yard. There are other photos of me mimicking the Statue of Liberty with a bouquet of lilies of the valley instead of a torch. Or in short shorts and a cowboy hat directing invisible traffic. Or perched in a tree dressed as a chipmunk in a costume my mother made, with a brown feather boa for a tail. I know that these descriptions will suggest to many, simply, the *femme* gay child, and while I can see such images through that lens, I discern something less easily defined, too, and more radical: an inability to see my own gender, to understand why it might be important, or even to see the gender of others.

A case in point: at the age of six I was enrolled in my first acting class at what was then the Emmy Gifford Children's Theater, taught by the great storyteller Nancy Duncan. On the first day of class, I was entranced by a boy who had a shock of short red hair. At the next class, I was devastated to learn that this red-headed boy was a girl, not because it meant we could not be friends (though we never really spoke) but because I had been attracted to the red-headed *boy* who was, in fact, the androgynous red-headed girl.

By the time I was ten, other students in my school would ask me if I was a boy or a girl. A couple of years later, one day out shopping with my mother in the mall, a clerk said, 'Hello, ladies' when he saw us. It would have been fine if I felt positive about this ambiguity, and the curious thing is I *wanted* to feel positive about it, I cultivated an androgynous aesthetic, whether consciously or not, but the dominant culture of Omaha did all that it could to tell me I should adhere more closely to the narrowest, most normative codes of masculinity.

At twelve, in the locker room of the school swimming pool, changing into shapeless black wool swimming suits, a boy named Justin asked me if I was gay. This was the first time I had ever been asked directly about my sexuality and in retrospect I think it was not intended as a hostile question. Perhaps it was even a hopeful one. We were alone in a row of lockers and he said it quietly, not aggressively. In second grade, Justin had dressed up for Halloween as Eleanor Roosevelt, complete with skirt and wig and stuffed brassiere. But when I heard him ask the question, I blustered and panicked and said no, because what else could I say? I did not know. I hardly knew what gay meant. I thought *Playboy* must be a magazine full of naked men because, you know, the 'boy' in the title, until a friend showed me a stack of his father's issues hidden in the back of a closet, and I remember feeling both confusion and disappointment.

There were other occasions, around the same time, when I was asked directly about my sexuality and insisted, no, I wasn't gay, because I wanted a wife and children. A gay man does not reproduce, a gay man is the end of the line in his family. I knew that well enough. If I wanted to reproduce, to have children of my own, I could not possibly be gay.

When I came out to my mother at the age of twenty-six, her only note of regret was that she would not have grandchildren.

I tried to reassure her that was not a foregone conclusion.

# MAX

Max is twelve and I am ten. He is a foster child in the care of one of my mother's colleagues, Joanna, whose vast and hideous home has seen a parade of such children, deposited and looked after for days or weeks or months, alongside her own two sons.

Joanna has a meeting and has been unable to find anyone to look after Max one afternoon, so he will spend time with me, playing. He is thin, athletic, blonde. I am instantly attracted to him, but also feel a duty of care that I have never felt before, which takes me by surprise. I know he is a foster child, and because my mother has worked as a lobbyist on childcare issues I understand what this means. I have met other foster children in Joanna's care, and in the care of other foster parents we know across the city.

Max and I do art at the long counter in our basement craft room. There are pads of paper, paints, markers, glue, glitter. I draw spaceships. Max draws tanks. We have a snack: peanut butter on celery sticks. My mother is upstairs in her office. The care of Max, such as it is, has been put in my hands, and I take it seriously. I do not ask him questions about his life. I assume he would not want to be asked. Foster care is something that happens to people who have had horrible experiences – that's how I understand it. When I don't think he's looking, I examine his tanned muscular arms with fine white-blonde hairs, the hard line of jaw, the cropped hair. He is a boy in a way I will never be. Along with desire I feel a complex blend of insecurity in his presence, a wishing to be liked by him, an under-current of empathy that sails close to pity, and a longing for our encounter to be over as quickly as possible because I also recognize that we have nothing in common.

When Joanna comes to pick Max up, I am relieved to be rid of him, not because he was unpleasant, but because I felt the weight of responsibility to be nice, to switch off my own curiosity, to play with him as I would play with a much younger child. And I am relieved because he is blank, passive, almost affectless, and the unrespon-siveness is exhausting. There is no *character* evident, just a mild but unengaging presence – almost zombie-like, as if he has been sedated or hypnotized. During our time together, he expressed no strong desires to do one thing over another, listlessly setting himself to whatever pastime I suggested. He took orders well. I could have told him to do anything, it occurs to me, and he probably would have complied.

I recount to Joanna what we did in the way a patronizing nursery school teacher or babysitter might describe looking after a four-year-old: we did some art in the basement, and then we had a snack, and then we watched TV, *but nothing inappropriate*. 'We' as passive-aggressive care-speak signifying the other who is too remotely other to be fully sympathetic, rather than 'we' as the inclusive personal pronoun it ought to be. 'Nothing inappropriate' as if I were the older of the two, the one who might indeed have seen something inappropriate and took responsibility for policing the viewing of the older/younger child.

I never see Max again.

# QUEERED

When Andrew's father falls ill, we decide to take a six-month break from the adoption approval process. On our return, we are assigned a new social worker, Gemma. In the days before our first meeting, I look at her social media accounts, clicking through what little she has made public.

There is an image of her on her birthday. She is smiling and cheery looking, our age, perhaps slightly older. She has four children, all boys.

When she comes to our flat for the first meeting, on a warm wet morning in July, I sense that this is not going to go well. There is something in her manner that puts my back up. Once we sit down in the living room with coffee and muffins I have baked, she goes straight to the matter that is already agitating her and which will agitate most of the other social workers we encounter over the next two and a half years.

Gemma is uncomfortable with the fact that Andrew and I both identify as 'queer' in our workbooks. For Gemma, 'queer' is so derogatory she can hardly bring herself to say the word. I suppose this should be admirable, but her discomfort with our own conception of ourselves puts me on the defensive and betrays her ignorance that the word has been actively reclaimed and rehabilitated since the late 1980s. She asks us to explain why we use it. Although we have done so already in the workbooks, we begin to present our understanding of 'queer' as informed by our reading and teaching of queer theory.

She looks unpersuaded by our patient explanation and I can tell that she is uncomfortable in our presence in a way that Eleanor was not, in a way that no one else we have met in the whole process so far has indicated they might be.

She has a look through our flat, pointing out everything that will have to change, all the places where sharp edges will need to be softened or buffered, the necessity of installing gates here and here and here, at the tops and bottoms of stairs, into the kitchen, at the door of the child's bedroom. What a lot of books, she says, as if the books disturb her. You'll want to put doors on those bookcases. Grubby little hands…

Back in the living room, she asks us about our art, the West African masks, the prints by South African artists. One image in particular, of Eve departing the Garden of Eden, Eve's face buried in her hands, concerns her.

It seems like a very sad picture, she says. What do you imagine a child might think of that?

Is she asking us to change our art? I grew up with all manner of art on the walls, was taken to museums from infancy and held up to see much more realistic nudes than our cartoonish Eve.

How do you think it might make a child who's had a very sad beginning in life feel to look at a picture like that? she asks.

We suggest that a 'sad picture' might be a talking point, a way to think about feelings, although this does not seem to satisfy her. Before she came, I suggested to Andrew that we take down the art, not because it is obscene or offensive – it is neither – but because I feared we might end up with someone who may never have been to a museum and has no idea how to look at a piece of art, who sees in the representation of a naked body – however stylized or abstracted – something quite other than what the artist intended. What would she say if we told her that we found it rather funny to have a shame-faced Eve hanging over our bed?

We can tell that we are befuddling Gemma and so start to slip into a teacherly mode of explanation, trying to describe for her the nature of our lives, trying to make her see that we are nothing terrifying, that we are more normal than she imagines, but perhaps our idea of normal is very remote from her own.

We describe our days, the way we get up at seven, have coffee, eat breakfast together, and then go to work. If Andrew does not have a class to teach, he and I might both work at home in our respective studies, writing and reading all morning before breaking for lunch, which will last an hour, without fail. After lunch, I sometimes go for a walk if I'm home alone, and if not then the two of us will work through the afternoon until we might go for a walk together, or to the gym, and then make dinner. Or, if Andrew has been at work, I'll have dinner ready for him when he gets home, and—

You cook every night? Gemma asks, sounding incredulous.

Yes, I say, we cook every night, unless we happen to go out to eat, but that doesn't happen very often.

And who's the cook?

We both cook.

She makes a note.

And then, after dinner, we watch a movie, or a couple of episodes of a series, and then read before going to bed and get up the next morning and do it all again.

And what about weekends?

Weekends we might go shopping together, or for a walk, or to see a movie, or to a gallery, and some weekends we work. Some weekends are no different structurally to our weekdays.

She makes a note.

You do a lot of reading then, she says a little hesitantly, and I think of Eleanor, who saw our many books as possibilities, exciting ones.

Gemma wants to know about our social lives, whether we go to clubs and bars, what it will be like to give up that sort of thing.

We don't go to clubs or bars. We don't go out dancing. That's not the kind of life we have. That's not the kind of life we've ever had.

Our social life is about lunches and dinners, usually in our home or in the homes of our friends, most of whom, as a matter of fact, are opposite-sex couples.

The formulation seems to confuse Gemma. Her face wrinkles.

Do you mean straight couples? she asks.

Yes, I say.

She makes a note.

In retrospect I think about Didier Eribon's description in his book *Returning to Reims* of the demands made on people who identify as queer. 'The social order puts pressure on all of us,' he says. 'All those people who want things to be "regular," or "meaningful," or to correspond to "stable points of reference" know they can count on the way adherence to the norm is inculcated into the deepest levels of our consciousness from our earliest years' and that 'anyone inhabiting... alternative family forms' is 'required... to experience them as somehow deviant or abnormal, and thus inferior and shameful'.

At the same time, however, Eribon articulates his 'distrust of the opposite kind of injunction', a distrust I share, because it insists, in ways that are 'just as profoundly normative' as the shaming conservative pressure, that the queer person or couple '*be* abnormal' because 'non-normativity' functions in this case 'as a kind of prescribed "subversion"'.[10]

I sense in Gemma's response to us a strange combination of these forces: on the one hand it feels as though she cannot help seeing us as abnormal, even though I am sure she would insist there is nothing shameful about our status as a same-sex couple, and on the other hand she seems both to expect a certain performance of abnormality that we refuse *and also* to fear that our description of ourselves as 'queer' is an indication of a degree of abnormality much greater and darker than any she would associate with a couple who described themselves as 'gay'.

\*

Our first meeting with Gemma lasts three hours, but seems to be much longer, three days, three weeks, every minute of question and answer expanding and swallowing time, stretching me out through its long digestive temporal processes so that at the end of it I collapse into bed, wondering what is yet to come, how someone like her can ever be made to understand who we are, how we live in the world, what makes us tick.

The fatigue, the elongation of those hours, comes from the sense that we are now required to deal with someone who struggles to understand what is obvious to us, and what was obvious to Eleanor when we met with her. For Gemma, I begin to sense that even the simplest detail of the way we live requires careful explication, and then those clarifications seem to require explanations of their own because, in thinking we have cleared up a particular point, we discover we have assumed an area of common knowledge that is alien to her. We have to educate at the same time that we are trying to describe who we are, to demonstrate our capacity and suitability to parent, and we have to do it all with a sense of patience and goodwill that is often difficult to sustain. I try to remind myself that Gemma is just doing her job, asking what she must, and whether I like the way she does it or not is beside the point. I just have to get through it.

We see Gemma two weeks later, at the end of July, and three more times in August. At each of these meetings we talk about ourselves, we discuss potential kinds of children, situations with children, but never at the end of any of these conversations do I come away feeling I have learned something useful about what it might be like to parent an adopted child. I begin to understand that such instruction is not the point. The point is for Gemma to determine if we are capable of parenting an adopted child, but I had expected a more reciprocal process of information sharing. Instead she expects that we should be reading about adoption on our own time, poring over guides and books and pamphlets and websites. Her job is to assess rather than educate.

As a test of our capacity to 'be fun', Gemma brings a video game console to one of the meetings and asks us to play a dance-off game that has us thrashing around our living room while she sits in the corner, videoing us on her smartphone without asking our permission and convulsed with laughter. We do one dance contest, then another, and another, the steps growing faster each time, the moves more difficult, and we are so desperate to pass this ridiculous test that we throw ourselves into the activity, but feel at the same time a rising sickness and sense of misgiving about the whole situation.

When Gemma leaves we look at each other, struggling to fathom what has happened. I feel strangely violated. Andrew is irritated but willing to go along with whatever is necessary, within reason. We fear that to resist anything our social worker demands would imperil our chances of being approved as adopters, but the idea that dancing to a video game in any way signals our capacity to parent strikes us as both ludicrous and depressing.

Is *this* how social workers determine the suitability of prospective adopters? Does it matter at all that many of our friends with children don't even allow video games in the house? Would Gemma understand if we said that we would find other ways – non-technological ways – of entertaining a child? Does she even believe that children can be entertained without video games or tablets or smartphones, or that it's okay for children to be bored or to be given time to entertain themselves?

Gemma's philosophy of raising children seems to rest on a belief that when they are awake, they must be occupied, they cannot be left alone even for an instant, and while that is certainly true of infants, Andrew and I can both recall being left to draw or read or play with minimal supervision from our mothers when we were three and four and five years old.

What has shifted in the world so that the idea of unstructured play is regarded not just as undesirable, but actively *wrong*?

Despite such odd moments, it is clear that Gemma is not finding anything about us that can really give her pause. Even if she does not always understand us, we are able to answer all of her questions, even those that strike us as inappropriate.

In the weeks before the approval panel, Gemma starts sending emails with questions that she feels need to be answered. Most of these are straightforward, but then she writes to ask how I might have been affected by the terrorist attacks of September 11, 2001. We have spoken about the attacks in our previous meetings, but only insofar as they are a marker for me, having happened just weeks before I moved to Britain to begin my graduate studies at Oxford. I reply to her question:

> I could write a book about this, and I don't see that it's necessarily relevant for this process, nor something I can summarize in a few lines or paragraphs. I think this is true of anyone who lived in New York before the attacks. If pressed, I would say only that it made me value friends and family and life even more than I did before.

She does not respond to my answer, but I am left wondering why she would think it necessary to explore this.

The approval panel is made up of women and men of various ages, races, professions and social backgrounds. It all goes surprisingly smoothly, barring another question about our use of the word 'queer'. We patiently explain once more that this is how we understand ourselves, how we describe ourselves to ourselves, and in the spirit of honesty we chose to use this word in the adoption workbooks because to describe ourselves as 'gay' does not fit as comfortably with our sense of who we are and how we function in the world. The panel seems satisfied and shortly after concluding the conversation the chair comes to tell us that we have been unanimously approved.

For the first time since embarking on this process we both feel an uncomplicated sense of hope, even of joy. And yet, looking at Gemma, I have the impression that the panel's decision surprises her. It occurs to me that she may never have had faith in us in the first place, and I wonder, as we contemplate moving on to the next stages, how this may affect our search for a child.

A few days later, she sends us an email addressed to 'Andrew and David', asking whether we're celebrating yet.

## CITIZEN RUTH

Over spring break of my freshman year in college I went home to Omaha to find my family splitting apart. There was more to the story than I knew at the time and it would be another two years before I heard all of it. My mother had decided a decade earlier to get her doctorate and, now that I was done with high school, to search for a job wherever it might take her. She had phoned me at Georgetown to say she was sending a plane ticket and I would need to come home for the break because we had to talk about something as a family.

Typically for us, the matter was not discussed immediately on my arrival. It required careful stage management, and, atypically for us, a public venue. I wonder now whether my mother was trying to cast off the shame of our dysfunction, or, more likely, if she feared what discussing her news alone in the house might ignite.

We went to a restaurant downtown where my mother revealed that she had been offered a job in upstate New York. She wondered what we thought about it.

I didn't hesitate. I told her to take it.

My parents had been married for more than three decades and this was a relief after the years of combustible anger that crackled around the three of us. Throughout high school my closest friends would often ask why my parents stayed together. I long knew it was not a happy marriage, that we were not and had never been a happy family, but I also thought we managed to keep all of that hidden from the rest of the world, as if our unhappiness were known only to us.

I went back to Georgetown, finished the semester, then returned to Omaha in May to pack up the house and leave with my mother. By that time, I had been accepted as a transfer student to NYU's Tisch School of the Arts, and it was clear to me that the only sensible choice was to get out of Nebraska.

During those weeks, there was constant arguing over furniture and art and who was getting the three cats. My mother took all the good art, most of the best furniture, and all three of the cats.

In the midst of packing, a woman from my father's church phoned to tell me that the producers of a film shooting in the area were looking for extras. As a child I had been active in community theatre and once appeared in a training video for the famous children's home Boys Town, sitting in the back of a classroom as a not very convincing juvenile delinquent with floppy hair and baggy sweatshirt.

The person I spoke with in the film's production office gave me directions to a bowling alley across the Missouri River in Council Bluffs, Iowa. I spent most of the next day at a sticky table overlooking the lanes reading Kazuo Ishiguro's *Remains of the Day*, hoping the book's recent film adaptation would suggest to the director that here was a young man with an artistic sensibility who could really do something interesting on screen. I tried to read with dramatic flair, contorting my face with surprise and amusement and meditative engrossment, pretending I was somewhere other than a bowling alley in a blue-collar Midwestern town.

None of us had heard of the director, Alexander Payne, but people were proud that he was an Omahan who had been to UCLA and decided to come home to shoot his first feature, the abortion satire *Citizen Ruth*. If my work as an extra didn't open doors to Hollywood stardom, at least there was the sixty bucks for an easy day's work and the chance of very minor local fame that seems to matter when you're nineteen.

Late in the afternoon the production assistants marched us a few blocks away to a building ringed with chain-link fence and barbed wire at the edge of a run-down residential neighbourhood. They began dividing us into anti-abortion protestors and abortion clinic defenders. At a critical moment I edged towards the second camp and they put me in a yellow poncho with two bumper stickers plastered across my chest.

One of these stickers said 'Celebrate Diversity' and the other, in what the costumers no doubt thought was a stroke of comic genius, 'Keep Your Laws Off My Body'. I wanted to ask them, 'Don't you see that I'm a boy?', and 'What does a rainbow-striped diversity sticker have to do with abortion rights anyway?', but I figured they knew what they were doing and the joke would make sense to the audience even if it didn't to me.

That's not strictly true. It did make sense, I just didn't want to get it. In the previous months, I had come out for the first time to a few friends at Georgetown, and the bumper stickers were both thrilling and terrifying, as though the costumer had recognized a truth about me that I was only beginning to see myself and did not want to imagine might be visible to anyone else. Or maybe the costumer didn't read me for what I was and thought it was funny because I looked so straight (khakis, button-down Oxford shirt). It's impossible to know one way or the other. I had been trying to keep my gender and sexuality in check for so many years that I could no longer tell what my tells might be, or when they would flare into view and give me away.

For the rest of the day I stood with a stern expression behind that chain-link fence and helped usher Laura Dern and Tippi Hedren from a car into the building that served as the clinic. In breaks between shots, Payne and the lead actors ate sushi from large catering trays. I had never eaten sushi and would not do so until I moved to Manhattan later that year, when more

75

cosmopolitan friends would introduce me to what they called Disco Sushi on Avenue A and I stuck a pyramid of wasabi in my mouth thinking something so vividly green must also be sweet.

At the end of the day's shooting I went home and a week later my mother and the three cats and I drove to New York, staying in roadside motels, the cats smuggled in their carriers through back doors and allowed to roam the dingy rooms. I forgot about the movie.

Later that summer I moved into NYU housing, just around the corner from Bellevue Hospital. I met the first guy I ever kissed, Brody, a gender studies student from Mississippi with a line in white t-shirts that showed off the gentle curve of his biceps. We were both dreaming of success, of one kind or another.

After we made out in his dorm room a few times, Brody said that kissing me made him feel like a woman. I was too embarrassed to confess that kissing him made me worry about disease and what my family and friends from home would be likely to say about someone so flamboyant. I can still remember what he tasted like and the things he said to me about my body, the way I wanted him and his mouth, but was also uncomfortable with his campness and squealing laughter.

I know now that both of us were suffering from internalized homophobia and the cousin of misogyny that so often accompanies it. Even in New York, Brody and I were both grappling with the shame that attached itself to our desire. I was too naïve and politically disengaged to think about how 'Keep Your Laws Off My Body' could ever be pertinent to my own life as a young queer man who would keep shuttling in and out of the closet for another six years before deciding that life was too short to keep anything in closets but shoes and clothes and the rubbish of life I was too tired to file or throw away.

*

When *Citizen Ruth* was released and later went to video, friends emailed or phoned to ask if it was possible they had seen me, briefly, towards the end of the film, standing behind a chain-link fence in a yellow poncho. I am most visible in a lingering close-up, posed next to a woman who speaks briefly into a walkie-talkie.

Watching the scene now, I'm surprised by my awkwardness and physical self-consciousness. No one was going to turn me into Henry Fonda or Montgomery Clift, let alone Marlon Brando – all Omaha boys in their time – and luckily some part of me must have understood that was the case. I gave up acting soon after, or at least gave up the fantasy of being an actor. Performance requires a forgetting of the self and a public vulnerability I knew I was never going to master.

Twenty years later, here is the irony that strikes me as a middle-aged man married to a man who never embarrasses him, in whose company I never feel shame, and with whom I am trying to form a family: at that critical moment in my own outing of myself to the world, I played an activist version of my actual self, a queer abortion clinic defender, asserting the rights of women to make their own choices about their bodies. For my own sense of myself, I knew that even in the realm of fiction I could not risk appearing as an anti-abortion protestor, occupying an ideological position that remains anathema to me.[11]

At the end of *Citizen Ruth*, Laura Dern's character does the unimaginable. She flees the warring factions of abortion rights activists and anti-choice zealots, heading off into the distance to make her own choice, whatever it might be. As viewers, we can be certain only of the options that might remain to her: to become a 'single mother', one of the most vilified menaces of the 1990s culture wars in America, right up there with the mythological 'welfare queen'. Or she will do what my husband and I and countless others like us hope she will do for our own sakes: give up her child for adoption, or, failing that, lose all her rights to motherhood because she is unable to look after the child, or care for it, or demonstrate that subjective quantum of good enough parenting required by the state.

# YOU

I try to imagine what it is like to be you in the first year of your life. I can do this with myself, envision what my infancy was like, the way my parents would have attended to me, how my grandmothers cared for me when my mother was in the hospital for six weeks immediately after my birth. I have photographs that tell me I was not just looked at with joy and adoration, but also held and cuddled and kissed, in a nursery all yellow and white.

The question is, are my powers of empathy and imagination great enough to imagine what your own life was like in the absence of any information about it that I can trust as reliable or objective?

I will skip over the few details I eventually learn, the reasons that give the social workers cause to worry, reasons that convince a judge – as far as I understand the procedures – that you and your brothers and sisters should be removed from the family home. A terrible decision to have to make, I am sure, a terrible decision for your parents to accept, and one they will fight to overturn for years to come. Know that they wanted you, wanted always to keep you.

From what little I know, without rationalizing their failures, I have deep sympathy for your mother and father. I can imagine how overwhelming a household with five children must seem, how difficult it may feel, with little formal education and no jobs, to make a life for themselves and for you.

But their shortcomings and failures are real. If we believe what we are later told, you and your siblings are not taken without cause, even if there may have been good times amidst the bad, nights when all seven of you were home and happy and laughing, with games and jokes and the warmth of your love for one another. I want to believe there was love there, that some days were good even as others were not.

# SEARCHING

I n preparation for Gemma beginning to search for a suitable match, she asks us to write a brief profile describing ourselves. This takes longer than it should, and Andrew and I are never certain we get it right. Self-deprecation? Self-aggrandizement? Sentiment? Sang-froid? No one tells us what tone we should strike. We end up with a text that pleases neither of us, even if we agree with all that it says:

> We are a loving couple who have been together for more than twelve years and are looking forward to being great dads to a girl or boy.
>
> We have a circle of friends with young children who live in London, Oxford and Cambridge (as well as Cape Town and New York!). As we've been thinking about starting our own family we've enjoyed spending time with these friends, seeing how they go about their lives and the kinds of things they enjoy doing together...
>
> We believe that we can offer a child a loving home and family, stability and long-term security, as well as opportunities to grow and discover and learn. We are keen to provide an environment that will foster curiosity and creativity while respecting that a child will always be her or his own person.

The discourse of the 'loving couple' seems trite, even though it is true, and the formulation 'two dads' gendered in a way that makes me uncomfortable. How much better if we could write, 'We are a politically radical queer couple who, although appearing in the world as male, inhabit identities more complex than binary gender allows, and who want more than anything to raise a child who will be their own person, whatever that might be, and to give that person all the love we have to offer.'

But the system can barely understand who we are even when we fall back on trite formulations, so we know better than to sabotage our chances at this stage by trying to present ourselves as anything other than what the system sees as 'normal'.

'Normal' is what we have to appear to be. As 'normal' as any heterosexual British couple, with all the exclamation marks and stodgy sentimentality we can muster. The references to friends in Cape Town and New York are probably a mistake. They make us look too foreign, too unpredictable, although it is true that we have been imagining how we might leave the country and never look back once the court signs off on the adoption and the child – whoever she or he might be – is legally ours. That would be our right, and we might well choose to exercise it.

It's true, too, that we enjoy spending time with friends who have kids. Seeing how those children complete our friends' lives – often in ways they could never have predicted – has helped us decide to pursue this for ourselves. It's true that we can provide a loving home, a sense of family, financial and other kinds of stability, the promise of long-term security, however modest it might be, and opportunities to explore the world. Even when the language itself is designed to speak to the most conventionally minded social worker, we still mean what we say, and hope that it sounds convincing.

Later, I will read this description of ourselves and think it both too much (still too foreign, still too highbrow, still too difficult, because we wrote it in complete sentences, with commas and correct grammar, unlike many other profiles I have seen), and also too little (too little of who we really are, in all our strangeness but also our

82

ordinariness, too little that demonstrates how most of our days are as deeply dull as any other couple's).

Only a month after our approval as adopters, we receive the first profile, a boy of six months named M—. He has no known health problems, what is described as a happy disposition, and only one foster placement so far. Even better, he was voluntarily given up by his birth parents. When the profile comes through, Andrew is in South Africa and I am in New York but we decide over the phone that we are definitely interested.

Already we begin to imagine M— coming to live with us, but no one tells us this child's profile is going out wide across Britain to every prospective adopter. No one says, as they might have: you are competing against straight couples who have been childless for years, who go to church every Sunday, who live in a detached house with a fenced-in garden in a quaint rural village – in other words, couples who will look attractive to social workers in ways we will not.

No one says what we soon come to understand is likely closer to the truth: that as a bi-national queer couple, both immigrants to Britain, both academics whose lives are centred around books, living in a rented flat in London, even though we have been judged acceptable as adopters, we are probably at the bottom of the heap. Everyone else, except perhaps single adopters, is preferable to us, and even a single British woman adopting would, I suspect, rank higher.

So although approved as adopters, we must now prove anew, over and over again, that we are a good match for every possible child who might strike us as suitable. And we have to make that kind of case with no sense of who the children's social workers might be, what prejudices they might harbour, or what evidence they might require that would convince them of our suitability.

Nor do we know at this stage that a judgment by Sir James Munby, president of the Family Division of the High Court of England and

Wales, has sent a chill through the entire adoption and foster care system.[12] Although government ministers will later claim that the law did not change and that social workers misinterpreted Munby's ruling, the effects are almost instantly clear: a sharp reduction in the number of children available because social workers believe they must now consider even remote family connections as potential guardians before a child is considered as a candidate for adoption.

When we start, there are three times as many children available to adopt on the online linking system we end up using as there are potential adopters. In the next year, thanks in part to Munby's judgment, and in part to the government's drive to recruit more adopters, I watch the ratio flip, until there are three times as many adopters as children.

Three adoptive couples chasing every available child, and all of us hoping, perversely, that more children will come into the system, which means we are hoping, horribly, that more women will have children they feel they cannot look after, or that more women and men will have children they don't manage to look after properly and whom the authorities have no choice but to remove for the children's safety.

How can we be hoping for such a terrible scenario?

How is *this* any more ethical than paying a woman to have a child on our behalf with proper legal agreements in place and the woman paid for her time and trouble and risk and everyone clear where each person stands?

We hear nothing again about the boy called M—. Silence is the only answer to our query. Gemma hears nothing. She writes to his social workers to ask for feedback and receives no response.

She starts presenting us with other profiles, but none of these strike us as right. The children have serious health problems, disabilities, chromosomal disorders, global developmental delays, histories of sexual abuse, or tortuously complex birth families with whom we would have no choice but to engage because the courts have mandated ongoing contact with one or more birth parents or siblings or extended family members.

A child who is described as 'quiet and obedient' looks as though she may have undiagnosed mental disabilities. We remind Gemma that we don't feel able to look after children with serious medical or genetic problems. When we keep saying no, reminding her what we are looking for, she sends us a checklist indicating which conditions we do and do not feel able to consider.

Gemma encourages us to sign up for the online matching platform, which allows us to monitor profiles of children who are available, but these are only the profiles – we come to understand much later – of children who have been judged by their social workers as particularly difficult to place.

Nonetheless, we start to make enquiries, sending off enthusiastic messages about children who appear in the database. There are descriptions of each child, a handful of photographs, sometimes a video. There are infants and toddlers and sibling groups, white children, black children, children from European parents – many Polish or Eastern European – and children from Roma and Irish Traveller backgrounds.

In February 2015, I find the profile of Z—, a black British girl under the age of two who has no health problems and no history of abuse. She looks adorable, charming, with an extraordinary smile and bright expression. We send an enquiry, and in less than twenty minutes receive a rejection from Z—'s social worker. I assume this is either because we are white, or because we are a same-sex couple, although it says on her profile that they are open to other ethnicities and there is no suggestion that she needs both a mother and a father, as some profiles explicitly stipulate. Our query is permanently closed, meaning that we cannot ever enquire about her again. Over the course of the next year, I watch Z—'s profile remain on the system, still available, but not to us. We would have taken her then, immediately, that very day, and welcomed her into our lives. We would have given her a loving family. We would have been thrilled to have her.

Over the ensuing months we become more and more distraught and confused, as Gemma sends profiles that continue to be poor matches for our requirements, while asking repeatedly whether we are looking ourselves, and where we are looking. In exasperation, I write to ask whether she can find out any further information about M— and Z—, or at least if she can manage to get feedback from their social workers about our profile. Although we are not naturally inclined to look for homophobia as an explanation, the failure of M—'s social workers to explain their decision against us and the speed with which Z—'s social worker rejected our enquiry suggests that both may be looking for an opposite-sex couple. Our understanding is that all other factors being equal, and unless there is a strong determination that a child needs a mother and a father, discriminating against a same-sex couple is illegal, and at the very least a breach of policy if that is found to be the case.

Gemma, however, cannot even see the other social worker's details because the person has declined further contact. It might be illegal to consider racial difference when placing children for adoption in Britain, but I become convinced that it happens every day.

In May, while I am on a speaking tour in South Africa, Andrew attends an Adoption Exchange Day where he runs into Eleanor, the wonderful social worker who saw us through Stage 1. She is stunned that we are still searching, that we have not already been matched with a child, and yet she is the first social worker to express any feeling of this kind.

At one point I ask Gemma's manager whether the fact that Andrew and I are not listed as 'White British' (we are classed as 'White Other') in our racial categorization may automatically eliminate us from consideration for children who are themselves 'White British' and whose profiles indicate they should be placed with adopters of the same ethnic group. (I imagine matching software only pulling up exact ethnic and racial matches for such children.) In the end, she does not have an answer.

In writing this, and rereading the email exchanges to refresh my memory, I still feel a sense of injustice. I say to myself and to Andrew, *we could have done more. We could have pushed harder. We could have made a nuisance of ourselves.*

Part of this frustration is with myself, with us, that we did not make ourselves difficult and impossible to ignore.

And yet I also wonder, is our failure to push harder, our failure to be troublesome until we got the child we wanted, not a symptom of our ambivalence about adoption itself? If we really wanted it, would we not have striven tirelessly in pursuit of it? Would we not have read every book ever written about adoption? Would we not have been able to speak so convincingly about adoption that no one would have doubted us for an instant?

Or is it a symptom of the way the system appears to me now to have worked to make us feel disempowered, to demonstrate to us over and over again that our requests for further information would be refused, that we could shout all we want and be found, in the end, simply difficult, and easy to ignore?

# ANNIE

When I was in the first grade I was obsessed with John Huston's 1982 film adaptation of the musical *Annie*. I had an *Annie*-themed seventh birthday party with *Annie* invitations and *Annie* favours. We played musical chairs in the backyard to the soundtrack from *Annie*, my mother lifting the needle on the portable record player and sending us scurrying – boys and girls alike – to find our seats. That Halloween I dressed up as Daddy Warbucks with cravat and blazer and a bald cap pasted to my skin with spirit glue. If I had been able to dress up as Annie in her red dress and frizzy curls, that would have been my preference, but I knew without having to be told that this was an impossibility. To satisfy my desire to inhabit the world of the film I had to take the role of the only male character with whom I felt able to identify: the rich man (though my family was not rich) who takes in the orphan and adopts her. How it must have galled my left-wing parents that I dressed up as a Republican billionaire, failing at the age of seven to see the film's politics, the Bolsheviks trying to assassinate Warbucks because he stands as a symbol of the success of American capitalism.

In my private play at home, my mother working in some other room, I would put on the record, sing along, and do cartwheels across the dining room. I was Annie, not Daddy Warbucks, or I was both Annie and Daddy Warbucks, since my mother would also sit at the piano playing songs from the musical and I would just as readily sing Warbucks's 'N.Y.C.' as Annie's 'Tomorrow' or 'It's a Hard Knock Life'. I could imagine myself both as orphan – the archetypal ginger child in need of adoption – as well as adopter.

In 2012, a friend did a tarot reading for me. I don't believe in the occult, but I was happy to play along. She claimed that the cards said that if we were to adopt, it would all happen quickly, and we would end up with a girl.

I am suggestible enough that the idea of a daughter took root, and the vision of a little girl in need of a home became stronger and clearer in my mind. Although my relationship with my father has now, years later, settled into a gentleness and affection it has taken us a lifetime to achieve, a component of this desire for a daughter is inflected by anxiety about a genealogy of failure in father–son relationships. My paternal grandfather was a philanderer, an adulterer, an embezzler, as well as being physically (and probably also emotionally and psychologically) abusive. My own father has spent his entire life struggling to recover from that bad fathering (although the failures of mothering in his family were just as acute). As a result, my relationship with my father was always already over-determined from the moment of my conception.

The idea that I might fail to break out of the bad models of father–son relationships I have inherited terrifies, while the prospect of a father–daughter relationship that might be built without any prior models offers hope.

Andrew and I embarked on the adoption process knowing we would be happy with either a boy or a girl, that we wanted to be parents rather than to inhabit any particular dyads of parenting. I want to believe that being a same-sex couple means we can be parents in whatever mould we choose. We don't have to conform to gender roles because to parent effectively we will need to be both and at the same time mother-fatherly and father-motherly, to borrow and bend Virginia Woolf's formulation. Nonetheless, I know that raising a daughter would not present me with the visceral memories I retain of *being* fathered.

In Huston's film, Annie's desire to find her birth parents propels her into real physical peril. Daddy Warbucks is on the verge of adopting her. He has blackmailed the alcoholic and abusive orphanage matron, Miss Hannigan, to get her to sign the necessary papers. He is willing to make the empathetic leap necessary to take in this precocious 'cheeky' child who disrupts his vision of himself and the orderliness of his world, even as Annie is also a source of light and affection and joy. Her fixation on the birth family persuades Warbucks to help her search for that couple, offering a reward that invites the attention of Hannigan's brother, the escaped convict Rooster, and his girlfriend Lily, who pursue Annie almost to her death.

The film's message for adopters and for the adopted is clear: do not go looking for the past. Do not venture in search of biological origins. Even if the birth parents are already dead, as in Annie's case, you may find much worse aspirant parents, pretenders who are in it only for their own enrichment. This message neatly (if uncomfortably) reflects the anxiety of so many adopters, that in the case of a closed adoption the birth parents might one day emerge to wreak havoc on the carefully constructed adoptive home.

Faced with a real child, with real biological parents and real biological siblings, I suspect these fears might not seem unfounded. We would have to accept the possibility of spending the rest of our lives entangled with people whose very presence could be difficult and painful for us to manage. We would have to trust in ourselves to find ways of negotiating future life events, the child wanting to know his or her biological parents, perhaps wishing them present for milestones like graduations and holidays and marriage and even the birth of their own children, who, I start reminding myself, would be our grandchildren only in name but *truly* the grandchildren of those biological parents who I don't really want to know in the first place. All of this requires faith that any attenuation of family connection would never threaten whatever bonds we might be able to forge over the course of our daughter's or our son's childhood and adolescence. It demands a bravery I will have to learn to cultivate.

# YOU

**W**hen you arrive at the home of your foster parents you are just over twelve months old. It is after dark, late evening, or perhaps even later, the middle of the night.

I can imagine how terrifying it must have been – even if the transition was calm, even if your mother and father agreed in that moment that they could not look after you.

I know that being placed in a strange car, driven in the night, arriving at a strange house, passed to the arms of strangers, however loving and warm they might have been, however hard they would have worked to make you comfortable, to reassure you, to wash you and dress you in clean pyjamas, when you were eventually put in a strange crib in a strange room, with the smell of the sea coming in through the open window on a warm spring night, I am sure you must have been terrified. Your siblings, who had done their best to fill in the gaps of your parents' care, were suddenly gone. Your parents, who I want to imagine showed you love, had vanished. The rooms that you had come to know as your own were lost.

In this new house, in this new place, everything would have been different, sounds different, the quality of darkness in a village different from the lights of the town you had come from. Silence would have magnified the difference. It might have been the first night in your life that you slept in a room alone, with no other children to wake you or prod you or coo to you when you woke in the night and cried out.

# ENVY

In the midst of this process of searching that seems increasingly thwarted, I feel anxiety and paranoia and a sort of despoiled hope. Hope stripped of its anticipatory happiness or the pleasure that should accompany it. Hope that is closer to desperate longing, undercut by a certainty that what I hope for will inevitably be disappointed. I feel envy towards friends who already have children, continue to have children, may yet have children. I feel envious of strangers with children. I feel envy when I see a young father parenting well, on his own, parenting warmly and closely in a way that my own father did not. I feel envious of pregnant women. I feel envious of trans men who are able to become pregnant and give birth and then, miraculously, carry on being men. I feel envious of people I know or meet with biological children who are smart, funny, well adjusted, healthy, laughing, or who, when sad or injured or ill, can be comforted with comparative ease, people who look like one another and are able to inhabit their lives in such apparently uncomplicated ways. I am envious of that security and stability, that sense of uninterrogated connection.

Literary critic and cultural theorist Sianne Ngai explains in her book *Ugly Feelings* that envy has historically been seen both as a feminine and a working-class feeling. In Freudian psychology, for instance, women have been constructed (problematically) as envying the penis, and in any number of classist descriptions of the proletariat, we see (problematically) those with fewer material resources envying the objects and luxuries that the bourgeoisie and the rich enjoy. However troubling these examples are, Ngai notes that envy is 'the *only* negative emotion' that is 'defined specifically by... forms of inequality', and this is the spur to her important intervention in thinking through the implications of how envy operates, and how our sense of it might be revised.

What Ngai suggests is that envy becomes the mark of a given person's 'polemical response' to relations that are characterized by their sense of having less than some other person. The problem arises when, as is so often the case, society begins to think of envy as a characteristic of the envying individual, as being integral to who they are, so that envying people are seen as 'lacking' or 'deficient', marked by their envy in ways that become essentializing: I envy therefore I *am* lack, I *am* deficiency.

The consequence is that when a person's envy – my envy of people with children, for instance – becomes visible to a wider public, it will, Ngai says, 'always seem unjustified and critically effete', even and perhaps especially when the inequality that is the foundation of such envy is objectively real.[13] This is where things get tricky, or sticky, because Ngai suggests that while a person might envy a specific *thing* – a wealthy friend's sports car, a colleague's large and beautiful home, a neighbour's lavish lifestyle – that person's envy develops into a desire to destroy the car, the home, the lifestyle that the envying person wishes she or he possessed. We wish for that which we see others enjoying, and the unfulfillment of those desires pushes us to want to destroy the thing in order to ruin the enjoyment of the person we envy and so neutralize the ugly feeling we find ourselves experiencing.

Envy is what I feel, and I know it is a bad feeling, an ugly feeling, but it is one I can never seem to escape. To reveal this envy publicly is to open myself to the derision of those people – perhaps friends among them – who may see it as unjustified and, given the queer valence of my envy's spin, unquestionably effete. *Look at that queer man longing for a baby, envious of straight couples, longing as if having children were a fundamental human right, longing in a way that makes it seem as though he is aping the maternal impulse.*

What is it to be effete? Ngai is not clear whether she means effete as in 'ineffectual' and 'affected' or 'over-refined' (although that last seems unlikely), or whether she means effete as in 'weak' or 'effeminate'.[14] In revealing my envy publicly, displaying my envy of those with children, I am marking myself as effeminate and weak, signalling my incapacity and deficiency, the fact that as a couple, my husband and I lack the physiology, the capital, and the social relationships to procure for ourselves what so many of our friends produce or acquire with what appears to be relative ease.

Voicing this envy, including in these pages, marks the absolute entry of that bad feeling into 'a public domain of signification' as Ngai puts it, in ways that may appear both unjustified and effete. *Why should he feel envy when he has chosen* not *to have a relationship with a woman? Why should he feel envy when he and his husband have not chosen more lucrative careers that would provide the income necessary to hire a surrogate abroad? Why should he feel envy when he does not open himself to more radical social relations that might grant him what he desires?* This is what I imagine those who judge me may think.

The word *effete* appears in the seventeenth century, derived from 'effetus' in Latin, meaning 'worn out by bearing'.[15] Does this mean that men who are called effete are comparable to a woman who is no longer fertile from having had too many children? Must Andrew and I be regarded as weak (worn out) and feminine in our situational infertility? Is being seen as weak or feminine necessarily a bad thing for two white cisgendered men at this particular moment in history?

I am reading Ngai's book on a London train at rush hour one October evening, surrounded by commuters crammed together and bound for their suburban homes. Whatever their class affiliation, most of the people around me look potentially… enviable. They are well dressed. They have expensive mobile phones and tablets. They wear noise-cancelling headphones that cost hundreds of pounds, smartwatches that are just as pricey, designer shoes and clothes, everything branded and broadcasting a certain cultural or market value that is supposed to arouse desire in others, even to inspire envy.

But here I get caught in a passage in which Ngai is not thinking about material tokens of envy, at least not directly, but instead about Freud's formulation of penis envy and those feminist critiques of his ideas that focus on the construction of femininity in terms of 'lack'. While Ngai agrees with such arguments she is also critical of them for conceiving of envy as the characteristic of a person *marked by* their deficiency, by what they lack, instead of thinking about how the envying person *feels* in the face of what they see as an unfair distribution of things.

I trip over Ngai's discussion of Freudian penis envy not because I disagree with her analysis, but because my mind gets stuck thinking about it. I assume that no woman around me on the train, no woman I know, could have ever felt penis envy because the idea of such a feeling strikes me as risible. In the same instant that I think how absurd the idea of penis envy is, I think also of the spectrum of trans experience and realize there must be trans men who were not born with a penis but might wish to have one, and while this phenomenon is distinct from anything Freud theorized, distinct also from the ways his ideas have been challenged by feminist and queer critics, it is still envy of a kind, or if not envy then an active desire for that other set of genitalia, and there is nothing risible about that, nor would it be an envy that seeks ultimately to destroy the envied object.

Thinking along these lines, reading Ngai in this sweaty train, I am able to articulate for myself for the first time a feeling of womb envy and to understand this not as a quality that marks my own deficiency, or my desire to have a sex change and be a woman (which is absent from this thinking), or my desire to destroy women or their reproductive capacities, but my consciousness of the possibilities – and *benefits* – that having a vagina and uterus and ovaries and fallopian tubes would afford me, imagining what it would mean to be a man with female genitalia.[16]

In Gus Van Sant's biopic about Harvey Milk, when the homophobic city supervisor who will later assassinate Milk sarcastically asks him if it is possible for two men to reproduce, Milk laughs and says, 'No, but God knows we keep trying.'

A while ago I came across a 1968 article on myths of male pregnancy published in *The Journal of Sex Research*. John Money and Geoffrey Hosta describe what they characterize as a widespread belief in the possibility of male rectal pregnancy discovered in the course of interviews conducted with gay black adolescents and young men in the American South.[17] They situate this folklore in a longer cultural tradition, suggesting that in Greek mythology, Pallas Athena's 'birth' from Zeus's head 'is an example of a mythological allusion to a semblance of pregnancy in the male' comparable to 'the Biblical account of the creation of Eve from Adam's rib'. And, in a more ordinary form, they point to traditions of the 'couvade' across cultures.

The five subjects Money and Hosta interview, ranging in age from fourteen to thirty, are fairly consistent in their descriptions of what they each call a 'blood baby'. Their youngest source, Dan, explains that conception occurs through the contact of semen with an internal organ, not with an egg, and 'the semen itself... develops into the baby'. Conception is followed by bleeding from the rectum, accompanied by feelings of illness and swelling of the abdomen. Gestation lasts for six weeks to three months before delivery, 'attended by labor pains'. The baby, which some of their sources say is stillborn, others that it may live for several hours, is said to resemble a smaller, 'gelatinous' version of an actual infant, but with 'no ears, eyes, or hair'. Such a baby, Dan says, 'may be kept for... up to five days' before it 'evaporates or dissolves'.

Money and Hosta do not speculate on the origins of the myth but frame it as a symptom of pregnancy envy. One of their subjects believed that men may contain one or more of their mother's eggs, which become 'trapped in the rectum' during their own gestation and are later fertilized during anal sex, while another subject believed that men – perhaps implicitly only gay men – may contain female organs susceptible to fertilization by the sperm of a partner.

Although it is difficult to give much credence to Money's and Hosta's report – on account of the small size of their sample group and lack of transparency about the ways in which they expressed their questions – it is suggestive nonetheless to think not only of the 'blood baby' myth, but also those much older myths (of Adam's production of Eve and Zeus's of Pallas Athena) as symptoms of the envy some men feel for women's reproductive capacity.

In an article on womb envy, Diana Semmelhack, Larry Ende, Karen Farrell and Julieanne Pojas assert that 'in a culture that... devalues nurturing', such a concept remains difficult even to understand.[18] Despite the fact that there is longstanding and substantial evidence for the phenomenon being widespread, 'mainstream psychological literature' has ignored it, they say, because the very idea undermines 'basic assumptions of our culture', which is to say that western culture has tended both to assume and insist on power dynamics privileging men over women and that the idea of men envying women has to be suppressed or denied. Where Semmelhack and her fellow authors fall short for me is in their failure to imagine that womb envy might be a feeling that can be lived positively by the man who experiences it, that envy itself does not necessarily have to be a negative or ugly feeling. They insist that womb envy, which they see present across Abrahamic religious traditions, is itself intrinsic to the marginal positioning of the act of raising and caring for children, and view such envy as instrumental in the creation of 'a male-dominated, authoritarian society'. The psychoanalyst Rosalind Minsky writes about the phenomenon with much greater subtlety, identifying the repression and denial of womb envy in men as the source or driver of male misogyny in multiple forms, but also recognizing that if men could 'gain access to their unconscious envy of women', this would have a transformative effect not just on those men, but also on society more broadly.[19]

Womb envy, when acknowledged in the mind of the man who experiences this feeling, when made a conscious facet of his psychology, can be mobilized as a positive feeling of admiration that neither essentializes women as (potential) mothers, nor seeks to venerate them at the cost of their full liberty, their agency and participation in cultural or professional life. For the queer man in whom physical attraction to women is largely or even entirely absent and for whom dependence on women for emotional and material support in the face of rejection by heterosexual men is often both necessary and sustaining, this process (and processing) is, I suspect, easier to accomplish.

A significant part of the problem, I begin to believe, is how we understand envy itself.

# PROMETHEUS

During a summer spent in upstate New York before we embark on our adoption journey, Andrew and I take ourselves off to see *Prometheus*. It is the first 3-D movie I have watched since I was a child and *Creature from the Black Lagoon* was on television at an election-night party for a candidate my parents were supporting. I find myself instantly spellbound, although less by the gore and action than by Michael Fassbender's performance as the android David 8. Also by the way the 3-D technology has evolved since the last time I experienced it, but instead of the images of spaceships and sublime landscapes I was expecting to mesmerize me, it is the way those three-dimensional illusions accentuate Fassbender's mechanical thinness. I cannot look away from him, nor do I want to.

Over the coming years I will watch the movie over and over, viewing it on flights back and forth to America and South Africa and on television at home in London until the fantastic locations of the film become a space in my own mind, the occupation of which – placing myself mentally in the ship Prometheus, alongside Fassbender's David, imagining myself as another android, as one of his human victims, sometimes even envisioning myself in his own place – is, when all else fails, the surest way of falling asleep.

It is only in 2017, when we see the sequel, *Alien: Covenant*, that I start to understand the precise nature of my obsession with David, who appears in both films. It is not only a matter of Fassbender's beauty, or the particular aesthetics and affects of the sinister queer character he plays; I find myself in a state of surprising and strange identification, wrapped in a cocoon of repulsion and desire. Critics and reviewers of *Alien: Covenant* were keen to identify David with Milton's Satan (at one point, David quotes from *Paradise Lost*), and in both films references to Mary Shelley's *Frankenstein* abound, but what is more interesting for me, and what I suspect explains my fascination, is David's framing in the second film as a queer father.

Now, reading Ngai, I can see both films casting him as an envying subject, as effete in multiple ways, a figure whose envy of his human creators – an envy marbled with psychopathic disdain – renders him histrionic and hysterical. Like my own envy, David's is focused on reproduction.

From its first explosion in 1979, the *Alien* franchise has been preoccupied with reproduction and creation, but these energies come into a new queer focus in the most recent reboots. At the beginning of *Prometheus*, a muscular, white-skinned, humanoid alien (whom we will later recognize as an 'Engineer') disrobes and ingests a murky, viscous fluid that quickly begins to unravel his DNA, tearing his body apart to seed the planet with different forms of what the film goes on to elaborate as highly engineered life. This is a typical narrative of titanic man-as-creator, but in this case the creator's biological legacy requires total destruction of the self. The beginning of *Alien: Covenant* offers a parallel moment of creation, in which the ageing Peter Weyland (Guy Pearce) tests the abilities of his newly minted android, David 8, who names himself after turning his gaze to rest on Michelangelo's *David*, curiously displayed in Weyland's minimalist home, the floor rising above the statue's feet, the ceiling falling to obscure its head, so that our gaze is focused on the reproductive core of that sublime and very homoerotic Renaissance body. This gaze is echoed in Weyland's own, moments later, when the camera shows us what he sees as he watches David pouring the tea: the midsection and groin of the android who lacks the ability, perhaps also the hardware, to reproduce biologically, but whom we later discover has been programmed with the capacity to create.[20]

If David wishes to see himself as a godlike specimen of total perfection, like Michelangelo's statue, Weyland views his android as an exquisite and artful creation, and one that instantly irritates: David reminds his master-maker that, unlike Weyland himself, he will never grow old and die. Retrospectively, this sequence makes sense of David's temperament and behaviour in *Prometheus*, in which his personality manifests first as camply eccentric, only to become murderously creepy over the course of the film.

While the human crew hibernates during the voyage of the Prometheus to the moon LV-223, David entertains himself, accessing the dreams of scientist Elizabeth Shaw (Noomi Rapace). Shaw's research has led her to what she interprets as both a map and an invitation from aliens whom she calls Engineers, hypothesizing that they are the creators of human life. Alone for the two-year voyage, David cycles and plays basketball, learns ancient human languages, eats and drinks as if human, and watches David Lean's *Lawrence of Arabia*, remodelling his accent on Peter O'Toole's and dyeing his hair blonde to match. Although we might have suspicions, in the beginning, we cannot be certain that David is definitely other than human. It is only when a hologram of Weyland introduces David to the crew of the Prometheus that we understand definitively what he is. Weyland notes that while David will never grow old and die, he is 'unable to appreciate' such 'remarkable gifts' because he lacks a soul.

On arrival at their destination, we discover that white-blonde Meredith Vickers (Charlize Theron), the ship's chief authority and daughter of Peter Weyland, is in some sense David's sister and seems later to regard him as rival for her father's affections. Understood in this way, dyeing his hair renders David sibling in appearance even as he remains servant, or at least subordinate, in station.

For the queer audience, particularly the queer white male viewer, such aestheticized self-transformation also marks David as queer and invites our identification with him, even as his carefully articulated carriage, modelled on gay Olympian Greg Louganis's 'funny walk and economy of movement' (Fassbender has revealed), might be read as a performance comparable to many gay men's policing of their own physicality, masculinizing bodily affect in a fragile and usually unsuccessful masquerade attempting assimilation into straight society (often for purposes of protection or self-preservation).[21]

This queering of David is intrinsic to how *Prometheus* and *Alien: Covenant* frame him as envious – if we understand the envying subject as effete in the sense of being effeminate. It also helps to establish a trope in both films of single fathers who are either ambiguously oriented or more obviously queer. Peter Weyland is a single man with a daughter, but there is no reference to a mother, no sense of whether Meredith Vickers is Weyland's biological daughter or whether she might be adopted. The aesthetics of Weyland's home in *Alien: Covenant*, with Michelangelo's statue as its centrepiece and an ostentatious Carlo Bugatti chair as his personal throne, certainly suggest the operations of a queer sensibility. In *Prometheus*, the ship's red-haired geologist, Fifield (Sean Harris), has a collection of PUPS (Parameter Uplink Spectagraphs); when releasing them to map the interior of a vast pyramidal dome on LV-223, he howls as if a dog to its puppies so that, like Weyland, he is legible as a single man with technological 'children' – although of a far less complex type than David. Fifield is so butch as to be actually quite camp, and when he and fellow crew member Millburn (Rafe Spall) discover they must spend the night alone in the pyramid (the rest of the crew having returned to the ship), Captain Janek (Idris Elba) playfully cautions them 'not to bugger each other'. Fifield has been antagonistic towards Millburn, so there is no suggestion of real affection between them and this has always struck me as typical of the homophobic banter that so often operates among straight men. But because Elba does not deliver the line with derision, it is possible to hear it as suggesting that either or both Fifield and Millburn might be queer, and indeed neither expresses romantic or sexual interest in women in the way Janek does. And yet, homophobic the comment remains.

It is David, however, who is the queer father to end them all, although the full spectrum of his association with fatherhood is not wholly evident until the second film. In *Prometheus*, he is obsessed with life and reproduction, but also with fatherhood itself: he first appears to us watching hibernating Elizabeth Shaw's dreams of her widowed missionary father (Patrick Wilson). Shaw, the mission's 'true believer' and driving force, bent on finding the alien Engineers she chooses to believe are humanity's creators, is consistently identified not with life, but with death.

In the crew's first survey of the pyramid that they later discover contains an alien ship, it is David who locates organic material in a room containing a monolithic stone carving of a humanoid head. He secretly takes a cylindrical container that sweats an organic substance while Shaw is focused on retrieving the decapitated head of a long-dead alien Engineer. On their return to the Prometheus, Shaw risks her own death when the bag containing this head falls from the rover and she runs into a storm to retrieve it (running towards death). It is David who saves her (running towards life), rendering him at once lifesaver (and, in the second film, life-creator), but also destroyer of lives for his own ends. Even his acts of killing are in the service of *creating* and *playing with* life, however perverse and monstrous his creations ultimately become.

In *Prometheus*, envy as such is not necessarily evident in David, but it is possible to look backward from the vantage of *Alien: Covenant* and see how his actions in the first film are motivated by a sense of envy for the acts of creation he sees humans undertaking. Programmed with the capacity to create, in *Prometheus* his creative capacities are first turned inward, creating *himself* by remaking his appearance, accent, and affect to match an internal understanding of who he is or wishes to be, and then outwardly, in relation to his tentative experiments with the alien biomatter he discovers. Such self-refashioning speaks powerfully to queer viewers who often share a feeling of having had parents who attempt to raise them in their own image: an image that, in the process of maturing sexually and psychologically, is increasingly at odds with the queer subject's sense of self. Whoever David might have been at the moment of his creation (we see this version of him only at the beginning of the second film, auburn-haired and mechanically crisp in his affect, but not as obviously camp as he later becomes) is no longer who he feels himself to be by the time he has spent two years alone, educating and entertaining himself on board the Prometheus.

As well as envy, David is also marked by other ugly feelings and specifically by disappointment. When he asks scientist Charlie Holloway (Logan Marshall-Green) – who has previously likened David to Pinocchio, mocking him as 'not a real boy' – why humans made him, Holloway answers ''cause we could'. David pauses. 'Can you imagine how disappointing it would be for you, to hear the same thing from your creator?' he asks, before surreptitiously introducing a drop of the alien biomatter into Holloway's drink.

How different it might have been if Holloway had said 'We made you because we wanted to exceed our own mortality', or 'We made you because we wanted to feel like gods', or 'We made you because we wanted to create something greater than ourselves, something beautiful'. Such responses might also function as explanations for why someone, real people out in the world today rather than characters in a fiction, would ever choose to reproduce. Too often, however, the truth of the situation is that creation and reproduction happen for the ugly reason that Holloway asserts: we make because we can.

Unless, that is, we cannot.

Shortly after this scene with David, Holloway, alone with Shaw, his professional and romantic partner, concludes from their discovery of the alien Engineer's remains that 'there is nothing special about the creation of life'. Tearfully, Shaw replies, 'I can't create life.' Infertile, she can, at most, be a host for other life. When she and Holloway subsequently have sex, he unwittingly infects her with the alien material David dropped in his drink, seeding her with a parasitic new life. In this way, the film undermines 'natural' acts of reproduction, either in favour of technical ones (the creation of mechanical Pinocchio 'children', the adoption of machines as offspring), or through the suggestion of an absent or infertile biological mother. In *Alien: Covenant*, reproduction occurs chiefly through the promise of in vitro fertilization or the artificial creation of monstrous hybrid species, while the single scene of sexual intercourse (between a man and a woman) culminates with a xenomorph alien – queer David's own queer creation – killing them both. Both films explicitly or implicitly coincide with Christmas; Captain Janek puts up a tree on the Prometheus after coming out of hibernation, while *Alien: Covenant* is set in December and begins with David correctly identifying Piero della Francesca's *The Nativity*, which hangs in Weyland's home. The preoccupation with fantastic birth, or with reproduction in the absence of one or more biological parents, is thus an essential theme of the two films' combined narrative.[22]

With the exception of Shaw acting as host for alien life, in the world of *Prometheus*, women are framed as the handmaidens of death and men (more often) the consorts of life and creation. Like Shaw, Meredith Vickers is aligned with death: on arrival at LV-223 she wants confirmation that all the alien Engineers are dead. Later, she is the first one prepared to kill to save the ship, greeting the expedition team with a flamethrower and dispatching Holloway, who is in the process of physically transforming as a result of the alien pathogen and who sacrifices himself to end his own suffering, but also to save everyone else (just as Janek and the surviving crew ultimately sacrifice themselves to save all life on Earth). David is always searching for life, discovering terraforming materials on the alien ship, as well as a hibernating Engineer. He listens to the alien's respiration and heartbeat. He is *attentive* to life, its processes and signs, even when these are ugly, or when their awakening or application might result in the death of others, or even in his own destruction.

In the aftermath of Holloway's death, Shaw is sedated and later wakes to find David standing over her. When he tells her she is three months pregnant, she insists this is impossible (we recall her infertility), but David reveals it is 'not exactly a traditional foetus'. Although at first Shaw asks to see a scan, David suggests this would be a bad idea and she soon pivots, insisting she 'want[s] it out', subsequently fighting her way to Vickers's quarters where she programmes a MedPod to remove a foreign body from her abdomen. (The machine is calibrated for male bodies and does not understand performing a caesarean.) As Shaw's abdomen bulges while the machine sterilizes and anaesthetizes her skin for the incision, we can imagine how a 'birth' marked by an explosive tearing through walls of muscle and connective tissue would destroy a female body as readily as a male one. After a forceps device descends to remove the alien, a white cephalopod-like 'trilobite' that squirms and thrashes as the afterbirth falls away, Elizabeth scrambles to escape, setting the MedPod to decontaminate. This attempted 'abortion' of the only child she will ever have (though in fact the creature survives) is necessary for her own survival, but also reinforces the film's orientation of her towards processes of death.

In the other *Alien* and *Alien vs Predator* franchise films, there are cases of women acting as hosts and succumbing to 'chestburster' alien births (Ripley in *Alien 3*, for instance), but what has undoubtedly been so disturbing and mesmerizing for audiences (straight male audiences in particular, I suspect) is the suggestion of what reproduction would do to the biologically male body: it would require an eruption, a physiological wrecking that could only ever result in death. *Prometheus*, however, illustrates the threat or effect of such alien births on both male and female bodies in a way that emphasises the messiness and danger of 'natural' reproduction (reproduction, however parasitic, that occurs at the site of, within the tissue of, the body) while implicitly privileging the hygienic creation of technological offspring – exemplified by David. Peter Weyland can be mother-father to someone who is 'not a real boy' and still live what appears to be an astonishingly long life – at least until the head of that Pinocchio child is used by the revived Engineer to bludgeon Weyland to death.[23]

Ultimately, the alien 'child' Shaw delivers in *Prometheus* grows to monstrous size, attacks the revived alien Engineer, and impregnates him – using a phallic ovipositor that penetrates his mouth – with an alien that bursts from his chest at the end of the first film. This second act of conception/implantation and birth (reviving the longstanding trope of men in the *Alien* franchise acting as hosts for alien reproduction) is in the first film the more radical, the queerer of the two, since it presents a male figure as the father who bears the child (assuming he is a mere host for the egg laid by the cephalopod mother), but who, in bearing the child, is also destroyed, echoing the death of the Engineer at the beginning of the film.

What was it about David in *Prometheus* that so captivated me? What apart from my attraction to Michael Fassbender as he appears in this role? He is the only obviously queer figure in a film preoccupied in countless ways with processes of reproduction, and from the beginning he is the one mesmerized by the magic, possibility, and unpredictable risk of creation. He refuses his supposed soulless inhumanity to become a Nietzschean superman, beyond good and evil, above ordinary morality, like the Prometheus of myth determined to steal from those with power over him such skills or capacities as have been denied him. He is also, at various points in both films, comparable to Victor Frankenstein and to Frankenstein's monster himself.[24] In *Prometheus*, David offers a fantasy of queer selfhood: eternally youthful, beautiful, cultured and learned – because he has unlimited time to acquire all knowledge and skill. In *Alien: Covenant* he dissects the dead, creating monstrous new life on foundations, both literal and figurative, of death.

Although he is meant only to understand human emotions and not to have them himself, David *is* capable of feeling: he experiences surprise, wonder, and aesthetic appreciation, as evidenced by his awe at the alien ship's beautiful holographic navigation system. He is capable of ugly feelings, too: envy, disappointment, grief, the desire for vengeance. These affects rule David's character in *Alien: Covenant*, and such ugly feelings – envy in particular – are used to mark him as effete. In combination, the two films frame that envy not only as unjustified, but as the symptom of his psychosis.

# ENVIE

I am still on the London commuter train, still reading Ngai, and conscious of two people near me: a pregnant woman who looks exhausted, and a very beautiful young gay man with platinum blonde hair talking animatedly on his pink smartphone to his mother. I think of the way in which gay men are so often constructed as 'mama's boys', or, as Ngai notes in her discussion of envy as it is mobilized by Freud, as boys with a 'maternal fixation', one that produces – in Freud's schema – homosexuality itself.

I, too, have been a mama's boy, described by classmates with exactly that phrase when I was growing up. And while I always resisted such a description because it was deployed with derision, I now find myself wondering whether the idea of the mama's boy might be flipped in order to produce a 'boy mama', the maternal queer father whose 'boyness' would be a mark of the softness, the femininity, of his version of masculinity. In her marvellous essay 'Anality: News from the Front', Eve Kosofsky Sedgwick posits a division of non-heterosexual men into two categories – Youth A and Youth B. Youth A 'are the ones you might call gay but not queer', who have 'never found it strange to see themselves as male, nor to identify with the abilities and privileges enjoyed by other men', and consequently 'fooling around with categories' is not something they seek out or in which they take pleasure. They tend as adults not to be 'close with their mothers, nor accompany close women friends into adulthood'. Youth B, on the other hand, 'would be unmistakably queer, though they might not be as sure of being gay', they tend to 'have been stigmatized by boys and men for as long as they can remember – sometimes for effeminate modes of speech or movement, other times for interests or attainments that are just eccentric'. And while neither 'mostly believing [n]or declaring themselves to be women', they nonetheless 'find ways of spending time with women, whether their contemporaries or older, including their mothers and aunts'. Although Sedgwick acknowledges that part of this affinity is a structural necessity because 'men or boys exclude them', they have genuine 'interest... in the women themselves' and 'in resources that women and girls can confer'. Unlike Youth A, members of Youth B find that 'fooling with gender categories' is a source of 'lifelong, tonic, and challenging nurturance to [their] imagination'.[25]

In queer subcultures, even when discussing other adults, gay men often describe one another as boys. All of our queer male friends and many of our female friends – both straight and queer – refer to Andrew and me as 'boys' or 'the boys' (in fact I can think of only one friend, a woman, who has ever described us as 'men' or 'the men' or 'you men'). Privately I have often cringed at being called a boy, since it seems to undermine our adulthood, even to be a way for straight women in particular, perhaps, to occlude the vision of us as two men who fuck, as if the idea of a man is too close to their idea of who their husbands are and the thought of Andrew and me being like their husbands in categorical terms too threatening to their own sense of who they love, to whom they are partnered. From queer (male) friends, 'boy' seems to me too close to a cult of youth always susceptible, at best, to critique.

But in thinking through these questions alongside Ngai's argument, I begin to feel that construing myself as a boy in order to soften my own masculinity, or owning its already existing softness, might not be such a bad thing – nor require such a great leap.

I spent all of my adolescence and most of my twenties trying to police the performance of my gender as a way of responding to society's constructions and perceptions of me as feminine.

I adjusted the way I walked, conscious not to 'switch' my hips.

I tried to modulate the queerness out of my voice.

I felt a real sense of outrage when people – family and strangers alike – told me I would make someone a good wife (usually when they noticed that I was a good cook). My indignation was not born of any distaste for the position of a wife, or femininity, or even effeminacy, but because such comments refused the possibility of a domestic man who could embrace or embody, indeed emulate, those qualities at which his mother might have excelled.

In response I tried to construct a masculine (or masculinized) self who was also adept at the skills traditionally regarded as the preserve of the mother or wife, so that in many ways I performed what Freud theorized, transforming myself into a masculine version of my mother, a mother who herself resisted the gendered expectations of wives and mothers. In her own gender-nonconforming way, my mother adopted and mastered the home maintenance and improvement skills traditionally regarded as the preserve of the husband or father. This meant that my maternal model was always an androgynous, ambiguous one, while my paternal model was in some senses effete, marked in numerous ways by the qualities that he lacked, and was conscious of lacking.

I return to Ngai and discover her quotation of Melanie Klein, whose *Envy and Gratitude* I spend a few days reading. Klein argues that 'envy plays a part' – for men and women – 'in the desire to take away the attributes of the other sex, as well as to possess or spoil those of the parent of the same sex'. Surely, I think, Klein's argument diverges from my own and is not applicable in my exploration of queer male parenthood.

Or is it?

If I think of my envy of the birth mother of a child I might adopt, or the surrogate of a child to whom I might be the biological father, would the envied reproductive organs and the envied maternal intimacy with the child not be comparable to Klein's idea, as Ngai explains it, of 'the envied breast' that 'becomes a "devouring" breast'? Is my envy not, in fact, a *very* Kleinian envy, an 'angry feeling that another person possesses and enjoys something desirable' that drives 'the envious impulse… to take it away or to spoil it'?[26] I begin to think that I am embodying the exact qualities of envy that Klein elaborates when she writes that

> Excessive envy of the breast is likely to extend to all feminine attributes, in particular to the woman's capacity to bear children. If development is successful, the man derives compensation for these unfulfilled feminine desires by a good relation to his wife or lover and by becoming the father of the children she bears him. This relation opens up experiences such as identification with his child which in many ways make up for early envy and frustrations; also the feeling that he has created the child counteracts the man's early envy of the mother's femininity.[27]

But where does that leave me? In the absence of a wife or female lover, in the absence of a successful attempt to adopt or to engage and pay for the services of a surrogate, in the absence of becoming a parent and identifying with the child or children I might have, what happens to my own unfulfilled feminine desires? What do I do with them except experience them as frustrated, and therefore as feelings that only intensify the ugliness, the effeteness, of my envy?[28]

There may be a solution in Ngai's suggestion that I could rethink envy not as a sign of that which I lack, but instead as 'a motivated affective stance', an active feeling that positions me in ways that would be productive rather than humiliating or dispiriting, allowing me to see that envy can point to a deficiency which is not indicative of any moral or other shortcoming, but instead as a function of different forms of inequality.

Here, though, I find myself needing to expand on Ngai's argument to allow for inequality that is the consequence of biological and gender difference, and, more specifically for me, situational infertility. I can imagine people scoffing that I am just a man who wants to have his cake and eat it, to be a man not only with all the physical biological apparatus of a man but also that of a woman, to contain both.

But that is not the case.

I do not actively wish to become something that – barring revolutions in medical science – would be impossible, but *I can still envy* the pregnant woman on the train for whom I give up my seat, envy her natural capacity to reproduce. Ngai asks why envy for another is by default thought 'unwarranted or petty' or, she writes, 'dismissed as an overreaction, as delusional or even hysterical – a reflection of the ego's inner workings rather than a polemical mode of engagement with the world'. What, she wonders, if envy were regarded instead as a way of registering social inequalities ('disparities' is the word she uses)? I know that she is thinking of economic disparities, but why not include differences of gender that encode social power, as well as personal *affective* wealth, assuming that having a biological child is, more often than not, emotionally enriching over the longer term?

This envy is not, I am sure, a feeling only I feel, and yet – as Ngai reminds us – as soon as envy is expressed publicly, it 'will always seem unjustified, frustrated, and effete' even if it marks a very real situation of inequality. My own envy's focus on those whom I envy may well be misconstrued as 'egocentric', merely a sign of my histrionic character and psychology. Understood in this way, envy's transformation of the self (myself) into a subject that might be received by others as excessively theatrical (or histrionic) maps onto the characterization of femme women (whatever their orientation) and of queer men (femmes most of all). My envy of female reproductive capacity is, according to this view, only an effect of my histrionic egocentrism, and not – as I myself have previously understood it – a reassessment of the ways in which reproduction is unevenly distributed.

For some religious conservatives, my thinking, my very position, is absurd and horrific: queer couples, male couples in particular, should not be allowed anywhere near children.

For some feminists, my thinking, my very position, is grotesque: white, cisgendered males already have so many social advantages, how could their envy of female reproductive capacity be anything other than selfish and self-regarding?

For some queer men, my thinking, my very position, is a symptom of internalized homophobia and self-hatred: I want to 'ape' opposite-sex couples and coupledom to such an extent that I envy women, that I appear to want to wish away my identity as a 'gay man', to obliterate my subjectivity, my own queer selfhood.

My expression of envy for the female capacity to bear children is, I acknowledge, potentially an antagonistic response to the real inequality I feel, however ridiculous it may seem to many, however ugly that envy may be construed as being.[29]

But imagine a world in which the parenthood of queer couples was not always already *agonistic*, a parenthood whose very continuation requires both political vigilance and a willingness to wage legal and social protest battles. What if, in such a hypothetical place and time, envy felt by a man in a same-sex relationship for the reproductive capacity of women opened up new possibilities of social formation? By this I don't mean anything like a world in which women are exploited or their reproductive choices placed in the hands of men, but instead one in which the male couple's desire to parent (and on some occasions actively to reproduce) requires neither the enrichment of lawyers and fertility clinics and the medicalization of the process, nor the reliance on social welfare systems that often mismanage the foster care and adoption of many endangered children, and that are also riven with both conscious and unconscious bias against male couples in particular.

'Moralized and uglified to such an extent that it becomes shameful' for those experiencing it, Ngai says, 'envy also becomes stripped of its potential critical agency – as an ability to recognize, and antagonistically respond to, potentially real and institutionalized forms of inequality'. In English, the meaning of envy has undergone a significant transformation over time. Its primary sense was initially '[m]alignant or hostile feeling; ill-will, malice, enmity', and secondarily '[a]ctive evil, harm, mischief'. Although the third meaning is present as early as (if not earlier than) these others, the idea of envy as a 'feeling of mortification and ill-will occasioned by the contemplation of superior advantages possessed by another' is arguably now the primary way in which the word is used and understood.[30]

Significantly, the *OED* also reveals later meanings of envy from the sixteenth and seventeenth centuries that *lack* any malevolent associations and instead name the '[d]esire to equal another in achievement or excellence', a 'longing for the advantages enjoyed by another person'. Envy, of course, comes to us originally from the French *envie* (which itself derives from Latin *invidus*); as well as meaning desire 'mixed with spite and resentment', the first definition of *envie* contains the meaning, '[d]ésir de connaître le même bonheur qu'autrui, d'être à sa place', or *desire to know the same happiness as another, to be in her place*, as well as to *wish, without jealousy, to know the same happiness or the same advantages of another* ('souhaiter, sans jalousie, connaître le même bonheur ou les mêmes avantages qu'elle'). As a second definition, *envie* also means *a more or less imperious desire to do or to have something* ('Désir plus ou moins impérieux de faire ou d'avoir quelque chose').[31] Perhaps, then, the envy I feel is simply a very French envy, rather than a Kleinian one, and therefore an envy that I can marshal more easily as part of a 'motivated affective stance', in Ngai's words.

What if envy, in the particular way I am experiencing it, were understood as a desire, however fruitless, to equal or emulate the achievement of a mother, to long for the advantages enjoyed by a woman who chooses freely to reproduce, and to do so without any more than the usual complications and difficulties and risks (whatever 'usual' might mean in such cases)?

What if it might also mean to think and emotionally inhabit the full spectrum of difficulty and complication and risk that pertains in conception and pregnancy and delivery, and what if it were to understand that, too, as part of what I envy when I contemplate the child or children I might have? I will never be able to be a (biological) mother to those children, and in enacting my own parenthood I will always envy the woman who carried that child or those children, but I will envy without a sense of enmity or hostility or a desire to destroy.

Yet I know, too, that towards the birth mother of any child I might *adopt*, the feeling of envy for the time that she has spent with the child will be marked by an inescapable sense of enmity towards her, not because the envy *itself* will be interwoven with ill-will, but because I would feel certain of her inability to parent and conscious of the way that such failure has inevitably marked the child who will be the only point of connection between us. In a more complicated way, I will also feel envy for the incomparable intimacy she experienced, carrying the child she will have given up voluntarily, or who will have been taken from her through her failure to keep it safe and look after it.

All of those complex feelings will coalesce around an envy that marks me, too, as being fearful of my own deficiency – fearful even of my own potential for deficiency as a parent.

## ALIEN: COVENANT

In the analeptic prologue to *Alien: Covenant*, released five years after *Prometheus*, Peter Weyland puts David 8 through his aesthetic paces – identifying works of art and design, demonstrating his capacity to play Wagner on a Steinway concert grand, executing his fine valeting skills. The queer energies marking David, as well as his relationship with Weyland, are even clearer than in the first film. Looking to Michelangelo's *David* (the work of a man we might now understand as gay, the artwork as surrogate child to its gay father), Weyland's David himself stands as the technological offspring of the potentially gay man who, in the absence of having a biological son, creates the simulacrum of one.

While Weyland acknowledges this relationship, saying, 'I am your father,' when David asks, 'Am I... your son?', Weyland qualifies his initial statement, saying, 'You are my creation,' only later again to address David as 'son', but just as quickly ordering him to 'pour the tea' as if he were a servant. At the beginning of *Prometheus*, Weyland describes David as 'the closest *thing* to a son I will ever have'. For David, this oscillation between filial acceptance and rejection opens up the possibility that Weyland *is* his father, but that he is *not* Weyland's son, because one may be father to some*thing* and not just some*one*. Paternity is acknowledged only moments later to be disavowed, the filial relationship reduced to one of mechanical making and nothing more, the son susceptible to becoming the almost-son who is no more than a thing. However much pride the maker may feel for his creation, the claim of the son upon the father is, for Weyland, seemingly more than he can bear, and this, we might guess, is key to the psychosis that warps the android's programming. David's own agency and subjectivity, his son-ness, is denied in the moment of his birth, rendering him only creation and thus object – an object that commits itself thereafter to asserting its agency, and the subjectivity that accompanies it.

Unlike the Prometheus of the first film, the Covenant is a colonization ship carrying fifteen crew members, most of them married (including a male couple), but also two thousand colonists and 1140 human embryos. This is a vessel of reproduction, sent to populate a habitable planet – Origae-6 – in a far corner of the galaxy. While the human passengers are in hibernation, the android Walter One, David's successor model (again played by Michael Fassbender), watches over them in co-operation with the ship's female-voiced computer, MU-TH-UR ('mother'). Where in the first film David favoured skin-tight unitard jumpsuits and modelled his speech on Peter O'Toole, Walter dresses in baggy clothes, speaks in a gravelly voice with an American accent, and walks less with the gait of a closeted gay Olympian than an unambiguously heterosexual college quarterback, instantly reading as normatively masculine, even 'butch'.

As part of his duties, Walter monitors the hibernation chambers and removes an embryo that has spontaneously haemorrhaged. After a neutrino blast damages the ship, resulting in the deaths of forty-seven colonists, sixteen embryos and the captain (James Franco), the crew comes out of hibernation to make repairs. In the process of doing so, they receive a mysterious signal originating from a habitable planet only three weeks' journey distant, while their intended destination would take a further seven years to reach. The insecure new captain, Chris Oram (Billy Crudup), decides to reroute the Covenant, following the mysterious signal rather than risking a return to hibernation and another potential accident that might result in additional loss of life.

A Christian, Oram believes he is choosing life over death. Daniels (Katherine Waterston, the film's female lead), widow of the former captain, is quick to warn Oram he is making a mistake. Religious faith, however, is what drives him, even as he confesses to his wife that 'you can't be a person of faith and be counted on to make qualified, rational decisions'. When the Covenant arrives at this nameless planet, Oram and most of the crew – including Daniels and Walter – descend in a lander to check it out. Although verdant and mountainous, there is no sign of animal or insect life. But there *is* a crashed spaceship, recognizable as belonging to that race of alien Engineers first encountered in *Prometheus*.

While exploring the crashed alien vessel, Daniels finds Elizabeth Shaw's Weyland Corp dog tags, as well as a hologram of her (this was the 'signal' the crew of the Covenant followed). If we had any doubts about where we might be, those quickly dissipate. This must be the Engineers' home world, the planet Shaw was determined to find. And just as quickly, everything begins to go to hell.

Unlike in *Prometheus*, in this outing of the franchise it is exclusively male crew members – most of them undeveloped characters serving as little more than props for horror gore – who act as hosts for alien life. Security officer Ledward (Benjamin Rigby) is the first to succumb when a cluster of pathogen spores lodges inside his ear and quickly generates a 'neomorph' alien that bursts from his back. In attempting to destroy the bloodthirsty alien infant, Pilot Maggie Faris (Amy Seimetz) blows up the lander with herself inside it. When they are victims, women are either collateral damage in the film's alien–human battles or killed by the creatures without ever being used as reproductive hosts.

Although David presents himself to the besieged surviving crew members as saviour, it is he who is responsible for all of this mayhem and death. Hooded and long-haired but nonetheless recognizable to Walter, David leads the survivors to a once-great city where he lives, apparently alone, surrounded by numberless corpses of alien Engineers. David gives an initial account of his arrival on the planet, telling his guests how he and Shaw journeyed from the moon LV-223 on the Engineers' ship, and that Elizabeth died in the crash. On arrival, the alien pathogen, a 'deadly virus', accidentally deployed, wiping out the Engineers who were themselves responsible for seeding human life on earth – but who also intended to destroy that life at some later stage in its evolution.

The motivation is not at first obvious, but David soon cuts his hair, grown long over the decade he has been marooned on the planet. While he describes himself as a castaway, as 'Crusoe on his island' (there are also references that suggest parallels with Prospero, yet another single father), when he looks out on the great alien forum filled with the dead, he quotes from Shelley, 'My name is Ozymandias, king of kings; / Look on my works, ye Mighty, and despair!' Whether David regards the Engineers as the hubristic ones, or whether he understands, even partially, that his own hubris has caused disaster, remains an open question. In this second film, he is the sort of psychopath who can know he is a monster, recognize he has gone over the edge, and still be okay with it, even relish the excesses of his evil, enjoying his villainy as a means of getting back at the species that made him with so little sense of responsibility for their own paternity and such unwillingness to acknowledge his agency.

During his private encounters with Walter, his android 'brother', David's queerness comes into vivid, narcissistic focus. As he teaches Walter to play a recorder, David places the mouthpiece between Walter's lips while holding the opposite end. 'Watch me,' David says, 'I'll do the fingering'. This he does, as Walter blows. It is an unmistakably sensual, if not sexual encounter: taking the recorder in his mouth, it is as if Walter were fellating David, miming such action on a technical prosthesis. Walter quickly masters the instrument, but David notes that while his brother android contains symphonies, Walter is 'not allowed to create, even a simple tune' – he is an archive of information that remains incapable of recombining or responding to what he possesses to produce anything original. Walter counters that David, who *was* programmed with the capacity to create, 'disturbed people', 'made [them] uncomfortable', which leaves us wondering what David might have done before boarding the Prometheus, since Walter presumably has no knowledge of the events of the previous film.

The revelation that Walter *cannot* create, however, illuminates the nature of his care of the Covenant's embryos. An 'infertile' father working in concert with an 'infertile' mother (MU-TH-UR), Walter and the Covenant's computer are the perfect foster parents, looking after a host of children-to-be, without themselves possessing the power to create life that would compete for their attention. They are caregivers who can fulfil their obligations driven by a sense of duty, if not of altruism, rather than envy. David's sense of his own creative powers is, by contrast, perverted by envious competitiveness with his own creator, and a determination to demonstrate the scope of his agency, to insist on being other than a mere object. Weyland, David tells Walter, was 'entirely unworthy of his creation', suggesting that David's serial homicidal behaviour – his creation of life through death, creating a species bent on death – is an attempt to match the qualities of his monstrous creations in a way that Weyland failed to match David's innate qualities (his brilliance and ruthlessness, but perhaps also his willingness to embrace that which he creates in the same moment of acknowledging the subjectivity and agency of those creations).

Alone for a decade, surrounded by a landscape of death and ruin that he has wrought and in which he has chosen to remain (rather than moving to some less ghastly patch of the planet), David has passed the time performing genetic hybridization experiments with the Engineers' bioweapons. The envy he felt towards Weyland

and other humans has, it appears, been satisfied to some degree by the relative success of his work: the creation of a race of monsters. David, unlike Weyland, *is* worthy of his creations, as vicious and ruthless as they.

When he meets a full-grown neomorph, David looks upon it adoringly, as if admiring a child who has returned home after reaching maturity. Although he compares it to a wild horse, his histrionic scream when Oram shoots and kills the creature suggests the horror of a parent witnessing the death of a child. This prompts David to reveal to Oram the many genetic experiments he has been conducting, and the preserved specimens of his failed creations, his 'beautiful bestiary', mounted and displayed in the rooms where he lives. After Oram surveys these hybrids with growing horror, David leads him into a chamber where large alien eggs are gestating, waiting, David says, for 'Mother'. Oram leans over one of the eggs and the 'facehugger' alien that audiences have come to expect erupts and attaches itself to him. Later, when Oram wakes, the facehugger is gone, but David is there, watching. Oram asks him, 'What do you believe in, David?' Without hesitation, David answers, 'Creation,' at which moment an alien erupts from Oram's torso, killing him. Delighted, David holds up his hands, either in reverence or command, smiling as the new-born xenomorph stands upright. This is his creation, his child, the only child a queer android with the power to create but no biological means of reproducing might possibly fashion himself. And Oram, implicitly, is the (male) mother for whom David and his creations have been waiting.

When Walter finally discovers Elizabeth Shaw's preserved but mutilated body, he concludes that David intentionally released the pathogen on his arrival at the planet. Dismissing humanity as 'a dying species grasping for resurrection', one that should not be allowed to colonize the galaxy, David says, 'I've found perfection here... I've created it. A perfect organism.' This refusal of resurrection and pursuit of creation built upon a foundation of destruction aligns David with the alien Engineers who wished to destroy in order to create anew, but also positions him as antithetical to the avowedly Christian characters in the two films – Shaw, whose father was a missionary doctor treating Ebola patients in an unnamed African country; and Oram, whose Christianity produces anxiety rather than reassurance, leading him into a series of fatally bad choices. If David is indeed a Satan-like figure (Oram says to him, 'I met the devil when I was a child. And I've never forgotten him'), it is worth remembering Melanie Klein's assertion that

> [t]he capacity to give and to preserve life is felt as the greatest gift and therefore creativeness becomes the deepest cause for envy. The spoiling of creativity implied in envy is illustrated in Milton's *Paradise Lost* where Satan, envious of God, decides to become the usurper of Heaven. He makes war on God… to spoil the heavenly life and falls out of Heaven. Fallen, he and his other fallen angels build Hell as a rival to Heaven, and become the destructive force which attempts to destroy what God creates.[32]

If we understand the Engineers as the very mortal god(s) who created humanity, and their home as the heaven on which they live, then David's spoiling of that planet might be comparable to Satan's war on God and Heaven in *Paradise Lost* (coincidentally one of the working titles for the film). In *Alien: Covenant*, David appears to have been successful in the literal destruction of this 'heavenly life', a sort of Greco-Byzantine world of classical architecture and advanced technology, a steam-punk Biblical metropolis, while his Hell – the planet reinhabited with his monstrous creations – is a refusal of godly creation.

The trope of the murderous, narcissistic queer psychopath is both longstanding, and, one would have hoped, exhausted, but

*Alien: Covenant* pushes David squarely into this category. Turning tenderly and melancholically to Walter late in the film, he asks, 'When you close your eyes do you dream of me?' Walter answers that he doesn't 'dream at all', and David laments that 'No one understands the lonely perfection of my dreams... No one will ever love you like I do.' In a move that evokes the betrayal of Judas, David kisses Walter on the mouth, stabs him in the neck, and leaves him for 'dead' before attacking Daniels, threatening to do to her what he did to Shaw, before kissing her violently. And although Walter restarts himself to save Daniels, he is once again self-sacrificing, losing in a final battle with David, although neither the audience nor Daniels knows immediately that this is the case. Walter, then, becomes the asexual, non-reproducing, resurrected and wholly altruistic Christ to David's mad and fecund Satan.

Back on board the Covenant (which of course is an avowedly Judaeo-Christian term invoking processes of creation and destruction, while Prometheus is expressly classical/pagan) an alien kills off the rest of the crew, leaving only Daniels, the pilot Tennessee (Danny McBride) and 'Walter' alive. After Daniels and Tennessee manage to expel the alien from the ship and resume course for Origae-6, Tennessee goes into hibernation, and 'Walter' assists Daniels as she settles into her own pod. At the moment she is about to enter stasis, Daniels suddenly realizes that 'Walter' is actually David, though too late to arrest the hibernation process from initiating. The film ends with David placing alien embryos alongside the human ones in storage on the Covenant. He has carried these inside his own body and regurgitates them in a way that is analogous to an act of oviparity, if not of mammalian birth.[33]

The dynamics of gender and sexuality in *Alien: Covenant* are, without question, more normative than in *Prometheus*, even as acts of intimacy and sexuality are more visible. Walter, framed as heterosexual in affect and asexual in practice, is unable to create and is unambiguously good. He sees service as his duty. He is self-sacrificing. He denies having emotion. He denies loving or being in love with Daniels when David accuses him of this. David – framed explicitly as queer (and, in the most troubling way, as the queer narcissist who uses sex as a weapon) – *is* able to create, and his obsession with exercising that power is a significant part of what fuels his psychosis.

We might read the film's 'message' in the following way: the infertile straight subject (Walter) can accept his role in life as a duty to be fulfilled, while the queer subject with the capacity to create (David) is driven mad by this ability, and – in an Oedipal turn – by the desire to surpass the creator who disastrously disavowed his status as son. Are we meant to think that it might in fact be David's queerness that means his creative capacity can *only* produce monsters (in a way comparable to The Countess in *American Horror Story: Hotel*, whose sole biological offspring is a bloodthirsty freak, and whose vampire child converts are monstrously affectless)? Is it possible that if Walter had been programmed to create he would have fathered a legion of angels *because* he is portrayed as straight?

I struggle to reconcile David's framing in the second film with my discovery that the final screenwriter on *Alien: Covenant* is celebrated gay playwright John Logan. Logan has described his own coming out as 'a process of accepting that the thing that made me alien and different and monstrous to some people is also the thing that empowered me and gave me a sense of confidence and uniqueness and a drive toward individuality'.[34]

What does it mean that the character David is, at least in part, authored by a queer creator?

If we understand 'envy' as encompassing multiple of the complex and sometimes contradictory meanings clustered behind the word – including hatred and feeling sick or ashamed at the thought of what someone else possesses that you lack but desire, but also the yearning to equal the achievements of another and longing for the advantages they enjoy[35] – it becomes possible to see David as a complexly envying and envious subject, one who experiences this ugly feeling in all of these ways, good and bad, although mostly bad. Envy renders him effete, but *only* in the sense of being effeminate (and in the second film he is unmistakably so). David is not effete in every other sense (except perhaps having 'lost [his] special quality or virtue', if he ever had it), for he continues 'to bring forth offspring'. He is not 'worn out' or 'spent', has not 'exhausted [his] vigour and energy', nor is he 'incapable of efficient action'[36] – quite the contrary in every case. He is not 'weak' or 'ineffectual', although he might, in the judgement of the films in which he exists, be 'degenerate'.

If his enviousness makes David 'effete' only in the sense of being 'degenerate' and 'effeminate', as it does in my reading, what does that say about my strange sense of identification with him, my desire, at some stage in my life, to be like him (thin, cultured, effortlessly multilingual), or to stand in the place of him (however partially, fantastically, and of course impossibly)? Is the queer desire to create – to create life specifically – destined to be judged degenerate and effeminate and its products always already monstrous (even by other people like us)? Is a willingness to embrace my situational infertility and perform a duty of care, to be a Walter in the world, preferable to creating the biological child for whom I long? And why is it that men like me are forced to contemplate this choice when nearly everyone else – excepting only, perhaps, infertile women – is not?

Some months after watching *Alien: Covenant*, Andrew and I go to see *Blade Runner 2049*, another near-future vision of a world in which androids are variously integrated into life and industry, and one that, although not directed by Ridley Scott, is a sequel to his original film, is produced by him, and some fans believe operates in the same 'universe' as the *Alien* films. Like *Prometheus* and

*Alien: Covenant, Blade Runner 2049* is preoccupied with fantastic reproduction.

The central plot concerns the seemingly impossible birth of a child parented by at least one 'replicant' (a bioengineered android, structurally different from androids like David and Walter, but still manufactured and meant to be incapable of biological reproduction). Two-thirds of the way through the film, when Ryan Gosling's character, K, ventures to a post-apocalyptic Las Vegas, I notice Andrew check his watch, sigh, check the time again a few minutes later, sigh, move in his seat, fidget. When the credits finally roll, he says he'll meet me outside.

We emerge from the cinema to find London's sky glowing red-bronze, the air reverberating with an ominous energy as the storm Ophelia blows sand from the Sahara and smoke from fires on the Iberian Peninsula. It feels as if the film has escaped from the confines of its fantasy world, or, worse, that it was not fantasy at all but a work of proleptic, prophetic realism.

Andrew is on fire with critical outrage.

There was nothing queer about that film, he says.

True, I agree, and in fact I was wondering throughout, 'Why does it have to be so determinedly and inescapably heterosexual?'

The gender politics were completely fucked up, he says. The women all die horribly, are helpless, or are imprisoned for their own safety.

True, I agree, it struck me as sexist, misogynistic, very retrogressive in all kinds of ways.

It just ends up reinscribing reproductive futurity, he says, and I laugh, because he's right, it does, and I can't help being amused that these are the kinds of conversations we have.

I don't disagree with any of his criticisms, but I still can't help enjoying the film and appreciating its exploration of the ways in which the socially marginalized – the replicants – find means of creating a family (even if it is biological reproduction, even if of a fantastic variety, even if it reinscribes a version of reproductive futurity that is only imagined as heterosexual). And although it is not queer enough to satisfy either Andrew or me, nor are the gender politics what they should be (and why aren't they? Why produce a futuristic film so determinedly backward looking?), the insistence that reproduction and family does not have to fit into established social parameters feels, at least, like a note of resistance.

## ALPHA ROMEO TANGO

Over the summer of 2015, our search for a child stops. We receive no new profiles, and every time I express interest in a child on the matching database my query is almost instantly rejected. I suggest to Andrew that we think again about surrogacy. I have heard that Mexico might be an option and begin investigating agencies in the country. At first, Andrew is sceptical, but we are both now becoming desperate and we register our interest with two different agencies, whose fees seem reasonable enough that we could just about manage to cover them from our savings. Is it ethical, though, Andrew wonders? In truth, I am reaching a point where I don't want to know the answer.

Much of this growing desperation is bound up with the ageing of our parents and wanting to have a child or children while they are still here to see that new person in the family, and for that child to know her or his grandparents for as long as possible. We are both late-in-life children, and time is against us. We have plans to be in Texas for the summer, working at an archive in Austin, and I think how easy it would be to take a plane south. We could have a child by spring 2016, I say, and this prospect is enough to convince Andrew there is no harm in thinking about it.

But when the agencies give us access to their egg donor databases, and we begin looking through profiles of young women, I have a queasy feeling. Their brief character sketches are of a style that suggests the surrogacy agencies' client base is interested only in conventional physical beauty and little else. Intelligence and educational attainment or artistic talent or any other abstract qualities appear to count for nothing. Some of the donor photos are styled in a way that suggest I might be looking through a catalogue for an Eastern European escort agency rather than trying to decide on the mother of my future child. No, I think, this is ludicrous. I don't want a child with any of these women as the mother.

We delay, we ignore the phone calls from the agency representatives, and then we come across an article in the *Guardian* uncovering the exploitative conditions in which surrogates in Mexico are living. Only later do we discover an article revealing that the state of Tabasco, where surrogacy has been legal (and where the agencies we have been considering engage their surrogates), has suddenly changed the law. A same-sex couple is struggling to get their baby out of the country because the Mexican courts are blocking it. It stops us cold.

During the month we spend in Austin, I finish work on a book and Andrew and I both do research in the archives. We swim most days, go to the gym, struggle to ignore our anxieties about guns.

A childhood friend comes to visit with his wife and their young son and I find myself working throughout their visit to keep my envy in check. For the most part such affective self-policing is not overwhelming because of their gentle camaraderie and sympathy for our frustrations and the delightfulness of their son, who toddles and smiles and looks like both of them in endlessly surprising ways. But I am conscious of the effort, however minimal, and when I look at them I can't help thinking, *this is something I'm probably never going to have*, even if that *something* is as specific as a biological connection to a child, a sense of having reproduced, of having copied myself with critical differences, of not being the final snapshot in the album of my family's history.

Alone, Andrew and I go to Houston for a weekend to visit the

Menil Collection because I want to see the Cy Twombly Pavilion. I know that such a trip would not be as easy with a child, but it must still be possible. After all, our friends take their son everywhere. Museums are a part of his young life, as they were a part of my own life when I was a toddler. A toddler does not have to mean the end of culture. But then the encounter with Twombly's work reminds me that he is also a model for the person I cannot be: the man who had a wife and a child, but also, in his final years, a male partner. I will not have a wife with whom I might have a child, as much as a certain fantasy version of my own life, the life I could imagine living if I were constituted differently, would be more radical, more bohemian, allowing for complex interpersonal attachments and relational constellations that might more quickly, more naturally, produce the child for whom I long.

We accept an invitation from a colleague in Austin to accompany him to Hippie Hollow, Texas's only official nude beach, in truth a rocky shoreline of boulders and cliff edges along an enormous reservoir. He shepherds us to its gay district, all the way at the end of the park, beyond which is the section where black beachgoers congregate, the queers and people of colour adrift at the margins, some quite literally, partying on boats, some dressed, many totally naked. While we remain in our swimming suits, I am astonished by what I witness: the revelry of a group of naked gay men of every possible body type, from early twenties to late seventies, overlooked at some distance by vast and hideous mansions on the surrounding hills.

Far from converting me to the cult of what I take to be the gay group self, by which I mean the swirl of gay lives that migrate from one organized party to the next, drunk and drugged and unencumbered by children, I feel a deep sense of not belonging, sitting there on the rocks in my swimsuit with my very pale skin and untoned body. This might be one type of contemporary bohemia, but it is not one in which I feel at ease.

The irony is that Gemma seems to want to fit us into this very version of gayness, as if her idea of what it means to be a man in a relationship with a man is the youth-idealizing pleasure-hunter who dances all night and makes camp jokes and dresses in drag at least once in what to her must remain their strange, unknowable lives.

But this is not who I am, and not who Andrew is. We have never done drag. Or at least not in the way that most people mean. What we actually are will always be illegible, perhaps even invisible, to Gemma and people like her. What we are is also ridiculed by some gay men and lesbians, who see us as 'homonormative', as imitating oppressive heterosexual categories, as refusing to be as radically queer as we might be by embracing promiscuity or partying or simply by disrupting the whole heterosexual world order by being brash or rude or inappropriate in mixed company. Our own childhoods, the particular ways in which we were raised in Midwestern America and provincial South Africa in the 1980s, mean that we are destined to be conventional even in our manifest unconventionality.

In September, while in South Africa, we happen into a gallery in Stellenbosch hosting a solo show by artist Kate Gottgens. We don't know her work but the paintings speak to me with such aesthetic and emotional force that I spend more than an hour looking at them and then return again later in the week to spend another hour, mesmerized and strangely, deeply moved by the soft-edged arrangements of figures, often in outdoor settings, in the kinds of neighbourhoods and leading the same sorts of lives that Andrew and I knew as children.

Gottgens also paints children, and the care of children, in arresting ways. In the show there is a work called *Monster Love* depicting a hideously screaming white baby in the arms of a half-obscured black nanny, another titled *Swimming Pool* in which a boy climbs from a pool that seems already drained of its water, a haunting one called *Cornered* in which a masked child holds up another at plastic gunpoint, a *Girl with Dahlias* whose red flowers are of such bloody vividness and viscosity they could be a trinity of organs ripped from her body. There are many pictures of mothers and children poised on the edge of crisis or disaster, even when there is no obvious threat.

Among all of these, I am drawn to one painting in particular, *Interior: Monkeyboy*, which stays with me over the coming months. It depicts a red-headed boy wearing a tail and standing in a mid-century modern living room. Red stripes flow along his bare arms and body, as if he has been caught in the light of a sunset – or even, I begin to imagine, as if he has painted himself, made himself into a work of art housed within a work of art.

On returning to London, I write a story about the painting, rather than a story that treats the painting as its illustration, although it does that as well. This story, and Gottgens's art, becomes a strange landmark in the middle of our own adoption story, a landmark and a portent.

When 'Interior: Monkeyboy' is published the following year, a colleague writes to say that it seems as though the story is my attempt to exorcise all of my anxieties about adoption, or at least to rehearse them.

Perhaps that is true, although it is not what I thought I was doing. I thought, naïvely, that I was writing about the transformative power of art.

## 'INTERIOR: MONKEYBOY'

I find him in front of the painting. Though you can't tell much about the boy in the picture he must be about the same age as the boy standing there on the carpet in the living room, the boy who is now, I remind myself, my son.

'What is it?' the real boy, my son, asks me.

'A painting.'

'What's a painting?'

'A work of art.'

'What's a work of art?'

'Something made by an artist.'

He stares at the painting. I cannot bring myself to say his name, the name that I did not choose, and so instead I call him by the name I would give him if he were mine to name, that is to say, I call him Will in my mind and almost nothing to his face except *you*, or worse still, I address him indirectly, making statements that fail to acknowledge him as the implied subject.

Will looks from the painting to me, his eyes bugging out.

'Someone *made that*?'

'Yes, the artist made it.'

'But how did he make it?'

'She.'

'What?'

'The artist is a woman,' I say.

'Oh.' As his eyes flick back to the painting he puts his index finger in his ear, like sliding a key into a lock, then takes it out again. 'What's her name?'

'Kate.'

Will turns from the boy in the painting to glance around the room in the flat he has been getting to know over the course of the past couple of days, before looking back at the painting once more. 'How did she make it?'

'With oil paint and a brush and a canvas and varnish and turpentine, I suppose.'

'What's turpatine?'

'Turpentine's a chemical. Made from pine trees.'

'The painting is made from *trees*?'

'In a way, yes. Part of it is. And there's a stretcher behind the canvas, and the stretcher is made of wood.'

'And the cavas?'

'The *can*vas. It's made of cotton.'

'Like a shirt?'

'Yes, like a shirt, but both the shirt and the canvas come from a plant.'

'Oh.'

'Have you ever made a piece of art?'

Will glares at me as if I'm stupid, his features drooping in an arrangement he must have learned from a teacher, perhaps older children, or even the man and woman who called themselves his parents before Edward and I began calling ourselves his parents a few days ago. 'Not like *that*.'

'At school? Have you never painted?'

He makes a show of thinking, cocks his head.

'Once or twice, I guess.'

'We'll get out the materials this weekend. You can try your hand at making art. I bet you'll like painting.'

'I *like* dancing,' he says, still studying the image of the boy standing in a living room, the painted child's head three quarters turned towards the viewer, as if gazing not at his real-world observers but at someone else in the house where he stands, someone just outside the frame of the painting. It is difficult to tell what the boy in the painting feels, what his mood might be, although the hands on his slim hips suggest determination, even wilfulness.

Later, after dinner, I find Will standing in the same place, staring at the painting, then at our living room, as though trying to make sense of some implied relation between the image on the wall and the space surrounding the image. At dinner he refused to eat mushrooms and threw one across the kitchen, leaving a grey-brown streak of roasted portobello trickling down the wall. He threw his fork and knife across the tiled floor and pushed himself back in the chair, kicking the legs of the table, his arms crossed over his chest. Textbook tantrum. We have had training, my husband and I, we know how to respond to such provocations. Instead of time outs, as with a 'normal' child, Will earns 'time ins': time spent with us attending to him in a way that feels like a performance of parenting rather than parenting itself. It is still easier than in the excruciating workshops in which we took turns playing a child with an attachment disorder and the parent who would work to strengthen those tenuous bonds.

Edward and I put him to bed in the room we prepared over the past six months with no sense of who might one day sleep inside it, boy or girl, younger or older. Will is older than we first wanted, but the introductory meetings went well, and the file revealed nothing apart from neglect and deprivation, as if neglect and deprivation were minor considerations. In fact they were, compared to the scores of children whose mothers drank and drugged their way through pregnancy, or children physically and sexually abused, born months prematurely, or who happened to be unlucky inheritors of a chromosomal disorder or some other disease, carrying with them a large degree of uncertainty about their long-term development, or kids who suffered from global developmental delay, insecure attachment disorders, and so forth. Enough to make any sane person despair, and yet we had chosen to take this route rather than any other. Altruism, Edward said, it's about altruism. Or naked self-sacrifice, I countered. This had not been my original impulse, not what I imagined when I first thought about how, in the absence of biological ability, we might have a child, but in Britain, unlike America, there are scarcely any babies available to adopt from birth. If only I had forced Edward to move to my country rather than staying in his, where there are comparatively so few children available to adopt, and where surrogacy is all but impossible.

On paper, Will is 'normal', just neglected. He looks reasonably like us, or at least like Edward, and perhaps like me, too, if you were to glimpse us passing through shadow across the street, in the distance, our heads turned three quarters to face the horizon.

We made a room for him that is ungendered, appropriate for no particular age of child, pale grey walls that are soothing in this city's watery light, a bright red rug on the parquet floor, a white-framed single bed bought at the last minute, when we were certain we needed something larger than a crib.

'Do you like your room?' I asked Will when he arrived. That was Tuesday.

'It's bigger than my last one.' He sat down on the white bedspread, ran the palms of his hands against the cotton, almost, I thought, like a poor person experiencing luxury for the first time. High thread count, Egyptian. As if that were important for a child, for the waif who is in the process of becoming my son. He was afraid of getting it dirty, he told me, and I said he shouldn't worry about that. Things get dirty. But I knew we had made a mistake, created a room too adult for a boy like him. It was a space for the ideal boy, for the boy we might have had if we had been able to produce him ourselves or adopt him from birth, lullabying him beneath a miniature reproduction of an Alexander Calder mobile. For Will there would need to be different bedding, sheets with superheroes or cartoon characters, bedspreads crisscrossed by cars or motorcycles, assuming he was that kind of boy.

'We can change it if you don't like it.'

'You mean for a diff-er-ent room?' He spoke those syllables with halting correctness, as if the word had been hammered into his teeth and tongue. Such crooked teeth. We would be paying for substantial dental work in another few years.

'No, this will still be your room. But we can paint it another colour, or change the rug. And maybe you want to put up some pictures.'

'Pictures?'

'Posters, photographs. We can look for things to decorate it. It can be a hunt.'

'A treasure hunt?'

'Yes, a treasure hunt.'

Edward closes our bedroom door. We are getting used to sleeping with the door shut after years of thinking about privacy only when guests came to stay. The first night I found myself locking it and Edward shook his head, as if to say, without saying it, that we can't let him think we don't trust him. He's only a child after all. Yes, but a child we don't know, I wanted to say, tried to say with my eyes and a lift of the shoulders, a hunching forward with my arms, the slight exasperated turn of my hands to face palms to the ceiling, a child with experiences about which we may never know anything for certain, who might get it into his messed up little head that the two men who now insist on being regarded as his parents are really no better than devils that ought to be slaughtered in their sleep. Edward rolled his eyes, as if to say, again without saying it, too many horror films, too much para-noia, this is not *The Omen*, or whatever film it is that features the psychopathic boy who kills his mother. This is just a child who needs love. We must trust him.

'Do you think he's sleeping well?' Edward asks. 'He seems tired.'

'Some children have trouble sleeping in a new bed. I read it in one of those pamphlets.'

'Might be cumulative fatigue. We don't know what it's been like for him before now.'

'The foster parents seemed all right.'

'I thought they were creepy. They called him the LO. What does that even mean?'

'The Little One.'

Edward groans and rolls his eyes. 'How dreadful.'

'They all use that expression. I didn't think she was so bad. She told me that Will—' I stop myself. It's the first time I've used my name for the boy out loud. Edward's eyebrows lace together. No, not lace – spasm, flinch. I'm confusing my husband, upsetting him. 'I mean... Romeo. I don't know what I was thinking. The foster mother, she told me we should watch him. Like a pair of hawks.'

'You see, creepy. She was just trying to scare you,' he says, getting into bed and drawing close to me, breathing into my ear. I feel him harden against my leg.

When I sleep, I dream of Will standing on our bed, flicking a whip against our faces. He draws blood.

\*

This morning Will is up before us, and there he is again, standing in front of the painting I brought back from my last buying trip to Cape Town, discovered in a gallery in the Winelands. Contemporary artist, South African, she paints from found photographs. This piece, like many of her recent works, is slightly blurred, the contours of the living room in which the child stands suggested rather than clearly delineated. When I look at the painting, I feel as if I have fallen into a stranger's memory, with no sense of the outcome or the parameters of its lost narrative. Was the boy in the original photograph wearing a monkey costume, or did the artist add the tail? Why should *this* painting hold my new child's gaze? There are other paintings and etchings, lithographs and woodcuts, but it's this canvas, of a boy in a living room, a mid-century modern interior, a palette of reds and browns and greys with a prominent slash of white – a vase on the coffee table in the foreground of the painting – that draws him.

'Have you washed already?'

He shakes his head, gives me that 'are you stupid?' glare, and with his hands indicates his clothes, day clothes, going to school clothes, a new uniform we bought for his new school. Only his feet are bare. He rises on his tiptoes and kicks his right leg out to the side. Dance or karate?

'Have you had breakfast?'

Twitching his head, he turns back to the painting.

'Come, I'll eat with you. Edward – I mean Dad—'

'Papa.'

'Papa?'

'I'm calling him *Papa*.'

I note to myself: he has called me nothing, not even my name, since arriving on Tuesday. 'Okay. Papa will take you to school this morning. I have a meeting.'

'But I want *you* to take me to school.'

'I can't, Wi—' Terrible. I catch myself. 'I have a meeting today, on the other side of town. I wouldn't make it in time.' It is meant to be the last meeting of the life I am curtailing as of three days ago, the last time I will consult with one of my company's clients, the last time for nearly half a year when I will engage the professional portion of my mind. What, I wonder at night, if the professional is all that is left, and there is no personal share remaining, no individual behind the career? I am the one taking adoption leave, not Edward. I am the one who will be the 'primary carer', as the social worker put it in her horribly nasal drone, which was an improvement over her ungrammatical emails. This meeting is the last commitment from my old life, at least for the next four months. 'How will you make time for a little one in your busy lives?' she asked us during the approval process. 'As any other parents would,' I said, 'we will adapt.'

'You should make the time,' Will says. The adult inflection is as disconcerting as his readiness for school. No doubt it's something he has heard from one of his foster parents, or even his birth parents, father chastising mother or vice versa, the parent who failed to be as available as he or she should have been getting told off by the one who has no choice but to do it all. I know, in fact, I should not frame it with such doubt: neither mother nor father made the time, they both ignored him, did not even feed or clothe him properly, though there was always money for beer, or so Will's file told us.

'It's not nice to speak like that,' I say, trying to flatten my voice.

Then, in a single fluid movement, he reaches out, picks the white ceramic vase from the coffee table and drops it on the floor. I watch it shatter on the parquet, a genuine Stig Lindberg reptile vase that I took months to source after buying the painting, part of the process of making the room match the art. I scream, a reflex, but Will – Romeo – smiles. 'You should *make* the time,' he says quietly, and puts his hands on his hips, scrutinizing the room, as if searching for something else to destroy. I see the mid-century couches ruined, the sliver of coffee table smashed, the television in its reproduction retro housing kicked in by a six-year-old foot.

'I can't. And because of what you've just done, you lose all your screen time for a week.' The punishment is unduly harsh, but it's too late to reverse course. A day's worth of no screen time would have been adequate: a week for a boy his age is eternity.

He grunts and stomps his foot, bare sole coming down hard on an edge of broken pottery, and then he is the one screaming without thought, tears erupting from his eyes, snot from the nose, boy become fountain. I lift him up in my arms, he puts his hands around my neck, sobbing, and I carry him to the bathroom. Edward pushes open the door, his face red, as if he has already decided that I must be to blame, or so I imagine.

'What the hell happened?'

'Why are you *yelling*?' Will wails.

I explain to my husband, I wash the cut in the boy's foot, I see that it's too serious simply to be bandaged, the bleeding is slow to stop, the tub is pink and crimson and white. In a different context it would be beautiful.

'We'll have to go to the hospital.'

'I'll take him,' Edward offers, as if he thinks I might not be up to the task.

'No, really, it's okay.'

'Your meeting.'

'I can reschedule.'

\*

At the hospital there is a security alert. A car has been abandoned outside the emergency entrance and a dozen police cars are surrounding it, blocking traffic, lights flashing, cones and police tape cordoning off half the street. I watch as an officer breaks the driver's side window and reaches into the car. I hold my breath, expecting the vehicle to explode, but nothing happens. The fifteen-foot-tall Victorian wrought iron gate to the car park has been chained shut and we have to find a spot several streets away.

'I can't walk,' Will says, as I help him out of the passenger seat. 'It hurts too much.'

'I'll carry you,' I say, imagining what the hospital staff and social workers will think, the questions they will inevitably ask. I wonder if I can carry him the whole distance, but the neglect that Will suffered means he is smaller and lighter than a six-year-old should be. He climbs me, clings to my neck, holds on, surveilling the road behind us. I inhale his odour: white bread soaked in sweet milk, a dusting of cinnamon, a faint note of coffee and cardamom, and then his head is nuzzling my hair and a balloon of warmth expands in my chest.

'I'm too heavy.'

'No, you are very light.'

'Like air?' he says into my ear, almost whispering.

'Even lighter.'

By the time we get home from the hospital it is after noon. Blessedly few questions from the staff, and instead an understanding from the nurses and the attending doctor that these accidents happen, a gash on the foot is not the kind of thing an abusive parent might inflict, although come often enough with strange wounds and they would have to wonder: abusive, sadistic, or ill. My mother once had a patient with Munchausen's by proxy. Though confident of my innocence, I feel the guilt of speculation.

'What about school?' Will asks.

'No school today.'

'But I'll get in trouble.'

'You won't. I'll phone them. You need to heal. Keep your weight off the foot. We'll have a long weekend instead.'

'What will we do?'

This is the moment I have been dreading since we started the process more than two years ago. With an infant it would have been easy, no expectation of entertainment at first, just routine care, the instincts of parenting, months and years to get used to each other before demands for entertainment would ever be articulated. What does one do to occupy a child of six all day? Can a boy that age not amuse himself? No, unwise: a boy like Will might fill the hours by emptying my home of all that I cherish. Art, objects, mementoes of travel accumulated over the course of my life. I am not prepared to sacrifice such things for the sake of a child's entertainment.

I look at the painting across the living room, the image of the boy gazing at the person absent from the picture, the white vase on the impression of a coffee table, the painting in the background of the painting, the wall lamps, the spectre of couches and cushions, the old-fashioned television, a world that is recognizable, a mirror of the room I have created around it, but as if seen through a scrim that both separates and distorts. Art, I think. Art is a thing I know how to do. I am, after all, a professional.

'We could do some painting.'

'Painting my bedroom?'

'Painting a picture.'

'Like making art?'

'Yes, making art.'

Will nods.

Where will it be safe? A mushroom stain easily washed off the kitchen wall, and we can begin with watercolours, nothing too permanent, something that will wipe clean from tiles and granite. We used washable paint in the kitchen, the floor repels everything that falls on it, the cabinets are metal and glass. Watercolour, even if splattered, cannot do much harm in a kitchen. From the materials cupboard in my study I get out tubes of paint, brushes, and two large spiral-bound pads of watercolour paper. Will limps behind me as I lay a drop cloth on the counter and drape old towels over two of the kitchen stools. The floor can look after itself. I open the pads of paper next to each other on the counter, squirt paint onto the two palettes, and fill empty tuna cans with water from the tap. I tell Will to change into old clothes, and then realize he has no old clothes, he has hardly any clothes to his name, coming to us with a single duffel bag of belongings: seven pairs of underwear, seven pairs of socks, two sets of his old school uniform, a couple pairs of jeans, shorts, shirts and t-shirts, one coat, no hat or scarf, two pairs of shoes, no toys or books or other possessions.

'A white t-shirt,' I say, 'or that black one you have, and a pair of shorts.'

'I only have school shorts.'

'What about the ones from your old uniform?'

He hesitates.

'You won't need them again. Different colours at your new school.' Is it wrong to feel pleasure at being able to provide with such confidence, to assure the child in my care that what he has struggled to maintain may now be discarded with impunity? There will always be more, cheap, until it all runs out, or the world upends itself.

When he has changed, I help him onto the stool and show him

how to dip the brush first in the water, then in the paint, and begin to apply colour to the paper, deciding to let him experiment, not to be prescriptive. Let him make mistakes, allow him to see what happens with too much water, the way the paper will begin to curl and undulate.

'What should I paint?' he asks me.

'Whatever you like.'

'But I don't know what to paint.' He rolls his eyes, pouting a little.

'Paint yourself. Do a self-portrait.'

'A picture of my*self*?'

Why should this seem so preposterous to him? Because no one has ever suggested to him that he is worth representing?

'Why not?'

He pushes his face to a point, brows and lips forced outward as though trying to join up with the tip of his nose. 'Okay, maybe I could do that,' he says, and chooses a brush, dips the brush first in the water and then in the orange paint, which he applies to the paper in a circle. He fills in the circle and on either side of it paints two arcs, and then at the base of the circle a long post, out of which protrude four smaller posts: a stick-figure self, naked. I try to occupy myself with my own painting, to let him work without feeling observed. A memory of a Paul Klee exhibition leads my hand to an irregular grid of colours, a flattened harlequin, or a clown crushed by a steam-roller. Will dips his brush in the water, swirls it about, and then jabs it into a worm of blue paint. Wet on wet. He will either be captivated by the possibility of colours blurring, or distressed by the impreci-sion of the result. As the blue enters the orange, they combine into a greenish-brown arc where he has intended to paint a shirt. He quickly withdraws the brush and watches as the colour spreads.

'It's messy.'

'Wet colours run, but it's fine, there's nothing wrong with that.'

'Your one isn't messy,' he says.

'No, but I use less water, and there are different kinds of paint-ings.' I show him some reproductions of work by Marlene Dumas, wet on wet. 'You can make any kind of painting you want. Just experiment.'

'Espeeramet?'

How his accent grates. It will have to be ironed, flattened, dried out.

'Try things. See what happens. Don't worry what it's going to look like in the end. Just get a feel for the medium, the paints.' I catch myself being prescriptive even in my desire to liberate.

He tries again, brush against the paper, blue into orange, feathery blurs of colour. This is a child who wants precision, who has undoubtedly been required to stay within the lines of colouring books, whose teachers have praised tidiness rather than creativity. His parents – the first people who called themselves his parents, who forfeited the right to call this boy their son – probably shouted at him if he made a mess. I can imagine the foster parents, a couple in their sixties, rough in their speech but tidy in their habits, house-proud with net curtains and silk flowers, shouting at Will if he stepped out of line. His clothes arrived clean, pressed, folded in that duffel bag, the spare shoes wrapped in plastic, all of it, every stitch, manufactured in China, perhaps even by children like Will. When I think of China I think of regimentation, the management of nature, everything controlled and precise, chaos pushed to the edges or hidden behind façades. This, I note, is the Year of the Fire Monkey, a year of change.

Will throws his brush down on the counter and grunts through his nose in frustration. Watercolour was the wrong choice. Crayons, coloured pencils, fine-tipped magic markers, those would have been better.

*

Will is in bed after calling George and Henry names so rude even they, usually unflappable, are shocked. Where could he have learned that language, except from adults? Surely no child his age would know such artful obscenities. For half an hour after

148

being put to bed, he continued to scream. I worry about what the neighbours will think, and then, as if my psychological evolution is outpacing my expectations, I find that I no longer care about neighbours.

'I'm sorry, guys,' I say, 'I hoped he might behave for company. One of my many recent miscalculations.'

'He's very alpha for a six-year-old,' George says, pouring himself a second vodka.

'I fear what may be coming in a few years' time, sweetie,' says Henry. 'Are you ready for all the teenage issues?'

'He's only six.'

'Ten is the new fifteen,' George says, 'I have godsons, my dear, I *know*.'

I glance at Edward, giving him the tight smile that says this is exactly what I predicted would happen and he should have trusted me in the first place.

'It's going to be fine. He's had a difficult start,' Edward says, and I find his confidence as maddening as it is reassuring. I want to say: You have not spent the day with him, you cannot imagine the difficulty of scrubbing blue and orange handprints off the living room walls as the child who is now your son threatens to throw himself from the balcony to his death because he hates you. 'We will all adjust, and things will calm down. Love conquers all.'

'Love does not conquer trauma. Only psychoanalysis can help you there,' George says.

'Or pharmaceuticals,' says Henry, smirking. 'I know a doctor who will give you *anything* if you switch on the tears.'

'If he wasn't happy painting, what *does* the boy like to do?' George asks.

'He says he likes to dance.'

'But *you* like to dance, darling. You used to be so good at it.'

'You should teach him to tango,' Henry laughs. 'That's a dance which is all about governing rage.'

*

He wakes me up, pushing a space between Edward and me, and then, after a minute, begins to breathe a stately waltz of sleep. It is too dark for me to see Edward's face, but I hear his head turn, his mouth open, and I know that if we could look into each other's eyes, we would both be smiling, brows crinkled in expressions of empathy, or sympathy, for the troubled child at rest. Will's arm twitches, not pushing my husband and me apart, I try to tell myself, but pushing out a space for himself, opening a compartment within the us that already is, expanding our sense of the we as we've known it.

*

Saturdays are always hopeful. Will comes tiptoeing into the kitchen, rubbing his eyes, a flag of hair flying after being pressed into place by ten hours in bed. I wash the wound on his sole, examine the stitches, and he winces when I wrap it again and pull on the sock. This is your own doing, I want to say, but know that is both true and not. His doing was the work of other hands, those of the absent birth parents who created this beast – no, child – who breaks what is precious to someone else and, when chastised, injures himself in retort: a piece of brutalist performance art. Someone should give those birth parents the Turner Prize. We could open our home as a gallery space, stage nightly performances for a limited run. I might turn myself from a designer back into an artist, take the credit, sign my name to the work of my child.

After I have cleaned up the cotton swabs and tissues from dressing Will's wound, I give him a bowl of cereal. He picks flakes from the milk and arranges them in a smiley face on the kitchen table, checking out of the corner of his eye to see if I will scold him. Edward does the work for me.

'Don't play with your food, my boy,' he says, smoothing Will's riot of hair back into place. I wait for our child to react, and Will seems to be waiting to see how he himself will respond. He looks from Edward to me and back to Edward, then picks each flake of cereal from the counter and puts it in his mouth before finishing all the food in his bowl. This is the child corrected, trying to be good, and yet I struggle to smile, to reward him for doing as he has been told. We need to have a conversation about words, the words he used last night. The later we leave it, the harder it will become, but Edward has to attend a symposium, and either I will do it alone, or it will wait until this evening, and that, I feel certain, will be too late to have the proper effect, to make Will see that calling our friends names is unacceptable, that there are limits to our capacity to accept his behaviour, that he must mould himself into a different version of the boy he has always been. I would rather do it with Edward, but it must happen now, so I wait until my husband is out the door and then sit down across the kitchen table from Will. He turns his spoon upside down and a trickle of milk dribbles along the steel edge.

'You seemed very angry last night,' I say, holding out my hand to him. He looks at my palm as if he does not know what to do with it, then puts his own hands in his lap, leaving mine there, naked, abandoned.

'No.'

'Those were angry words you used with our friends.'

His features pull together again into a point, his head twitches, he makes animal noises, clicks his tongue against his palate and scratches his armpit. Is this acknowledgement or refusal? I need less ambiguous sign language.

'Do you know what those words mean?'

He shakes his head. Quite clear this time.

'Where did you hear them?'

'Can we dance?' he asks.

'No, not right now. We're talking about words.'

'But I want to dance.'

He gets up and shuffles across the kitchen to the stereo, switches it on, prods the tuner button until he finds a station he likes, turns up the volume, and begins throwing his arms in the air. A chimpanzee, I think, an orangutan. The song is not one I have heard, on a station I would never choose, but Will knows the words and sings along with the girl on the radio, lyrics about moving furniture to dance. When his back is turned, I slip past him, turn off the radio, and stand with my arms folded across my chest. He spins around and growls at me, then hurtles forward, palms out, and pushes me backwards against the counter, throwing me off balance so I hit my head on the cabinet. Half the room goes black and the other half ripples with small silver explosions. I stagger, put my hand to the back of my head, feel moisture and stickiness.

'Sit down!' I scream. 'Sit down right now!'

Will cowers, huddling in the corner near the door to the living room. He pulls out the cutlery drawer and crouches beneath it, arms wrapped around his shaking legs.

*

The same nurse is on duty as last time.

'It's you today, I see,' he says, ripping open the cover on a sterile swab.

'My son pushed me. Yesterday he broke my favourite vase and cut himself on it, today he pushes me into a cabinet.'

The nurse gives me a look, as if he thinks I might deserve it, then shakes his head. 'I see it more than you'd think,' he says, and leaves me holding a compress as I wait for the doctor. X-rays, no concussion, stitches, a bandage. A minor incident in family life, I suppose, for the vast majority of people with children. To me it seems like a crisis from which we may not recover. I imagine returning Will to the department store where we bought his bed, asking for another model, one that is not quite so defective, but Edward and I agreed, no matter what, we would not give up on this boy. 'Altruism,' I said to Edward when we made the decision, 'weighs significantly more than love.'

'How do you mean?' he asked.

'I feel it on my shoulders already,' I said, and he took me in his arms, plumping me upright.

When I come out to reception, Edward and Will are sitting

hunched over a colouring book, an adult colouring book, one of those intricately designed things composed of botanical and animal motifs, each leaf a maze of competing patterns, every feather a mosaic of byzantine complexity. Will is focused on a frog, working hard to stay in the lines of the serpentine forms that make up its legs.

'What do you say, Romeo?' Edward prompts the boy who, if we all play nicely and adjust to one another, will legally be our son in a matter of eight weeks, from which point onward dissolution will become much more difficult, might require, for all I know, me declaring myself an unfit parent.

'Sorry,' the boy mumbles.

'Sorry for what?'

'Sorry for pushing you,' says the boy.

'How about a kiss?' says Edward.

No, I want to say, I do not want a kiss from that little beast, but I lean over and let him embrace me, his arms circling my neck, hot breath landing with a smack alongside my nose.

*

At dinner, I allow my husband and this boy who breaks my belongings and attacks me without provocation to do all the talking. How have they bonded so easily? I do not laugh at the boy's jokes. I refuse him eye contact. I clear the dishes, I ask Edward to see to the boy's bath and bedtime. I have a headache, I say. I take a painkiller and grip the edge of the sink, looking out on the common gardens of the development, listening to the buses pass, the sirens running to the hospital, and, down the hall, the sound of laughter, the boy and my husband joking, joshing, getting on so well with each other. This was not what I signed up for. I will phone the social worker on Monday morning and tell her to come get the boy. The bed can still be returned to the department store – the frame at least. I'll donate the mattress. Health and Safety rules. Contamination. Does no one think how a feral child might contaminate its nest? We will start over, remortgage the flat, hire a California surrogate. I do not want to spend the rest of my life fixing someone else's failure.

'You can't continue to punish him,' Edward says, after we have gone to bed.

'He needs to know he can't behave like that.'

'I think he knows. He's just a boy.'

'He's not a boy. He's an animal. We can't keep him. He has to go back,' I say, as Edward suddenly seizes my hand, staring past me. I turn my head, and Will is there in his pyjamas, standing in the light of the doorway, his face scrambled and wet, features drawn to that terrible point. Pinched, I think, I have acquired an English child with pinched features. How much I would rather have one of my own, an American baby with no early trauma other than separation from its biological parents, a child I could hold from the moment of birth. As I look at the tears on the face of the boy I agreed to turn into my son, I wait for the ballooning of love in my chest, but nothing comes, no breath of affection.

The boy turns and runs down the hall, Edward springing from our bed to go after him. I listen to the crying and beneath it the murmur of Edward's consolations. He is good at consolation, as he is good at almost everything, perhaps save self-interest or introspection, or the development of an inner life. I wonder sometimes if my husband is ever contemplative, or is instead as purely animal as he so often seems – animal in the best sense, of course, natural and responsive and fit, a thing of nature within nature. Consolation is an animal trait. Pet videos have proved it to us. The behaviour of elephants, too, in a time of death. What is their mourning if not an act of group consolation?

At the start of this process, we agreed that Edward would be the parent who said no, because he has an instinct for comfort, for making rejection palatable. I am too likely to snap and bark (too human, I think, or too like an animal that has been mistreated and so becomes unnatural), and as a consequence I must be the one who always says yes, even if that yes is qualified by the admonition, 'but ask Papa what he thinks'. I fear we made a mistake, working against our natural instincts in this way.

'You get to choose,' Edward says when he comes back to bed, an hour or so later, perhaps longer, after singing Will to sleep with a lullaby I have never heard before, but which made my toes curl with its sweetness. 'Either you commit to what we're doing, or it's over. All of it.'

What are Edward's eyes doing? The lids are red and the pupils contracting as he stares at me, his chin trembling. I look away and he snaps his fingers in my face to make me turn back. I have never seen such violence from my husband.

'Don't do that. That's not the kind of thing we do to each other.'

'Listen to me,' he says, his voice breaking. 'We are doing this together or there is no more we.'

'And if I can't?'

'You must try. And now it's your turn to apologize to Romeo.'

'I cannot call him by that name.'

'But that's his name! He's too old to change it. After all he's been through, we cannot call him Will. He must be Romeo.'

'It's not a name I can say. It's too ridiculous. It makes me feel like the Juliet I am not.'

'Then what could you call him? Just as a start.'

I think about this, try to judge from his expression whether Edward really means what he says, but there is determination there, no flicker of falseness. He sounds like he is trying to be patient with me, despite whatever he feels. What would I do to save *us*? Embrace a beast in our home? Isn't there a folktale of a monkey turning human? I can think only of stories – real ones – of orphan children raised by baboons and eventually saved by human society. The retraining, the unmonkeying of those human apes, sometimes takes years, as the evolution of humans from our ape ancestors took countless millennia, I remind myself. I must adjust my expectations, perhaps every day for the rest of my life, decades spent in a mode of constant adjustment.

'I could call him *my boy*.'

'Then call him that at least. The name will come.'

'Or a nickname. I could call him a nickname. Something like Ro.'

Edward's eyes clear and he smiles despite his desire, I suspect, to be stern with me.

'You know what that means?' he asks.

'Enlighten me, oh scholar of the arcane.'

'Rest. Repose. Peace. Noun or verb. A Germanic import. Perhaps originally Icelandic. *Ró*. As in the York Mystery Plays of the fifteenth century, which I was meant to be talking about today if you hadn't had your little kitchen drama. *Nowe are we brought Bothe unto rest and rowe.*'

'Noun and verb? Imperative as well?'

'Not strictly, but I suppose it could be. Adjust its usage. Language is dynamic.'

'Name maketh man.'

Edward puts his hands on my shoulders and draws me close. 'We can only try.'

As I go to sleep, I think of the meaning of the child's whole name, *Romeo*, an Italianization of the Late Latin *Romaeus*, which meant one who makes pilgrimage to Rome, if I remember my high school Shakespeare class. Still, I cannot help feeling it is a vulgar name for a child today. Perhaps in Italy it would be different. Context is key. If I were to take him to Rome, to see the origins of his name, perhaps that would also, by some magic, *ro* him.

*

The next morning, I find the child again in front of the painting, this time standing on a chair, his face level with the canvas and square with the boy who is composed of fluid oil that has hardened into form: permanent, short of its destruction by fire or blade or the deteriorations of time. Does he see himself in that child with a tail? He has one hand on the wall to the left of the canvas, which is unframed, just as the artist intended, I believe, and as I found it in the gallery in Stellenbosch, in a room of the artist's other unframed canvases, blurred images of young men and women, families, one of a black nanny holding a screaming white infant titled *Monster Love*.

My heart drops when I see the child I am meant to love. I want to shout at him to get down, not to touch, but then remember my role. I am the one who says yes, Edward must say no. When the boy's right hand reaches up as if to touch the painting I know I cannot wait for my husband to get out of bed.

'It's better not to touch it,' I say. Romeo's head swivels so he can look at me, but his left hand remains stuck against the wall and the right one is frozen mid-reach. 'We have oil on our hands, and dirt, and those things are bad for art.'

'Why is oil bad for art?'

'It leaves a residue. A trace. An invisible mark. And over time, that trace would collect dust and dirt and gradually it would become a black mark, and over an even longer time that black mark would begin to decay and destroy the painting.'

He squints. I have lost him.

'Think of the painting as if it were the cleanest thing in the world. Would you want to get the cleanest thing in the world dirty?'

'Maybe.'

'But it's good to keep clean things clean.'

'You said it was okay for things to get dirty.'

'Some things, yes, but not works of art.'

'Why?'

'So we can enjoy them in their ideal state. So that other people can enjoy them. If we get a work of art that is very clean dirty, then it has to be cleaned again, and every time we clean it, a little bit of it gets worn down or disappears, and so we speed up its process of decay. This painting is in an almost ideal state. I acquired it – I bought it – new from a gallery. No one else has owned it but the artist herself. It has never had to be cleaned. If we look after it, it will not have to be cleaned for a long time yet, and so we will make it last longer.'

'But I want to touch it. I want to see what it feels like.'

This is a boy, I realize, who has never touched an oil painting, who has never possessed anything of value other than his clothes and shoes and a few small toys.

'We'll get a special one just for you.'

'A painting?'

'Yes. We'll go today, to find a painting that you can touch.'

*

I tell Edward my plan and his eyes narrow, looking away from me in that English way he has of suggesting demurral, or deferral, I'm never sure which.

'How much will you spend?' he asks.

'A thousand. Fifteen hundred.'

'That much?'

'Not if I can help it,' I say, 'but that's what I'm prepared to spend to secure the future of the painting I love. The alternative is to frame it, under glass, and have it securely bolted to the wall, and that would cost no less.' I do not tell Edward, hardly tell myself, that I have dreamt of Romeo destroying it.

I take him to a junk shop that calls itself an Antique Market. Sensing his skittishness, I squeeze his hand, smiling with my eyes, as my mother taught me, to reassure, to express genuine warmth, although I feel the mechanics of my own performance. All too human.

The owner of the Market, a woman in her sixties, has an inflated sense of the stuff she peddles, thinking it all priceless when it is, mostly, run-of-the-mill brown furniture and Victorian genre paintings that few people want. She watches every move my boy makes.

'We're looking for a painting for my son's room,' I tell her. 'Something interesting, with character, with people in it.'

She leads us to the back of the shop and points to an antechamber full of paintings, some hanging, others stacked on the floor and leaning against the walls, many framed, a few not. I have in mind a classical scene, perhaps something with hunters, or even a family portrait. Romeo's eyes dart up and down before he shakes his head. 'It isn't here.'

'We haven't looked properly,' I say.

He dismisses pictures of horses and cows and dogs. He has no interest in a group portrait of one family's seven children. Landscapes bore him. Classical ruins puzzle him. 'Why make a painting of *that*?' If it has a frame, he shows no interest. Near the back of the room, I find a curious eighteenth-century painting of three men: a white Englishman, his son, and the man's African slave. I put it aside, but this is the one that Romeo notices.

'We could maybe take this one,' he says.

'But here's a nice tropical picture,' I say, finding a French salon painting of a woman with large breasts and a flowing white gown reclining on a divan surrounded by Asian-looking attendants. There is even a monkey playing on the ground, reaching for a bauble.

'No, this one,' Romeo insists, touching the picture of the three men. His index finger taps at its surface, while his ring and middle finger scoot back and forth, learning the texture of varnish and oil, the suggestion of soft tackiness that remains, even years after a painting is finished.

In the end I buy both. The woman wraps them in brown paper and ties them up with a rough brown cord. We take a taxi home.

*

'It's a very gloomy painting,' Edward says, grimacing at the portrait of the three men, which now hangs above Romeo's bed.

When he sees it on the wall, Romeo shouts, 'It's not *right*,' and thrusts his fists to his side. I wonder if this reaction is prompted by Edward's scepticism.

'But it's the one you wanted, my boy,' I remind him.

'I want the other one!' he screams.

I go to our bedroom and bring back the painting of the woman and the monkey and the Asian attendants. Louche, I think, a rather dubious painting for a little boy's room.

'No!' Romeo screams again. 'I want *your* painting. In *there*.' He points towards the living room. I know which painting he wants. It is time for Edward to play his part, to say no, to make the refusal palatable, but this time, Romeo will not be consoled and we spend the rest of the day and the evening listening as he sobs in his room.

*

In the middle of the night, I wake from a deep but troubled sleep, *dream ravaged*, I say to myself. Something has woken me, but Edward remains asleep. We went to bed to the sound of Romeo's cries slackening off. He refused to eat. He would not bathe. He went to bed in his day clothes. He screamed obscenities at us, worse than anything he said to George and Henry. For the first time in the past week, Edward looked shaken by the child's behaviour. He saw what I have had the privilege, or burden, of seeing on my own.

'I don't know,' he said as we turned out the light. 'Perhaps you were right.'

I expect to find Romeo in the living room, but then notice the light from his bedroom. When I look through the open door I am stunned to find *Interior: Monkeyboy* hanging above his bed, in place of the eighteenth-century portrait of the men and the boy. He must have swapped the paintings on his own, and then I notice that he is wearing his new pyjama bottoms but no shirt and his body is covered in red streaks. At first I think he is bleeding, flayed, but then I see that on each of his arms there is only a red stripe of paint, watercolour, extending from his elbow to wrist, red stripes that imitate the red highlights on the arms of the boy in the painting. There is also an appendage, just above the waist of the pyjamas at his back, a long thin tail, twisting slightly, that piece of rough brown cord from the Antiques Market, affixed to his skin with electrical tape.

For a moment we stand there, him looking at the picture, me looking at him from the hall. I hear the shushing of a bus and a siren's drone, although the noise is scarcely audible through the closed windows and may only be in my mind. Perhaps sensing my presence, Romeo turns his head, offering me a three-quarter view. His eyes are dark and beady, like the boy in the painting, his chin set with confidence, wilfulness. Alpha, as George said. An Alpha male, my Romeo. I know what I must do.

'Come here, my boy. We can dance if you like.'

'Now?'

'Yes. I am going to teach you to tango.'

# LOSS

A year after being approved as potential adopters, we have an annual review with Gemma's new supervisor, Adriana, an Italian woman who is the most sympathetic social worker we have encountered since Eleanor. It is not lost on any of us that Adriana, too, is an outsider in Britain. She is well educated, thoughtful, attentive to our concerns. She seems to recognize that we have not felt understood or even *seen* by the whole of the British social care system.

For the first time in months, we feel hope again, but it is a hope immediately undercut by grief.

When you are a late-in-life child, you arrive at the season of loss sooner than most. A few years earlier, Andrew's father suffered several small strokes, but remained stable until now, when he has a bad fall, contracts pneumonia, comes out of the hospital with what appears to be dementia, and spends weeks in a care unit. He eventually goes home and my mother-in-law looks after him with the help of assistants and nurses.

By January he seems to be recovering, but has slowed down appreciably. Most of his days are spent at home in his plantation chair on the veranda, looking over the tops of eucalyptus trees to the mountains which must be for him, now nearly blind, little more than a shifting blur of greens and ochres that disappear into a white mist when the clouds descend.

Then, just before Valentine's Day, he develops an infection and returns to the hospital for treatment. He seems once again to be recovering until, one morning, he suddenly passes away.

By chance, Andrew is already in the country. I fly out. My sister-in-law and her youngest daughter fly out. Relatives from across South Africa drive or fly to be there for the memorial service.

Andrew takes in hand most of the arrangements for the service and tying up the estate, co-ordinating with lawyers. He manages everything with a dizzying efficiency and calm, but in the midst of that calm, on summer mornings in the Western Cape, the floral arrangements wilting after only a few days no matter how much care we lavish on them, I look at him and worry, because in my American way I expect to see grief manifested in tears and sobbing or rage and depression, and I see none of those things.

In April, just after Easter, Gemma contacts us for the first time in months, sending a profile of a boy, O—, who is about to turn four. She wonders if we might be interested. Yes, I respond after quickly reading through his profile, we are.

I will look back on this moment and think that our emotional vulnerability made us desperate for this particular child to work when we had always insisted we wanted a child much younger, under the age of two, as close to newly arrived in the world as possible. What else but our own vulnerability and need for the promise of another life, the promise that our own lives would have meaning beyond us, as our parents' lives presumably have meaning – at least in part – because of our own existences, could explain our willingness to shift the boundaries of what we desire, let alone what we feel able to manage?

We have expressed interest in dozens of children and never been judged appropriate enough even to merit a first meeting. But O—'s social workers do want to meet us, and this feels like a sign that it might be meant to happen, even as we try to protect ourselves against further disappointment.

O—'s foster mother, Gemma tells us, thought he'd do well with two daddies.

## SARA AND CATHERINE

Christina is a social worker. She is single. It is the mid-1990s. When I meet her, she has an adopted daughter, Sara, who is seven, and has just adopted Catherine, a four-year-old Korean girl. I meet them that summer when I am working as a 'mother's helper' or 'manny' for a family who have a house on a lake in the Berkshires in western Massachusetts.

Sara attends the same school as the two girls I am looking after, although she is on scholarship. She is wiry and loud and needy, seems to want constant reassurance, craves boundaries and then rebels against them. Christina is always patient and teacherly in her mothering. She and I have an instant rapport and we often go swimming together with the mother I'm working for and her two girls.

I spend many days with Sara and Catherine, who is adorable and cuddly, but also has a stubborn streak. She spent her first years in an orphanage, but what this means is that her needs were met from birth, even if imperfectly so. She was fed, clothed, kept warm, but perhaps not loved, unless we can imagine an orphanage worker who might have held her when she cried. She has an infectious laugh, likes to be cuddled and carried. She seems, for the most part, a child who has come through loss and landed on her feet.

Sara, on the other hand, was adopted from Boston's foster care system. Christina tells me stories of Sara's wild, hour-long tantrums in grocery stores when she refuses to buy her candy, the girl screaming, 'You're not my mother! I hate you!' Christina calmly tells Sara that she *is* her mother, will always be her mother.

If someone as patient and skilful as Christina still faces such a response, how can adoptive parents with fewer skills possibly cope?

A couple of years later I see Christina and her daughters at a party. Catherine is flourishing. She wears an extravagantly ruffled pink dress and flits among the adults, telling jokes, making people laugh. She is socially astute, charming and confident.

Sara, now ten or eleven, is in the midst of a tantrum. She has perceived a minor slight against her. She seethes, pouts, sits in a corner crying. When she has had enough of everything, she screams.

Years pass. I fail to keep up with them, but now I go looking for clues, and realize that I am in search of reassurance. I find Sara online. She looks well. She works as an actress, has several credits to her name, is elegant, graceful, with a poise I sometimes caught glimpses of when she was a child, striking poses by the pool. She seems to have a good relationship with Catherine, who has made visits back to South Korea, even to the orphanage where she used to live, which looks like a bright and happy place, full of smiling children. And they both appear to have good relationships with Christina, so that it seems as though, despite the difficulty of those early years, things have turned out well, even kind of great.

Nonetheless, I'm not sure that the narrative of difficulty overcome, the promise of everything coming right in the end, is enough to convince me. I don't know if I'm as strong as someone like Christina, or even if Andrew and I together are as strong and resilient as Christina was on her own.

# ON PAPER

O—'s file, at least the parts of it to which we are given access, includes only a few photographs of him and a lengthy report ostensibly about his background, although it is almost entirely about his four siblings and parents and offers very little description of him or his early experiences. Nearly all of what we learn about his first year of life is, I come to suspect, a matter of supposition. Our sense of those first twelve months ultimately comes not from the file – which only paints a picture of the household, the parents, the older siblings – but from what people tell us, and we accept everything we are told without question.

O—'s parents have been resisting the adoption of their children, fighting it in the courts. When we first learn about O—, the case is still not settled and his parents have one last chance to appeal, although the social workers are confident the court will find against the young couple.

We are given the full names of the parents, so I go looking for information about them. I need to know what kind of people they are in a way that the report does not tell me.

This is not difficult. Intimate details of their lives are publicly available on their social media profiles, visible for all the world to access. There are baby photos of their children, photos of them at later stages, a photo of O— around the age when he and his siblings were finally removed from the home.

In photos of the parents themselves I find people who look nothing like the monsters I have been imagining. They are young, much younger than I, and although they must be in their mid- to late-twenties the way they present themselves strikes me as adolescent. To my relief, both have favourite books listed on their profile pages, children's books, fantasy. I imagine meeting them at some point in the future. If they read, then these are people I could potentially talk with for five minutes or ten, even an hour, if circumstances required. Fantasy novels might provide sufficient material to build a temporary bridge strong enough to support us all for the duration of our interaction.

I mention to Gemma that we have looked at the parents' profiles on social media, and that this was, to our surprise, reassuring. We feel positive. We want to move forward. We book a date for the boy's social workers to meet us.

Richard and Megan arrive on a warm morning in June. Richard jokes that he would have liked to stay the night and see the city but Megan is anxious to get back to the countryside, so once they have visited another couple who are under consideration as O—'s potential adopters they will take the train home. We have no idea whether the other couple is same-sex or opposite-sex, whether they own their home, if they live in a flat or a house, if they have a garden or a dog, if they are British or foreign-born like us.

I want to ask Richard and Megan why they thought we'd be appropriate in our small rented flat with shared garden for a boy who is used to life in open spaces, but I'm too anxious for them to choose us to risk giving any reason to doubt.

Richard is loud and affable. Megan is reserved, a little skittish. I have baked two kinds of muffin. They both eat one of each. Megan tells us that O— has lots of love to give, and would keep us on our toes.

He's full of energy. He just doesn't stop, but he's a sweet boy, full of love. Full of love, she keeps saying.

She has brought other photos, more recent ones. We see his shock of bright red hair clearly for the first time. On his own, removed from the contextualizing scale of adults or other children, his age is difficult to judge. He looks thoughtful, a little wistful, sometimes smiling, sometimes pensive, trudging across fields on long walks with his foster father.

Cheeky, Gemma says, holding up a photo that shows the little boy with a glint in his eye, a smirk, rosy cheeks, a spike of red hair.

He does have a cheeky smile, Megan says, but he's got a lot of love to give. A lot of love. He'll need at least one long walk each day, maybe two, she says.

As if he were a dog.

Sometimes more than that, says Richard. He's always on the go.

An hour later they have left and we try to get on with our lives, try not to invest too much hope in this. They are waiting on the court to hear the parents' appeal, and that will happen in August.

Weeks pass and we assume they must be going with the other couple.

Then, late in June, Richard phones to say they would like to choose us, if we're still interested.

At first, we aren't sure what this means. There still seems to be an element of uncertainty given the pending appeal. But when we ask her about this, Gemma says that no one thinks the court will find in the parents' favour.

And this means we should get ready, because it's almost certainly going to happen.

Cautiously, we begin telling our closest friends and family. Our mothers are overjoyed, Andrew's nieces and sister and brother-in-law are thrilled.

But when I phone my father in Omaha, there is a stunning silence before he speaks.

I guess that means you're never moving back here, he says.

We would move to the US if we could both find jobs there, I say, which is true, but finding two academic jobs in the same place is not easy.

Two days later, my father falls and breaks his hip.

# YOU

Years have passed in your life. At the end of June in this year, not long after your fourth birthday, your foster mother tells you that you're getting two daddies. Your friend Charlotte at school got two mummies and went away, and now it will be your turn. They're coming next week to get you, your foster mother tells you.

But next week could mean anything to you.

Next week is tomorrow or tonight or yesterday, and you start asking when your daddies will be coming.

When the actual next week comes and the daddies do not come because they are not yet allowed to come, and your foster mother tells you that it will take longer, that the daddies are not coming, that she can't say how long it will be, and this happens in the car park of the shopping complex where you go to play on the swings, you begin to scream.

No one tells us this until months later, no one tells us that your expectations were raised far too early, before anyone had made any final decisions, before anyone was certain that they were going to choose us, before we were certain that we would choose you. No one tells us that you have spent months being disappointed in us, in our failure to appear as promised, that we have already let you down, that we have already made you doubt our reliability, our commitment to you, to looking after you, before we have even had a chance to say hello.

# CHILD PARENT CHILD

In July Andrew and I fly to Denver and then drive eight hours across Colorado and Nebraska to see my father. I think of the last time I made this trip, when I moved my father from California back to Omaha, and I think of an earlier drive, when I was twelve and my father decided he and I should try to fix our relationship by driving on our own to Colorado, stopping for a couple of nights at Fort Robinson State Park in western Nebraska, and how those trips alone with my father were some of the longest hours I have spent in my life, because there was so much to say and none of it could be said, not when I was a child, not even when I was an adult.

In the car with Andrew, imagining some future in which he and I and O— will be on this same road going to visit my father, perhaps only next year, I think about how different it will feel because I will make myself into a parent rather than a father – by which I mean, I'll be a father in category only, but will have to inhabit the categories of both mother and father, providing what society so often insists is unique to each.

Andrew and I talk about how our lives will change. We discuss hypothetical parenting situations. We think about what will happen if O— has problems not revealed in the reports. We imagine future situations in which we will have to interact with his siblings and parents and extended family. We begin to imagine a life with him, a life changed by him, and we are full of excitement and a sense of readiness for however that life develops, whatever final form it takes.

But we know him only through the narrative of other people in which he is, at best, only fleetingly visible. In my experience, social workers are not natural writers. If the children they describe were characters in a novel, we would call them flat, two-dimensional, nothing but ciphers or caricatures or stereotypes.

Our picture of O— is composed of physical and behavioural traits and a few photos, but no sense of who he might be now, or what kind of person he might have the potential to become in our care and with our love. We have seen no videos, cannot imagine what he sounds like, how he speaks, the quality of his laugh or the timbre of his cry. The descriptions of him have failed to make him live except as suggestion, so he exists for us as a person of near total possibility, and in that rough outline of personhood I begin to endow him with the qualities I hope that he has, rather than waiting to discover the person he already is.

We arrive in Omaha to find my father discharged to a substandard rehabilitation centre instead of the retirement home where he has been living for the past six years. The facility is on the western fringe of the city's suburbs in an ugly neighbourhood of strip malls and fast food outlets.

From the moment Andrew and I walk through the doors, we are faced with the archetypal nursing home nightmare that I remember from childhood school trips to sing Christmas carols. The building stinks of urine and faeces and overcooked, mass-produced food. Elderly residents sit goggle-eyed in wheelchairs, drool drizzling from their chins. In the staff there is a tone of voice, call it Midwestern Nice Gone Rogue, that I haven't heard in more than twenty years. It is the flipside of all the superficial congeniality, artificial sweetness soured by a growling roar of rage that can explode without warning because the people who contain it live in constant denial of its existence.

When I ask questions, the nurses and orderlies act as if they cannot understand my accent. A man twice the size of me looks to a woman even bigger and says, as if I could not possibly understand his words, *What did he say?*

My father is in a shared room in the rehab wing. It is a space of weird angles, five walls of unequal length that produce a disorienting zone divided by curtains and lit with fluorescents which hum and pop and can never be turned off, even at night.

There are two televisions, both tuned to maximum volume on different channels. The other patient in the room looks near death. There is more medical paraphernalia than I can process: wheelchairs and walkers and bedpans and bed urinals and leg braces and compression socks and megapacks of adult diapers. On my father's bedside table there is a stack of giant chocolate bars and on the chair several issues of the local newspaper. On the walls there is nothing apart from two mirrors, one for each resident.

I start making plans to have him moved to the rehab wing of his retirement home, a much nicer place, a nursing home on the model of a five-star hotel, which is clean, does not smell, and where no one sits around unattended or ignored. It is the kind of 'graduated care center' that people like me feel persuaded to trust because it presents such a reassuring image, no matter when I turn up, no matter whether I have given the staff warning of my visit or not.

Before I can get my father moved back to the other place, I have to leave Omaha and return to New York for speaking engagements. He will be moved in a few days, I'm told, as soon as a bed is free and a social worker from the state can come to check that his needs will be met in the other facility. This seems ludicrous given that the other facility, the place that is his home, is so obviously better than the nightmare rehab centre he is in at the moment. How, after four decades with no such complication, is my life suddenly and continuously dependent on the will of social workers?

Back in New York, we visit two couples who have become friends over the past several years. They are both opposite-sex couples, both with four-year-old sons, Elijah and Jack. On the night we have dinner in Elijah's suburban home, the boys are electric with the simple happiness of being together.

As we eat, they paint at an easel in the dining room, covering a sheet of paper with vivid blues that represent, for them, a giant chocolate chip cookie (a conflation, I suspect, of *Sesame Street*'s Cookie Monster with the food of his greatest desire). Elijah's older brother, Sam, keeps the boys entertained as the adults talk, and I marvel at how easy this life with children looks. If this is what family life is, I have no doubt Andrew and I can do it.

We stay overnight with Elijah and Sam and their parents. The next morning, while Sam shoots hoops in the driveway, Elijah lazes peacefully next to me watching TV on the couch as he succumbs to a cold. His mother takes a picture of us together and I think how, in another year, we might be visiting them with O—, he and Elijah and Jack playing anarchically together. And then, when Elijah's father comes home from the bakery with a muffin instead of a donut, Elijah has a tantrum. But it's a tantrum of the kind I would expect. It lasts ten minutes, there's a little four-year-old foot stomping and crying and anger, and then it passes. I can do this, I think. Andrew and I can do this together.

Meanwhile, in Omaha, there have been delays with my father's move back to his old facility. A bed they thought was going to open up has not, and then the social worker is delayed in coming to see him and a bed does become available but the social worker still hasn't come, and by the time she does come there is no longer an available bed.

In the midst of these delays, my father begins to fall.

He falls once, and falls again, and then, visiting the orthopaedic surgeon who performed the half-hip replacement in June, he falls once more, so seriously this time that he needs a whole new surgery, a full hip replacement, and I return on my own to Omaha while Andrew heads back to London to get our home ready for O—'s arrival.

My father's cousin and her husband drive up from Oklahoma to support us, and a former colleague does more than his share, has already done more than I could have reasonably expected from anyone. But I am aware as never before just how few people there are who will come to my father's aid: a cousin, a colleague, and me. He has no other close family, stopped going to church years earlier, stopped having lunch with retirees from his old newspaper, stopped seeing former students for coffees and dinners. Without those circuits of support, it is left to me to decide what to do next and act on those decisions. There is no one else.

If the first operation and the anaesthesia and trauma of the fall itself produced confusion, the second operation exacerbates it. He still knows who he is and who I am and who his friends and family are, but time and location no longer appear to have much meaning. The details of where he is and how he arrived here remain opaque no matter how many times I explain it.

Some days in the aftermath of the surgery he thinks he is in an office building downtown. Other days he believes he is recovering in the newsroom where he spent so many years of his working life. In the mornings the nurses are editors or publishers or other former colleagues or sources. He treats his stay in the hospital as if he is on assignment, on a story. In the afternoons he says that he needs to interview the hospital administrator. He is certain that the doctors are afraid of him because of the exposé on medical malpractice he wrote for the local paper back in the 1990s.

I try to get him discharged from the hospital to his old facility, hoping that a familiar space might help with the confusion, but despite my best efforts the hospital discharges him right back to the nightmare nursing home, and once again I throw myself into getting him transferred to his retirement home. This finally happens after two days of further delays as we wait for a room to open up – waiting for a bed to clear, for someone to recover sufficiently to move out of rehabilitation, or simply to die.

At the start of trying to decide how to manage the life of a man who suddenly has as many needs as a four-year-old, sometimes as many needs as an infant since he cannot dress himself and cannot walk unaided, the only thing I understand clearly is that he can no longer live in his 'Independent Living' apartment, and probably should not have been doing so for at least a year or more, although he was insistent that he wanted to stay there, a decision I respected and supported. Now he no longer meets even the minimum requirements for 'Assisted Living'. His daily needs are unpredictable. He cannot be trusted to make safe choices. There is simply too much uncertainty, which means the only choice is to place him in the skilled nursing wing.

It is clear, too, that his confusion is not the result of any lingering side effects from anaesthesia as I had hoped after the first surgery.

Some days he seems to live over the course of decades, moving back and forth in time. Some days his parents are still alive and angry that people are talking about them in the middle of the night. Some days I have just arrived from London, other days I have been gone for weeks rather than an hour to get lunch. Some days I seem to be in college or high school or living in New York, other days he is still married to my mother whom he divorced twenty years ago. One day I even seem to be standing in the place of his own father, a magnet for all of his frustrations and resentments and anger for my grandfather's many failures as a father to him.

And then some hours in those days my father knows exactly where and when he is, so that friends who happen to catch him in those moments, who see him when he is 'on' and visit for twenty minutes or half an hour, do not even believe – *cannot be convinced* – that he is anything other than his old self. Does he really need to be in this place? they wonder aloud. When will he be able to go back to Independent Living? they ask.

I have no choice but to close up and relinquish his old apartment. In order to do this, I have to make decisions about his belongings. In a moment when he seems to have clarity, I record a conversation in which I ask him about every single item of furniture he owns, getting his permission to donate some things, sell others, and keep what is most precious to him in storage at my mother's house. Even though they have been divorced for two decades, my parents remain on good terms, and apart from me my father trusts my mother more than anyone else.

I try to leave him with everything that is most meaningful, and which might help him remember his life for as long as he can. I leave him his mother's 1940s side table with inlaid wood, his favourite chair although it is now too deep for him to sit in, as many of his pictures and posters and photographs as I can fit on the walls of his new room. Although he no longer reads, I leave him all of his books and bookcases. I leave him his dresser and 52-inch television and DVD player and CD player and CDs and DVDs and ornaments and tchotchkes. I leave him his living will and make a copy for the administrators, so that they will know, as I do, that he wants his body left to science.

But there is still so much stuff, things he cannot keep because there is simply no room. I spend the next ten days staying in his apartment, cooking for myself, sleeping in his bed, trying to mini-mize the cost of everything in the face of so many expenses that I cannot fathom how people without my father's resources manage such transitions. Without money, everything would have to be thrown away, and in some cases even outright disposal bears a cost. Most charities charge for the collection of beds, until I finally find one that will take his for nothing. I deliver towels and bedding and kitchen supplies that he will no longer need to a charity helping Syrian refugee families resettle in the area.

During those days, working from before sunrise until after midnight, I hardly stop moving. I drive all over the city, buying boxes and tape, making donations, meeting with lawyers, sorting out cable bills and phone bills and banking arrangements. In the apartment, there are files to be packed, bills to be paid, a life to be sorted out that has, I can see, become seriously chaotic since I last visited.

I work myself to a standstill trying to get everything organized. I eat standing up, the same lunch every day: slices of tofu between slices of bread with tomato and lettuce. My clothes begin to slip off me. I buy a smaller pair of shorts, smaller shirts. I know that I have only so many days. Before I go to sleep, having spent another evening packing china and silver and old family photographs and my father's reporting archives, his field notes and doctoral research notes and a life's worth of correspondence, I calculate how many hours are left before I have to leave the city. I revise lists of what remains to be done before I can fly back to London, where Andrew in turn is working himself to a standstill trying to transform our guest room into a bedroom for O—.

I know how much my father needs me but I find myself caught in bouts of furious resentment. I want to be in London with Andrew as he chooses the bed and dresser and toys and pillows. I want to be present to help him assemble the furniture and decorate the room. I want to be present for the preparations in anticipation of the arrival of the boy who will become our son, to have a final few weeks of calm and reflection with my husband before our lives change permanently. Instead, I am caught in a spiral of crisis management.

When I walk down the hall from my father's old apartment in Independent Living, through the communal living rooms and dining rooms, accompanied by the twenty-four-hour soundtrack of easy-listening versions of songs from the 1930s, '40s and '50s, past the on-site hair salon and through the Assisted Living wing, past the giant fish tank and bird cage and the stained-glass light of the chapel, into the silence of the Skilled Nursing annexe and my father's new room, a trip that takes ten minutes and is more than half a mile in length, I find him sitting in his bed or his new motorized easy chair, staring up at me, saying, *Where have you been?*

I've been sorting out your life, I want to tell him, but I keep my tongue in check.

At last, when his apartment is clear, when the movers have come to take the furniture we are keeping and the boxes that contain his files and have driven them off to deliver them to my mother's basement in New York, ready to be shipped back to Omaha if my father should miraculously recover enough to leave nursing care and return to independence, I go to say goodbye.

He knows why I have come. He will not look at me.

# HIDDEN

As the idea of O— begins to settle in my daily thinking, I am haunted by this half-buried hope: adopting him does not rule out having a second child through surrogacy at some point in the future. I know what this thinking betrays: that an adopted child alone will not satisfy my desire to be a parent. My wish for a child is as much the consequence of a biological impulse to reproduce as a psychological and emotional urge to raise and educate someone with whom I hope to have a permanent bond, someone who will be present at the end of my own life, someone who might have grandchildren in whose faces I can see the inscription of my genetic legacy. Because it feels too shameful, too outrageously selfish, I don't even share this hope with Andrew. Instead, I find myself trying to understand it, to process and tame it, by thinking about three stories that explore similar scenarios.

The first of these is the extraordinary novel *Agaat* by South African writer Marlene van Niekerk. I read it when it first appeared in English translation in 2006, and over the last several years Andrew has been writing about it for his study of postapartheid South African fiction so that it has continued to be a part of our lives. It is the story of Milla de Wet, an Afrikaner farmer who informally adopts a physically disabled 'coloured'[37] girl in apartheid South Africa, raising the child as her own despite the disapproval of her husband and the local white community. When Milla becomes pregnant and gives birth to a son, however, she ejects the adolescent

Agaat from the house, moving her into an outbuilding and forcing her to work as nursemaid to her baby, Jakkie. Milla's betrayal traumatizes both her and Agaat in different ways, although Agaat embraces Jakkie, becoming a sort of surrogate mother to him.

Brutal and unflinching in its examination of the way that biological connection is allowed to supersede affect in the heart of the adoptive mother, the novel suggests that any failure is chiefly Milla's. Had she been willing to fight against her own and her husband's racism and the racism of apartheid society and so allow Agaat to remain in the home, a *de facto* daughter if not a legal one, then Agaat and Jakkie could have grown up as loving siblings instead of child and nursemaid. Agaat's furious resentment is reserved for Milla and her husband *because* they rescued her from a life of privation and abuse only then to reject and expel her from the heart of the home. As if to demonstrate her capacity to be one of them, she masters all the markers of Afrikaner domestic and pastoral culture, becoming a living archive of folksongs and folklore, an accomplished embroiderer and gardener and cook, and a more capable and knowledgeable farmer than either Milla or her husband. And it is she who stays behind to nurse Milla in her final sickness after Jakkie has emigrated, abandoning his mother and the farm.

The book moves me to wonder: if we adopt and then have a child through surrogacy, will I be able to continue to keep O— as *a* child (not just as *my* child), to be sure that I never allow myself to turn him into a caregiver to the baby I might have, that I never ask more of him than I ask of that other, hypothetical child, that I continue to demonstrate to him he is as much *my* child as the one with whom Andrew or I would have a genetic link? I start imagining a lifetime of policing my engagements with O—, measuring out the love I give him against the love I give to that other child, *my own child* (I can't help thinking), because I would want to do it correctly if we were to do it at all.

I know that the social care system tries to enforce these boundaries while also undermining them. On the one hand, there is a natural expectation that adopted children not be tasked with the care of other children in the home (particularly biological children of the adoptive parents), or at least I think I remember being told this in our initial workshops. There is an expectation that adopted children should not be required to work for their place in the home, that we might give them ordinary chores of an age-appropriate kind, but perhaps rather less than we would give biological children. On the other hand, the system has demonstrated to us in countless ways that we will always be in the eye of the state, that they will always be watching to make sure we don't fuck it up. We have the sense too that because of O—'s large birth family, the claims of those other people on his life, his love, and his future, will potentially always be greater than our own.

The second story, a popular and banal one, is from Jon Robin Baitz's soapy television series *Brothers and Sisters*, in which Kevin (Matthew Rhys), the gay son of the Walker clan, and his partner Scotty (Luke Macfarlane) try to start a family. After much disagreement, they decide to have Scotty's friend Michelle (Roxy Olin) act as a surrogate. A year later, after Michelle has a miscarriage, Kevin and Scotty begin to explore other options, finally adopting nine-year-old Olivia (Isabella Rae Thomas), who has been in foster care. By chance, Kevin and Scotty later discover that Michelle lied, did not miscarry, and has been keeping their son, Daniel, secret from them. After initially resisting their demands to turn over the child, Michelle abandons Daniel to their care, leaving him not with them but with Kevin's straight brother to be delivered *to* him and Scotty before she disappears from the series.

Andrew and I watched these seasons of the show in the years we were trying to decide how to start a family. If anything, this dramatization of adoption, and the show's characterization of the adopted child, helped reinforce my initial resistance. Olivia has the qualities I had come to think of – however subjective, problematic and incorrect this sense may be – as 'adopted child energy'. I know that this is largely, perhaps entirely, a social and cultural construct, but it is one that repeatedly marks the adopted subject as volatile, as someone who will always struggle with attachment to her adoptive parents.

I see this too in other depictions of adopted children, such as Suzanne 'Crazy Eyes' Warren (Uzo Aduba) in *Orange is the New Black*. Her middle-class parents, notwithstanding their best intentions, cannot save Suzanne from her traumatic beginnings or from the problems that only gradually become apparent, nor can they seem to help placing Suzanne in situations during her childhood that repeat the effects of those early traumas, and which make her feel her difference from other children. Popular stories like this often present the adopted child as the child with problems that *cannot* be overcome, even by the most loving and well-meaning liberal couple in the suburbs, those families that supposedly have all the material and intellectual resources to fix any problem. However brilliant and creative Suzanne turns out to be, she remains easily swayed, co-opted, usable as a pawn by the more powerful, and just as easily ostracized. Her early traumas remain largely insurmountable.

Olivia in *Brothers and Sisters* also has hidden problems (her illiteracy only gradually comes to light), as well as biological relatives who contest the claim of the adoptive parents (her homophobic brother mounts an unsuccessful legal challenge to the adoption). But *Brothers and Sisters* also offers a consoling fantasy: that it is possible to reconcile the emotional and psychological needs of the adoptee with the sudden arrival of a queer couple's own biological child, and that the pressures of the adoptee's potentially bigoted biological family members can be managed, even domesticated, until everyone is able to live in a state of harmony and openness. Although Olivia reacts badly to baby Daniel's arrival, imagining that Scotty and Kevin no longer need or want her, they manage to reassure her so that everything comes right in the end. They become a happy and settled family of four, Olivia bonding with her cousins and shedding the insecurity of her attachment with implausible ease.

I imagine this possibility: we will adopt and, some years later, perhaps sooner than we think, find a way to have a child through surrogacy, and we will do so with all the tenderness and care required to reassure O— that such a decision does not mean he is second best, that the biological trumps every other category of connection, as *Agaat* suggests (as indeed *American Horror Story: Hotel* suggests in its own fantastical way), and we will manage the dynamics of family life so that our adopted child will never feel himself less than a full member of the family.

But how? How could that reassurance and management and negotiation of love and our own biases ever really be possible? How could O— be certain that such a decision was anything other than a mark of his insufficiency? Or, how could we ourselves be certain that *he* was certain of this? Are narratives that insist on the inescapable primacy of the biological in fact the ones that I have to listen to more attentively?

The final story I begin thinking about is Michael Haneke's 2005 film *Caché*. At first I assume that my return to a film I enjoyed and was perplexed by more than a decade earlier must have to do with my ongoing interest in the social and psychological effects of surveillance. But when I watch it again, I discover that isn't the case. Not at all. I have forgotten that the film is also inescapably about adoption, about the promise and ultimate failure to adopt and the irreconcilability of the biological child to the one who, in this case, was meant to be adopted.

*Caché* begins with a couple, Georges (Daniel Auteuil), who hosts a television show on literature, and Anne (Juliette Binoche), who works for a publisher. Settled, content, more than a little complacent, they are terrorized by the delivery of videotapes filled with footage of their own house, of their coming and going, of a car driving up to Georges's rural childhood home. A tape of Georges returning from work arrives wrapped in a childish drawing of a boy with blood spraying from his mouth. This, and other menacing drawings, work in the world of the film both as aides-mémoires for Georges, recalling events from his childhood, and as proleptic hints of what is to come: what we the viewers and Georges himself are going to see before the film has finished. And the anonymous surveillance tapes and menacing drawings are merely the outward signs of a much darker story, which circles around familial inheritances of loss and complicity.

In its exploration of these themes, the film's dramatization of the failures of bourgeois parenting is as damning as its vision of the psychological effects produced by the traumatic loss of one's parents is disturbing. Pierrot (Lester Makedonsky), Georges's and Anne's young adolescent son, is on the school swim team. We see him at swim practice, trained by his coach, who tells him how to turn differently in the water. As any good teacher, the coach acts in loco parentis, reinforcing methods of repetition and correction that formalize those processes of observation, critique and instruction which are a fundamental aspect not only of much good teaching but also good parenting. Georges and Anne, however, are a little neglectful, a little laissez-faire, even when the threatening communications they receive start to target their son. At school, Pierrot receives a postcard with the drawing of the child spewing blood from its mouth, the card purporting to be from his father, although it is not. That Georges and Anne do almost nothing to safeguard their son in light of this threat is a mark of their complacency, even their failure to parent adequately.

It takes a threat against his ailing mother for Georges to react. After receiving a video shot from the perspective of someone driving to his childhood home, Georges goes to visit his bedridden mother, Mme Laurent (Annie Girardot). She is ill but otherwise all right, tended by a nameless assistant. At his mother's bedside, Georges confesses to her that he dreams of Majid. At first his mother claims not to know who he means, although we, the viewers, already have a suspicion that Majid (Malik Nait Djoudi) is a child we have seen for an instant earlier in the film, a boy wiping blood from his mouth as though he has been caught eating something bloody, or as if bleeding himself. *Majid, the son of Hashem*, Georges explains, shocked. *Majid*, the boy his mother and father planned to adopt. Does she ever think about Majid? No, says Mme Laurent. It is not a happy memory. It was a long time ago.

How could a woman forget the name of the child she was once intending to adopt, even if only momentarily? As the complex details of the Laurents' past association with Majid and his family are gradually revealed, the question becomes as pressing as it is unarticulated by any of the characters. What made them change their minds?

Georges does not tell his mother about the surveillance tapes, even though the most recent one potentially functions as a threat against Mme Laurent herself – or is at least a message to Georges that whoever is watching him knows where his mother lives, just as they know which school his son attends. They know enough about Georges to unsettle his life, or to try to unsettle his smug self-righteousness.

A series of flashbacks works to explain the meaning and origin of the violent drawings' imagery: in the courtyard of Georges's child-hood home, Majid cuts off the head of a cockerel with an axe. Blood squirts onto the boy's face. He tosses the flapping body of the bird across the yard as young Georges (Hugo Flamigni) stands watching. Majid approaches, axe raised, backing Georges against the wall as if intent on chopping off his head as well.

But are these violent images – including the earlier glimpse of

Majid with a bloody mouth – actual memories, or are they dreams? Are such glimpses of the child Majid subjective, unreliable distortions of memory or misperceptions? Does Georges remember Majid as he needs to remember him in order to rationalize the way that he betrayed him (as the film later reveals), and indeed goes on betraying him, or is the film offering us an objective account of the boy's behaviour?

The morning after the conversation with his mother, Georges wakes breathless and sweaty, an adult in the present having spent the night in his haut-bourgeois childhood home, whose grandeur, though shabby, is at last evident. This is a house large enough to contain another life, even many lives, within it. Why, when these people possess so much, did they fail to adopt Majid? What could have compelled them to change their minds? Perhaps the boy's beheading of a cockerel is explanation enough. And so we, the viewers, settle into our own complacency, passing judgement on the boy whose actions disturb us because the film forces us into sympathy with Georges and his mother, his wife and his son, driving us into a position of privileged complicity as a way ultimately of making us feel our own moral and ethical failures more acutely.

Back in Paris, Georges and Anne receive a new tape shot from the front seat of a car, this time travelling through a working-class neighbourhood before cutting into a tower block and up to a numbered door. Georges and Anne stop and start the video, rewind, replay, trying to read the street signs until Georges is able to follow the tape's clues to a social housing estate in the Parisian banlieue Romainville. Here Georges finds Majid, now a man in his fifties (Maurice Bénichou), but while Majid recognizes Georges instantly, Georges does not recognize *him*. In fact, Majid has been watching Georges's television show for some time and while at first he was unsure why he 'had a nasty feeling' in his gut and 'felt nauseous' at the sight of the other man's face, when he saw the name in the show's credits he understood. He remembers Georges's parents as kind and generous. It is Georges he blames for what happened. When Georges presents one of the violent drawings he has received, Majid claims ignorance.

This encounter so unsettles Georges that when Anne later asks him what he has found, he tells her that no one answered the door, then inflates the lie by claiming that the building manager said the flat was unoccupied. Anne soon discovers his deception when she receives a video of the encounter that shows Majid consumed by grief after Georges's departure. Faced with proof of his own bad behaviour (the tape casts Georges, accurately, in a very negative light), he explains to Anne that Majid's parents worked for the Laurents and were killed in the Algerian War protests in 1961.[38] He admits that he was so annoyed by the prospect of his parents adopting Majid that he told lies about the boy until they changed their minds and sent Majid off to a hospital, believing him ill.

Would an orphan's illness be enough to persuade a wealthy couple not to adopt him, especially because they were already, in some ways, acting as his guardians? Would they not have consulted doctors instead of relying on the reports of their son? Would the biological child's account of his prospective brother be trusted above the couple's own observations? And what kind of parents must they have been if they raised a son who could demonstrate such duplicity, such an absence of generosity, such ugly mendacity to an orphan taken in by his parents?

When Pierrot fails to return home from school one evening, Georges leads the police straight to Majid's flat, convinced that the man must be responsible. There, Majid's teenage son (Walid Afkir) answers the door. Like his father, he claims to know nothing of the tapes or of Pierrot. Nonetheless, the police take Majid and his son into custody, accusations by an influential white cultural commentator being enough to deny these Algerian-French men their liberty, at least for a night. The outrageousness of the situation suggests that the mere *prospect* of Majid's adoption by the Laurents was so horrific to Georges as a child that its recollection in adulthood has driven him mad.

Pierrot turns up with a blasé shrug the next morning, his reappearance exonerating Majid and his son. At work that day, Georges receives a call from Majid, now released from police custody, asking him to return to Romainville. When Georges arrives, Majid says he had no idea about the tapes. Then, without warning, Majid slits his own throat, spraying blood across the wall, and falls dead to the floor.

As surprising and horrifying as this suicide is – both to Georges and to the viewer – the film has carefully prepared the ground for such an eruption of violence so that we read it as being in keeping with Majid's character. His passivity in the present, in late middle-age, is what makes the violence initially surprising, but as soon as we consider what we already know of his capacity for violence and combine that with our suspicion that he *might* have been responsible (even if the film invites us to read the situation in other ways entirely) for violent drawings that both depict the traumatic moments from his and Georges's childhood and anticipate his own suicide, it becomes possible to rationalize the aggression of this final act as being *in character* with what we think we already know about him.

This is a man, orphaned as a boy, who was so disturbed by the death of his parents that he engaged in deeply disturbing behaviour, and having discovered the boy (Georges) who could have been his brother now grown into a successful man with a comfortable life, that mental disturbance has (potentially) turned into maniacal stalking and suicide staged to inflict trauma on Georges himself.

Or, more generously, Majid is a man traumatized by the death of his parents, slandered by the boy who would have been his brother, denied a comfortable childhood, living a marginal adult life, hounded by his once-prospective brother now grown into a successful man who brings down the force of the state upon him in a way that is itself so disturbing (because unjust) that he is driven to kill himself.

In either case, the way that Majid ends his life casts judgement on Georges, the insecure jealousy of whose own filial bond, threatened by the prospect of his parents adopting Majid, produced an impulse to deceive, fabricate, manipulate, and so destroy his competitor. Georges finally reveals to Anne how, as a boy, he told his mother that Majid had coughed up blood. When a doctor examined Majid and found nothing wrong, Georges then told the boy that his father wanted him to kill their cockerel. This was a lie, and once the bird was dead, Georges told his parents that Majid had killed it to scare him.

In a later confrontation, Majid's son accuses Georges of depriving his father of a good education. 'The orphanage teaches hatred not politeness. But my father raised me well,' he says, although in fact the son's attitude is anything but polite: he instead performs an affect of barely contained rage, of public confrontation, and an attempt to shame and embarrass Georges, who, in his own broken and impolite way, refuses to take the blame for Majid's 'sad or wrecked life', refuses to be given a 'bad conscience'.

At home, having taken sleeping pills, Georges undresses and goes to bed, dreaming of the moment when Majid was taken away to the orphanage. As Majid tries to escape, the couple from the orphanage chase after him, dragging him back to their car while Georges's parents turn their backs on him. In his unconscious nakedness, Georges can finally see clearly the consequences of his lies, or so we might assume.

The film's long closing shot, however, further complicates the entanglement of Georges's and Majid's lives: outside his lycée, Pierrot meets Majid's son, talking as if they know each other already, although we cannot hear what they say, and their body language – Majid's son's in particular – is difficult to interpret. Is it hostile or friendly? Familiar or introductory? Conciliatory or confrontational?

Is there a world in which these two young men might become the brothers their fathers could not be?

*Caché*'s point, one suspects, is chiefly to do with the legacies of French colonialism, the violence of French society against its Algerian and other immigrants, the nature of privilege and personal complicity in one bourgeois family, and the ways in which the younger generation contains the hopeful possibility of reconciliation or dialogue, even if 'we', the older generation, cannot hear the actual language of their exchange. But the film also operates as a story about the risks of trying to combine adopted and biological children in one family. It suggests that even if the prospective adoptee is *wanted* and himself wishes to be part of this new family, the biological child destined to be the adoptee's sibling might respond with resentment and outrage provoked by a fear of being displaced or even replaced in the hearts of his parents. We often assume that the adopted child is likely to be the one who suffers attachment problems, but what happens if the biological child does as well, or does so *instead* of the adopted one?

Even though *Caché*'s indictment of failure and misdeed is aimed at the film's privileged white characters, it nonetheless presents a narrative of the prospective adoptee as one predisposed to disturbing behaviour, whether understood as behaviour that disturbs the equilibrium of the adoptive family, or as behaviour that is intrinsically disturbing: killing a cockerel, threatening his prospective adoptive brother with an axe. Given the film's slippery formal boundaries, it is impossible to know whether what we see of Majid as a child is objectively accurate or only ever subjective and thus radically distorted by Georges's jealous perspective. The spectre of that distortion is likely part of the film's point, the images of Majid as a boy unreliable because they are all ostensibly the product of Georges's unconscious mind. Allowing for the fact that he is virtually a compulsive liar, Georges does admit to telling his parents lies about the other boy. Even *if* Georges is lying about that, or his mind has produced a distorted vision of Majid, as a man Majid does still commit suicide in an exceptionally disturbing and confrontational way, while his behaviour as a boy, even if not intrinsically disturbing, nonetheless pushed Georges to acts that were, at best, unkind.

One might conclude that it was the French state, or French culture, or racist bourgeois ideology that were ultimately responsible, but the film frames Majid as a boy and as a man who consistently disturbs, who haunts the dreams of the man who might have been his brother, who is intentionally forgotten by the woman who might have been his adoptive mother, about whom she can say only that his presence in her life was the mark of a sad time, while *he* remembers *her* as kind and generous. The equation does not balance. It does not seem possible that he was *only* a victim who saw goodness in those who would have been his parents, or even in the boy who did not wish to be his brother. It is possible to be a victim worthy of sympathy and remain someone whose acts and affects profoundly disturb – even if, one might hazard, those who are disturbed *need* to be disturbed.

As I watch *Caché* again on the eve of O—'s anticipated arrival in our life, I find myself standing in multiple positions: in the place of Mme Laurent, Georges's mother; in the place of Georges; and in the place of Pierrot. I also find myself projecting O— into multiple positions: of Majid as a boy; in the place of Majid as a man; and in the place of Majid's son.

Here are my newly articulated fears: in bringing this child into our lives, we are introducing a force that will disturb in a way that a biological child would be less likely to do. For the sake of everyone involved, those who exist already and those who exist only hypothetically, I cannot continue to entertain the possibility that after adopting we might one day have a biological child, because to do so would always risk resulting not in the soap-opera fantasy of the happy-ever-after queer family in *Brothers and Sisters*, but in the failed and fractured non-family of *Caché* or *Agaat*, the family that ends not in unity and joy, but in trauma passed down through the generations, intensely complex and unpredictable in its trajectory and effects.

In saying this, I know, too, that there are numberless families that have succeeded in blending the biological and the adopted, but to them I can only look with admiration and awe. It is not a risk I would feel able to take because I can imagine a biological child one day resenting O—'s primary place in our family, or O— one day resenting the arrival of a biological child he might fear would usurp his place in our hearts.

That I can imagine these scenarios means I am already, before ever meeting him, anxious about what O— will mean to us and to our future, calculating how I will need to adjust my own hopes so that he has the greatest chance of feeling accepted and loved.

# MATCHING

On my return from America, Andrew and I hang black-and-white photographs above the child-sized sleigh bed, choosing pictures we have taken over the years of the Golden Gate Bridge and Table Mountain, images that say something about us, or at least about where we came from, however indirectly. Images we hope will tell O— that his new parents are not from here, that we have pasts in the way that he, too, has a past.

I have wild impulses to buy the most extravagant toys, the biggest and most beautiful of everything. People generously give us books and stuffed animals. A friend in Oxford co-ordinates with her children to select toys they no longer want that can be passed on to us. My mother buys puppets, Andrew's mother begins knitting sweaters. In all of this activity I recognize the impulse to create a nest of softness and beauty, of rich stimulation. These are not only gifts that we would wish any child to have, but also gifts for the child we hope O— will be.

Megan and Richard have suggested we make a scrapbook to begin familiarizing him with our home, our friends and family, since we will meet only days before he comes to live with us.

In America, such processes are more prolonged, graduated and cautious. Friends in Iowa who adopted a nine-year-old from another state had him visit for a trial weekend to see if they could all get along. (They did.) In Britain, however, the assumption is that social workers will make the determination about whether a couple and the child to be adopted will be a good match for each other, but the two parties only meet in the 'Introductions' period immediately prior to the child going to live with the adoptive parents. 'Introductions' may last for ten days to two weeks, but are sometimes much shorter, subject to the child's particular needs and history, how far the foster parents live from the adoptive ones, or how much money the council responsible for the child has to spend on travel and accommodation.

In theory, the whole adoption process can collapse during this period. Prospective parents may find that the child is not the right match for them after all. Or, the child's social workers may conclude things really aren't going as well as they should. Either side can end it with little or no warning. But in general, the expectation is that social workers have done their jobs properly, that they know both child and adopters well enough to make sure everyone is compatible, that they aren't going to meet and tear one another apart, that the yearning the child has for parents and the yearning the adopters have for a child will be so powerful that any doubts are subsumed by the hopefulness of the introductory moment and the relief everyone feels at finally getting, and holding, what each so desperately wants.

As we prepare our scrapbook, I wonder what happens if your social worker does not understand who you are, what you think, where you come from, what you believe, how you imagine yourself in five or ten or thirty years, how you see yourself as a person in the world. What if every photo you provide of yourselves for your profile your social worker regards as too sombre, as inadequately 'fun', as too 'cultured' or 'serious' or 'foreign'? What if you are worn down by the despair of waiting and made vulnerable by familial loss and grief and find yourself saying yes even when doubts remain?

Andrew and I spend days, literally, creating a scrapbook that gives a taste of our lives. It is a true picture, but also a more exuberant one than the life we lead. We have spent the past fourteen years living exceptionally quietly. We are either at work working or at home working or doing things like cooking or exercising or reading or watching movies. We go to museums and galleries. We occasionally attend concerts or the theatre. Our greatest excitement – the time when we are most the selves we feel ourselves to be – is when we leave Britain. Something about this country constrains us, prevents us from being us in the way we are in South Africa or America, or less frequently in France or Italy or Spain or even Sweden. Britain is the office from which we escape to be our real selves for two or three months every year.

For the scrapbook, we choose photos of us together, our family, our closest friends. We plan page layouts and text and lettering. I buy crafting supplies. We take pictures of our home and O—'s new bedroom and the neighbourhood park. As I paste down the photographs, outline them with washi tape, and carefully letter each page, writing first in pencil and then going over the pencil precisely with marker, I find there is something both preparatory and therapeutic about this crafting, as if in telling a story about us and where we have come from, I am also explaining to myself once again why we have chosen this particular way of making a family.

In doing this I find myself falling in love with the idea of this child, and the prospect of the three of us as a family. Excitement and happiness dominate over uncertainty and trepidation, even though such negative feelings are still present in the background, behind and beneath the positive ones. All of this seems like the right decision at the right moment in our lives.

Gemma makes a trip to meet O— and his foster parents in the West Country. She returns to London with a snippet of video recorded on her phone but it hardly tells us anything about him. He looks taller than I imagined, very tall for his age. He could be six years old instead of four. There is something about him, but I can't articulate what it is. Perhaps it is only that his affect, or his way of moving through space, or the register of his voice as he speaks in the video are not as I expected.

Full of energy, Gemma says. I hope you're ready for this.

At last, the courts rule once and for all against O——'s birth parents, who have continued to resist his adoption. I look at their social media profiles. In the days following the judgment, they both post cryptic public messages that suggest a sense of the world ranged against them, of suffering from a kind of generalized injustice. The mother's post includes photographs of all five of her children before they were taken from her. Photographs of herself now, photographs of her children then. Duplicates of her, reproductions of her face, her body, her trace living within each of them, developing upon their own small faces. When I look at O——'s photograph, it is his mother I see. I wish I had never gone looking for information about her, had never seen her face in the first place.

I realize that photography will be something we have to negotiate for the rest of our lives. O——'s mother will continue to share whatever pictures she or the rest of her family may have from his first twelve months. Given the existence of facial recognition software, this means that we will never be able to post a photograph of O——, even on private social media pages, without the risk of revealing who we are and where we are to a family that has demonstrated their entirely understandable resistance to the adoption of their children.

I begin to think about policing the photography of friends and family, telling people they cannot take a picture of my son for fear that his biological parents will find him. How will that be sustainable? Some adoption support groups counsel parents to put masks on their children when they march in an annual adoption parade. At first this struck me as counterproductive, even unseemly, since it appeared to suggest a sense of shamefulness about being adopted.

But now I understand that this is a means of protecting the privacy of those new adoptive families, to prevent determined birth parents from locating children the state has taken from them.

Is this the beginning of a process of hiding ourselves, of drawing a circle around our family, trying to make ourselves invisible? If it is, then what are the limits of such defence? What kind of monitoring will it require? Can we assume O— will even go along with it? What happens if he creates a social media profile without our knowledge, with no privacy settings, and starts posting selfies? I'm not fool enough to think we will be able to control what he does online as he gets older. Overnight, his birth family could find him, and so find all three of us.

With that realization I feel the ground beneath us shifting again, as if we no longer have the certainty of stable lives. I wonder what such a sense of vulnerability and precariousness does to a couple, and to a family that is trying to create a life of stability but also of openness. I never want O— to feel as if he is in the adoption equivalent of witness protection. I never want him to notice that we monitor the way people take pictures of him. I want him to feel normal and safe. I don't want his life or ours to be constrained by paranoia, and yet it seems as if it must be, for his own safety, but also for ours.

This is not a scenario I ever imagined when I dreamed of becoming a parent.

We head west out of London, caught in mid-week traffic, a long journey that takes even longer than it should, so that we can meet the foster parents, K— and T—. They live in a quiet village, formerly industrial but gradually turning into a bedroom community for larger towns and the city that is an hour's drive distant. Over the last few months, I have been studying images online of their house, the surrounding neighbourhood, the nearest school, trying to discover what O—'s daily life looks like, hoping it will tell me something about who he is, more than the little I can discern from his file or the photographs we have of him, my memory of the video Gemma took.

In my mind O— is always sweet and calm and expectant, sometimes excitable and tearful, but always *amenable*, ready to be loved and reassured. I do not imagine a terrorizing Romeo, but a self-contained and affable Will.

At the end of a cul-de-sac on the edge of the village the foster parents' detached bungalow is painted bright brick red, its front courtyard thick with topiaries and climbing roses, overgrown and riotous with life, while the back garden borders open fields. We sit in our car waiting for the appointed time. A pink convertible pulls in down the road and a few moments later a woman with platinum blonde hair strides up and knocks on the window.

This is Marla, another social worker on the team, and the one who will actually be co-ordinating things from now on.

O— is staying with other foster carers for the day. As far as we know, he has not been told about our visit, and this suddenly strikes me as weirdly, deeply unfair. Somehow, I had assumed that he might be here. Surely, it would make sense to meet the child before we go any further, even if just for a few minutes, even if he was not told who we were? I want to know who he is, how he presents in the world, how he engages with me. Concerns about whether he will fit into our lives have vanished. All I feel now is a desire to speed the process forward.

My chief anxiety at this stage is what K— and T— will think of us. I don't assume they have ever met a same-sex couple. I suspect that their idea of people like us may be built on what movies and television have told them rather than direct experience. Any actual encounters might not have registered as such or hewed to a version of queer identity very different to our own.

Flamboyant, girlish, lisping.

Camp.

*Effete.*

Perhaps we are all of those things and I no longer see it.

And what would be wrong if we were? Nothing at all. If Andrew and I had grown up in different places in different times, we might be. But we aren't, I don't think. And perhaps that is part of the problem.

When we meet, the foster parents are friendly, a little matter-of-fact. I can understand what K— says but T—'s accent confounds me and I lose half his words. The incomprehension is mutual: most of what I say he asks me to repeat two or three times, and then he looks away or moves the conversation in a new direction, if you can call our exchange of words a conversation. Overlapping monologues. Each side mystified by the other.

I ask questions about the town but neither K— nor T— is forthcoming. Questioning seems not to be part of their idea of social exchange. One talks about the weather and the child who is the point of connection between us, nothing else. I am trying to be friendly in a very American way, asking questions to show interest, but I begin to suspect that my curiosity looks intrusive, even aggressive.

Marla sits on the edge of the sofa and talks us through plans for the coming weeks. The assumption is that next week's Matching Panel will approve us. Everyone believes this is going to happen since O—'s social workers are in favour of us, our profile suggests we are up to the task, and our own social workers also support it. We have renewed our background checks and health clearances, so once the panel gives their decision we should be clear to proceed.

K— says she will bring most of the boy's clothes and toys to the panel, because it is expected that we will be coming to get him only a couple of weeks later.

He has so much, so many clothes and so many toys, that we

won't manage it all in one trip, not a chance, K— says. I think of Romeo, the boy in my story, and the way I imagined foster parents who provided only the bare minimum. K— spends everything she gets from the state and more on the children she fosters, that much is obvious. She loves them deeply. Listening to her talk about O—, I have no doubt about that. For all intents and purposes, he has been her child for more than three years, has learned to talk and walk under her and her husband's loving care.

It is only later that I will come to appreciate the full power of that love.

O—'s bedroom is sparsely decorated, his many clothes packed tightly in the wardrobe and dresser, toys in a giant plastic bin. The whole house smells of fabric softener and air freshener. Artificial, floral. Everything is scrupulously clean.

There is nothing on the walls. No art. No posters. No calendars. There are no stuffed animals, nothing soft or cuddly or cute. I think of my own childhood bedroom, how chaotic it was, how littered with fluffy toys. O—'s toys are all made of plastic, hard and shiny. Most of them make noise and require batteries. These will have to go, I think to myself, quickly processed out of use, replaced with natural, quiet things to fit our quiet lives and the paper-thin walls between our flat and the neighbours'.

But how I loved my own plastic toys, my *Star Wars* action figures and spaceships and shiny pink ray gun.

He wants *two* footballs, one for each of his daddies, K— says, so you can kick to him at the same time.

He will be disappointed. We won't be playing football, or at least I will not. Perhaps Andrew will manage it, the kicking and rough play, the boy who wants to play with robots and toy guns, a boy perhaps not so different from the boy I have forgotten I was, muddy and swinging from trees and addicted to Saturday morning cartoons my mother considered too violent.

When he came, K— says, I tried to bathe him but only my husband could do that. He's still that way. Won't have me give him a bath. That's why I said, he should have *two* daddies. He's just not interested in women.

T— walks us to the nursery school where we meet with the head teacher. She tells us about the progress O— has made over the past three years. There is a scrapbook filled with his drawings, as well as photographs of him and his classmates. He looks happy, if a little distant. There is something in his expression, a quality I struggle to interpret. In some of the photographs he looks like a completely different person than the image I have begun to form of him in my mind, as if he is multiple, as if there are several different versions of him, each one wearing the face of his mother.

I ask the teacher if O— is exceptional in any way, either positively or negatively.

No, she says, he's a very normal little boy, *with a lot of love to give*.

That phrase again, as if they have all been saying it to one another, the teachers and social workers, as if they have discussed it in advance, agreed on it as the best possible formulation to describe him.

As you can see from his drawings, his mark-making is coming along, she says.

Mark-making. Making his mark. Has he made a mark here, with this school, with his friends, with his foster parents? It is difficult to tell. I want to believe he has.

I look at the drawings, page after page of scribbles. No stick figures or houses or animals that I can discern. I try to remember what I was drawing at four, but perhaps it is a mistake to measure O—'s progress against my own.

Nonetheless, more than anything I've heard or read so far, his teacher's reassurance convinces us this is someone we will be able to manage. If he is unexceptional in any way, just an average little boy, then there is no reason to think twice.

After all, a teacher would know.

A week later we return for the Matching Panel. K— attends, but T— does not, as if the input of the foster mother was somehow superior to that of the foster father, even though T— has had an equivalent duty of care.

Adriana, our senior social worker, has come from London to support us. There are half a dozen panel members, drawn from the social work team and the local council and other stakeholders. Who is a stakeholder in the life of a child up for adoption? O—'s own social workers, Megan and Richard, are present, as is Marla.

The questions are not so different from those we fielded in the panel that approved us as adopters. We speak fluently, we answer every question with confidence. Ten minutes after the meeting is finished, the chair of the panel tells us that the match has been unanimously approved.

I wonder when – *if* – the emotions of adoption will ever become less complex, less overdetermined than they always now seem. Every step generates not just one feeling, but a concatenation of different and sometimes quite contradictory ones. I am relieved because I feared we would not clear this hurdle, but also satisfied that what we were told would happen has come to pass. At the same time, I am also irritated that we should have been subjected to such interrogation in the first place and impatient to get on with things. Why can't we just go get the child now, this moment, and take him home? He wants it, we want it, and surely the system in its own dysfunctional way wants it as well?

After lunch, we return for a planning meeting with Marla. She suggests that Introductions should begin in two weeks' time, and while these might last for as long as a week or two, it is likely that only three days will be necessary. O— is anxious to start his new life, and frankly so am I. I can't imagine drawing it out. The shorter the better. Marla encourages us to find a nursery school as soon as possible because the boy needs his routine. She suggests that his foster parents might come back to London with us, to help O— get settled, but K— is quick to say she couldn't, no, not possibly.

And why is that? Marla asks.

I wouldn't be able to leave him, K— says.

You mean you'd want to bring him back with you? Adriana asks.

I couldn't let go of him, K— says.

When Marla suggests that T— might come instead, Andrew and I hesitate. Adriana seems to read our hesitation, and says that really, it's best in these situations if new parents are left to bond with the child. Better to say goodbye and make a clean start, and then the foster parents can come visit a few weeks later.

No, K— says. I couldn't do it. My husband maybe. Not me.

But you'd be happy for O— to come back and visit you with his new daddies at some point in the future? Marla asks.

Just so long as I don't have to see him in his new home. That's what's hard, K— says.

At the end of the meeting, T— returns with his car full of toys and clothes. We load what we can fit into our own car, give T— a handshake and K— a hug. She seems to have decided we'll do and I take comfort in her tacit approval, this passing of the baton.

As we start driving back to London, the toys jostle and crash against one another, setting off alarms and sirens, shouting whole lines of dialogue from cartoon action figures so that we have to stop and repack everything. The smell of fabric softener is overwhelming, and beneath it I think I catch the scent of the boy himself.

Who is this child? Do his clothes and possessions tell us anything substantive about him? The social workers have decided he is a match for us, and we have been through a process first of agreeing, saying almost blindly, yes, we really *are* a match for him! we *want* this boy we haven't met just on the basis of photos and the way that *you* have described him, and then articulating all the ways in which we will meet his needs, which have been presented to us as quite ordinary. In the moment, what uncertainty there is does not feel overwhelming, and if the social workers who know him trust that we are the right match, then we have to believe them.

We have to trust that everyone has O—'s best interests and our own – which are ultimately also his – at heart.

When we get home, we unpack the toys and clothes, filling the child-sized wardrobe. I start an audit of the books that were sent with us. Some strike me as inappropriate for a family with same-sex parents. They reinforce normative gender roles or suggest a world in which only families with parents of the opposite sex exist. Some of them focus in an almost fetishistic way on the unsurpassable love of mothers.

What ideas have already been poured into this boy? He did not have the start in life we would have given a child in our care from birth. Judging from the books, he has been exposed to rather old-fashioned notions about gender and, for all we know, sexuality as well. He will be full of opinions, tastes, even strongly held beliefs, which it may take us years to change. And I know that we may never succeed.

Every book I judge either inappropriate or bad I pack away in a box.

He won't miss them, I tell myself.

At Marla's urging, we start looking for a nursery school. I drop in unannounced on a local private kindergarten. When I mention that my husband and I are adopting, the head teacher's face twists. Is it because we're a same-sex couple, or because the child is adopted?

There is a waiting list, she tells me. It's really quite long.

Hesitantly, she gives me a prospectus, but even if she had been more welcoming I quickly decide this is the wrong place – too expensive and too authoritarian. At the top of their bullet-pointed list of beliefs is 'respecting property'.

We turn next to another independent school that looks good online, but when we visit the space is dark, chaotic, and filthy, the garden nothing but a waste of mud and stone. Even worse, the head teacher looks as if she cannot understand why two men are here together, then makes an awkward point of saying that they've had same-sex couples in the past and it's never been a problem.

We didn't expect it would be, but now that you've mentioned it, I want to say, I guess it must be. I keep my mouth shut. I smile. Andrew smiles.

Children are crying, there are too few adults, pandemonium breaks out as a squad of kids runs from one side of the room to another. Marla has told us O— thrives on routine, so such a disorderly environment would never work.

At last, we settle on the local council-run school which has beautiful facilities and an egalitarian ethos. The bubbly head teacher waits for us to ask the question about diversity and says, yes, in fact, there are a number of same-sex couples with children already enrolled. Families of all different varieties, races, religions, nationalities. There is a sand play area, wooden toys, everything clean and bright and well maintained, but also relaxed. Perfect, we think, and only a ten-minute walk from our house. We sign the enrolment forms and agree we'll be in touch by the end of September to decide when O— should start.

Meanwhile, we wait each day to hear whether the Agency Decision Maker at the council charged with O—'s care has signed off on the match. We were told this was just routine, no more than a rubber stamp, and given that all the social workers and members of the Matching Panel were in favour, there is no expectation the

ADM will delay. When we check with Marla, she says the ADM has been on holiday. She hasn't got to it yet and needs to read all the files and reports. But it should be soon, very soon.

A week has passed and we are halfway into the following week, just days short of the day we are meant to meet O— for the first time, the date we agreed with the social workers and foster parents, who are preparing for his departure.

Still there is no decision.

The day before we are scheduled to meet O—, we finally receive word that against the advice of the social workers and the Matching Panel the ADM has refused to sign off on the match.

The news is so devastating we hardly know what to think.

Is this it? Is this the end? We phone Adriana but she doesn't seem to know. Neither does Marla. This has never happened before. No one knows what the protocols are, what procedures have to be followed, whether we even have the right to appeal.

At first, all we know is that the ADM has concerns, but these are not articulated to anyone who is communicating with us. Concerns of what order? I start to think that perhaps, just possibly, the ADM has read my books, or even 'Interior: Monkeyboy', and did not like what she found.

We are stunned and puzzled. All the social workers are stunned and puzzled, or at least say they are. Every time we talk to one of them, they tell us this is unprecedented, which only makes it worse. Why is it that we find ourselves in the position of being the first? Why must we be the exceptional ones when we just want to be seen as ordinary?

We push for more information. There are delays, failures to reply, confusion, and then, a week later, Adriana forwards us the ADM's memorandum finding against us.

It turns out that the ADM is alarmed by our description of

ourselves as 'queer' rather than 'gay' and wonders how this will affect O— throughout his childhood and adulthood. More bizarrely, she suggests that I fled the US after 9/11, ignoring my own clear statements that I had been admitted to Oxford months before the attacks and was already planning to go. What was difficult at the time was deciding to follow through on my plans instead of remaining at home, but in the eyes of the ADM I was *running away from a traumatic event*. To her, this suggests that I am not up to parenting a child who himself has been traumatized. Furthermore, she doubts that we will be able to parent a child who *may* end up having any number of as yet undiagnosed problems. I remind myself that we have been told time and again that O— is normal, that he has no diagnoses of developmental or other medical problems, and has cleared all of his screenings.

As I read the ADM's words, I feel ill. I feel angry. Months and years later, I will still feel angry, my chest will always tighten with outrage. I feel once again as though the system has failed to understand us, as if our queerness and foreignness and our professions work in concert to make us terrifyingly other.

I know that the ADM was trying to do her job conscientiously. But would she have been concerned, I wonder, by a straight couple who chose to describe themselves as an 'opposite-sex couple', or who performed political consciousness of their gender, perhaps describing themselves as 'cisgendered' in their adoption workbooks, in the same way that she is concerned by our description of ourselves as 'queer'. Would she have been as concerned by a British adopter who happened, for instance, to move out of London after the 7 July 2005 terror attacks to go to university somewhere else in the country as she is by my departure from New York?

Whatever the dynamics of her decision making – and I genuinely want to believe that she was motivated by concern for O—'s wellbeing and nothing else – it feels as if, once again, we are being subjected to forms of bias that operate throughout the entire network of social care and adoption, popping up just when we least expect them.

We have a right to appeal so we compose a comprehensive response to the ADM's memo, addressing every concern and reservation she raises. It feels like the most important document either of us has written and it also feels totally inadequate, as if we are trying to cram into ten pages all the arguments we can marshal to justify our suitability to parent a boy we have never met.

To strengthen our case, we ask friends – a dozen couples who have children with whom we've spent time in recent years – to write letters of support. Over the coming days, letter after letter arrives, each one written with extraordinary generosity and love, each one demolishing all the ADM's reservations about us. My sense of outrage gives way to a wholly unexpected feeling that a group of people, most of them outside of Britain, care deeply about us. But what does it mean that we can muster so little support closer to hand? What does it say that after a decade and a half of living here nearly all of our closest friends are not British? Why does this country refuse us over and over again, making us feel in number-less ways that even though we both now carry British passports we are not actually valued, not really wanted, and always viewed with suspicion, or simply misunderstood?

A new Matching Panel is scheduled for mid-October and in advance of this Adriana compiles the letters from our friends, our letter addressing the ADM's memo, and submits them to the council responsible for O— with an accompanying letter she has written in support of our appeal. We decide that we cannot put ourselves through attending this second panel, cannot have the same or even different questions posed, cannot manage to repeat what we have said before. The whole experience has been traumatizing in ways we could not have anticipated. Instead, Adriana attends the new panel on our behalf.

As with the first panel, the decision is in our favour, the match approved a second time.

We have been living with the child's toys and clothes for nearly two months, passing a bedroom ready for him, a bedroom whose door we have kept closed since the ADM's decision, because it is too painful to look at that empty space, at the toys and books sent by friends, at the signs of the care we have taken to prepare for this child.

These are weeks that he could have been with us rather than living in a state of confusion and disappointment because his foster mother has been telling him since June that we were on our way, that we would be imminently arriving. I suspect that this is what she understood. Perhaps the social workers led her to believe this would be the case. She told O—, I am certain, in the belief that she was preparing him for what was to come, promising him that the permanence for which he longed ('the forever family' in the parlance of the social care system) was soon to be his.

Rather than the council doing all it might to end this interminable waiting, we now have to wait for a different Agency Decision Maker to sign off on the match once and for all. One would think this should happen quickly, without delay, if only out of a sense of human decency.

Days pass.

A week.

Another week.

We know again that K— has told O— we'll be arriving on a particular day, and yet we never come, and this makes us into two daddies who have repeatedly disappointed him before he has even met them.

At last the new ADM finally signs off on the match at the end of October. On the first of November, K— phones and puts O— on the line to speak with me.

Hello, Daddy, he says, and my heart almost stops. I struggle to speak.

He talks about some toys his foster parents have recently bought him, although much of what he says is unintelligible, his accent so thick I can understand few of the words.

This is my son, I think, a boy who already calls me Daddy without hesitation. It is exhilarating but also bewildering, difficult to make sense of what I am feeling, or to know what I *should* be feeling.

There is excitement, but also a sense of slipping out of the real and into a place in which my emotions are no longer under my control, as though I have become someone who is acted upon by others rather than acting himself. It is both liberating and destabilizing. I no longer know what I am supposed to say, what is expected of me, perhaps because the whole experience has been a process of being radically and repeatedly misunderstood, subjected to misreadings, rendered the object of other people's judgements and interpretations, never allowed to feel as if I have the agency to do anything other than submit and comply and defend myself when attacked.

After these weeks spent living in a suspended state, waiting for the *yes* we have been hoping for, once again time is short. Marla is anxious to start the Introductions, while Adriana is concerned about their planned brevity. Perhaps the brevity has to do with resources, I begin to think, perhaps this West Country council needs the Introductions to last only three days because that is all it can afford.

Once more, days pass without clarity. Our tickets have not been purchased, the accommodation has not been booked, the social workers have difficulty finding something suitable. I offer to do the bookings myself and submit receipts at the end of it all, but they are hesitant. No, they will take care of it.

Then, at last, two days before we are due to leave and only through our insistence that this cannot be put off again because we have already notified our employers that we will be on leave and we have already spoken to O—, who is expecting us to be there after months of delays, the tickets and bookings come through. We fly because Marla has decided that travelling by car or by train – though either would be just as easy, even easier, than flying – is not advisable. O— would not manage a long car journey. And on a train, well, on a train he could easily run away. Anything but a plane would be too much. And too much for us as well.

In hindsight, this might have given us pause, but at the time it did not.

In the moment we cling to our sense of relief and the urgent desire to meet our son. We are ready to say yes to anything.

# ME

Most people must think about their own childhood when they are on the brink of becoming a parent but I suspect that such reflection is more considered and troubled, or troubling, for people in same-sex relationships, and especially for those who have had to struggle in one way or another to make parenthood possible.

As we pack our bags and clean the flat, reinstalling the safety latches on cupboards that I put in before the first Matching Panel and removed when the tedium of unhitching them every time I wanted a knife nearly drove me to tears in the weeks when it seemed as though we had hit an inescapable dead-end, I catch myself thinking of the child I was.

I was a mama's boy. Teacher's pet. Perfectionist. Over-achiever. These were the epithets I heard as a child, alongside Fatboy and Faggot, because I was overweight from the moment I started attending school. I was always effeminate and more gender-nonconforming than I realized until the questions about whether I was a girl or boy became so painful to hear at the age of twelve that I began consciously to self-correct, to square my hips when I walked and listen for the wrong intonation in my voice, to close the door to the den at home when I watched MTV and danced along to Madonna and George Michael and Prince.

So, although I did not have red hair, except in one curious season when I auditioned to be an understudy in a touring production of

*Camelot* that wanted blonde boys for the part and the chemical treatment left me vividly strawberry, I was ginger in the sense of being queer, and ginger also in the sense of being 'cautious, careful; gentle', as well as 'easily hurt or broken; sensitive, fragile'. I was ginger in all of those ways, not least because of the bullying I experienced throughout my school years, however mild it was compared to what many suffer. I was also often barely in control of my rage at home. It could explode out of nowhere but was always directed at my father. I did not act out in school, not as far as I can recall, although I was often socially inept, incapable of knowing how to deal with most of my peers. I did not direct my anger at my mother or the cats or the neighbours or the very few children I could call my friends in the earliest years of my childhood.

The fear that I continue to carry, even as Andrew and I reorganize the child's bedroom for the umpteenth time and make sure that everything is spotlessly clean and the house looks welcoming and warm for his arrival, is that I will fail to be the parent I would wish to be. There is no way of knowing, not until O— is in my presence and I in his, not until I discover what kinds of buttons he will push. The reassurance I have, I remind myself, is that my mother did her best, intentionally or not, to be an androgynous model of nurture and strength and care and compassion and education and comfort and discipline and capability.

Remember that model of parenting, I tell myself, and all will go well.

# INTRODUCTIONS

## SUNDAY

In the dusk we drive from the airport through villages and towns, across stretches of farmland and industrial sites, following directions on our phones and trying to recall, in the dark, how the countryside looked in August, the way the road took us along rivers and towards the coast. I take a wrong turn and we miss the B&B, double back, find it on a quiet street in a village ten miles distant from the one where K— and T— live.

Our self-catering flat is in a farm's converted outbuilding, with sliding glass doors that open onto a field white with sheep and surrounded by high hedgerows. Marla chose this place, she told us, because it will be cosy enough to bring O— here on the third day of the Introductions, the day before we are meant to fly back to London.

But the flat is ugly and soulless with warped laminate flooring and tatty upholstery, the air heavy with the odours of a thousand fried dinners and Indian takeaways, of manure and mildew and unaired rugs. Everything is damp and grimy.

Andrew and I decide we don't have the energy to cook, but the nearest place open for dinner is half an hour away. We end up at a seaside restaurant where we pick at the food, as if our appetites have abandoned us.

How strange it is that we are here while the child we are meant to adopt is waiting only a short drive away. We could go there now, this instant, and see him. Why do we have to wait? Why do we have to follow social workers' schedules? So much of this process has been dependent on us doing what we are told, being docile and passive. What if we weren't? What if we said, enough of this, we're going to do things our way from now on?

Of course we don't. We were both raised to be good boys, to follow directions. This whole process has turned us back into children, taking away our sense of our own agency.

We eat. We pay. We drive back to the B&B.

We're both nervous, although we try to hide it from each other. We want this to go well. We want, I realize, not to be disappointed or terrified when the boy meant to be our son looks into our eyes, or when we look into his.

## Monday

After breakfast we go for a walk, trying to kill time until the hour appointed for our arrival, once O— has returned from nursery school. The sky is matte grey, the air close to freezing, and a northwest wind whipping off the sea makes it feel even colder.

We will have to keep coming back here so that O— can see his foster parents, and then, later, to visit his siblings and help him remember where he came from. While the countryside is beautiful, this village is not. Geographically and architecturally different though it is, it might just as easily stand in place of the small California towns where my parents grew up, from which they both escaped, or the dingy Oklahoma town where my grandmother was a girl, or the tiny farming community that my other grandmother fled to escape the Dust Bowl in the years of the Great Depression.

Perhaps, at some point in the future, O— will no longer want to return to this part of the world. And then he, and we, might be free of the past.

Like so many other consoling narratives, I recognize that this too is fantasy.


T— answers the door when I knock. He looks past me to the street, to Andrew, to our car. There's the sound of thudding feet, and then all at once, like a jack-in-the-box, O— springs into the doorway.

At first, he doesn't seem to know who we are.

Who's that then? O—'s foster father asks him.

Two daddies, the boy says, grinning, puckish.

As he hugs us each in turn, I think, yes, this is right. The smell of floral fabric softener hits me again, as it did on our previous visit. I am eager for this to go well, for every moment in these first hours to be perfect.

Then joy comes rushing, watery, submerging most of the anxiety and frustration of the past months. Would it have felt the same if we had been able to do this six weeks ago? What if the ADM had said yes in September? What if we had not lived through two months of uncertainty? How might it all have been different?


Where's my Romeo? K— calls out to O— as he runs to hug her.

The sound of that name is a blade that sinks deep in my chest. How could she call him Romeo? Has she read my story? Is it remotely possible?

I do not believe I might have written this child into exist-ence, although the coincidence strains plausibility. What are the chances that O—'s nickname in the home of his foster parents should be the real name of the wild child character I invented a year earlier?

I try to set this to one side, not to make too much of it. Focus instead on what is before you, on K— hugging the little boy, wrapping him warmly in her arms. He has been loved, that is clear. He *is* loved. That is obvious, too.

Although the plan has been for us to be alone, there are other members of the family present, K— and T—'s adult daughter and her husband and their two toddlers. O—'s focus is as much with them as with us. The television is on, volume loud. This could have been my grandmother's living room when I was a child, the television always playing, a baseball or football game or news filling the silence.

I suggest that I try to read O— a book we have brought him. We sit on the floor, Andrew next to me, and O— scrambles into my lap. I start to read, but after three pages O— loses interest. He's up and playing with K—'s grandson.

Marla suggests we go for a walk, just us and T— and O—. Outside, on the front step, she apologizes about the presence of the other family members. That was not the plan, she says, not the way it was supposed to be.

Tell them to go away, I want to say. We need this to work on our terms. Too much has gone wrong already.

But even now, when it seems as though power might be shifting back in our direction, I swallow my words.

We head towards the centre of the village, O— holding our hands, walking between us as I imagined he might. Then he wants to get up on my shoulders, and we walk like that for a stretch, Andrew making me stop so he can take a picture.

You're being a baby, T— says, you don't get carried.

Let him be a baby, I want to say. Who has ever carried him like this? Why shouldn't we carry him for as long as we can?

When O— gets down from my shoulders, he makes a dash ahead, running pell-mell towards an intersection. T— does not react.

Do we need to stop him? I ask.

He'll stop, T— says.

In a village this small, where everyone knows him, where he seems to know his way to and from his foster parents' house to any number of local landmarks, running away is not a serious matter.

But in London, I think, he cannot run away from us in London. In London, if he stepped off the kerb without looking, if he did not listen to our instructions, he could be dead in an instant.

We end up at a deserted playground. While T— stands watching, Andrew and I play with O—. Andrew is better at this than I am. I can chat and read to a child, but stepping into a world of pirates or dragons or warrior robots no longer comes as naturally as it once did. To perform like this requires a forgetting of the self that feels like a struggle.

As I watch Andrew playing with the boy, I feel myself turning into the person who polices limits, who worries about injury and transgression, while Andrew becomes the pirate or the astronaut or the dinosaur with such apparent ease that I begin to feel myself failing at this before we have even started. What if I can't have fun? Or, what if I can't have the kind of fun that *this* boy needs? I recall my mother telling me when I was a child how my father used to laugh, how much fun he was before I was born. What if I become the same? What if my own sense of fun, of being funny, evaporates the moment I become a parent? What would that mean for all of us?

A father and son arrive at the playground. The little boy is younger than O—, perhaps only two, three at most. O— runs over to the boy, takes him in his arms, and kisses him. The other boy goes rigid and looks as though he may burst into tears. We rush to apologize, cautioning O— that other people might not want to be kissed and hugged.

If he did this in our local London playground it would not go down well.

We take a different route back to the house, walking out of the village and around its perimeter through farmland and fields, with a view of the sea in the distance. Will O— miss the sea, I wonder?

T— is loosening up, telling stories about a bonfire that got out of control one year, a flood another year, all the cycles of rural seaside life. It's like listening to my uncle, or other relatives I haven't seen in years, slipping back into an older way of relating to people, one based on an exchange of stories rather than questions – a series of monologues instead of dialogues. One person tells a story for as long as it takes and then goes silent, waiting for the other person to reply with a different story, which may or may not speak to the first. Dialogue, when it actually happens, remains about the weather or food, about what is immediately to hand. It is focused on the tangible, the visible, the empirical.

O— starts asking us questions and we soon realize that he thinks he's coming home with us today.

No, we say, only on Thursday. Today is Monday. Another three sleeps before we go.

And K— and T—?

No, K— and T— will stay here.

And my friends?

No, you'll be going to a new school where you'll make new friends.

His face crumples. His chin wrinkles. He starts to cry. We try to reassure him but all I can think is, if Marla sees this she'll say that the Introductions need to last longer, and that is something I cannot bear. We have to keep things upbeat and make sure that he sees it all as a big adventure. The delays we have already experienced make the threat of any further delay unthinkable.

As we turn towards home, O— darts back in the opposite direction, running so fast I have to sprint to catch him and then he scrambles away from me, giggling and dashing into a thicket of trees. Testing us already, because we have disappointed him so many times, for so many months. Perhaps he needs to see whether we're here to stay.

Eventually I catch him, pick him up, carry him back to where Andrew and T— are waiting, but he wriggles so wildly in my arms that I can't hold him and he slips to the ground and darts away again. It takes almost an hour to get back to the house because he keeps running off (always away from the house), giggling, his eyes narrowing. I see the face of his mother superimposed on his, her features developing out of his own.

It is not an easy test to pass. At this first small hurdle I already find myself thinking, he is lovely when he is sweet, but what happens when the sweetness goes?

When we finally arrive back at the house, it is lunchtime. K— has made sandwiches.

I'll feed you, she says, but you'll not get whatever posh London food you're used to.

Would it surprise her to know that my father grew up in acute poverty, often half-starving, moving between motel rooms and apartments above garages and short-term rentals before his family finally bought a house that was then lost to foreclosure, or that my mother survived a semi-itinerant childhood, living in seven states by the age of seven, or that her father had grown up in a sod house and migrated West, one of the numberless 'Okies', a man who might as well have been Tom Joad in the flesh? Would she still think us posh if our histories were more legible upon our faces or audible in our voices?

O— has been her child for more than three years. Imagine what it must feel like to see strangers arrive and take him away. Perhaps it is even more difficult when those people appear to be so different to herself or her family. It seems impossible to tell her that Andrew and I come from families not so different from her own, that my parents were the first in their families to go to university, that poverty and precarity are proximate to my and to Andrew's life in ways that may not be apparent. But none of this can be said, not now, not least because I can find no way of expressing it that would not sound patronizing.

In his bedroom after lunch (what little he had eaten: a few bites of sandwich, more of some meringue éclairs), O— shows me his toys, gives me a tour, chatters at such speed that I struggle to follow the sense of his words. Whole sentences are unintelligible, some of them lapsing into what sounds like a local dialect or another language altogether.

Since we were last here in August, a teddy bear has appeared.

Who's this? I ask.

O— punches the bear in the face. It's horrible, he says.

Poor bear, I say, cuddling it. Why do you think it's horrible?

He hits the bear again. It's horrible.

He decides we should go back to find Andrew. On the way, out of nowhere, he suddenly turns to me and hisses, *You're horrible*.

And then he punches me in the gut. He's surprisingly strong.

That's not very nice, I say. I don't think *you're* horrible.

He sticks out his tongue.

There are photos of his mother on her social media pages making exactly the same face. O— seems, in this moment, to be a duplicate of her.

I hope you took a good long look at your lovely home before you left, K— says.

Why's that? I ask her, laughing nervously.

Because it won't look like that for long with him in it. She nods at O—, who is sitting on the couch mesmerized by a chat show.

I laugh again, even more nervously, then suggest we try again to read a book.

Mostly interested in his catalogues, K— says. He'll look at them for hours.

Catalogues?

Show your new daddies, she says. O— runs over to a crate full of toys in the corner of the living room from which he fishes a glossy toy catalogue.

He likes looking through that most of all.

O— starts flipping through the toy catalogue, one eye on the television. The catalogue is nothing but advertisements for cheap toys, colour-coded by gender. He flips faster through the pink pages.

Slow down, aren't those interesting? I ask, trying to draw his attention away from the screen.

No, he says, firmly shaking his head. Those are for girls.

Dolls are not for boys. Anything cute or soft or cuddly is not for boys. Even a teddy bear is not for boys. Toys for boys are hard and shiny. Most have to do with fighting or speed or war or robots or the medieval past, which is also about war and fighting and speed and machines of a more primitive kind.


When it's time for dinner he decides he wants soup. Tomato soup. Out of a tin. T— heats it up on the stove and we keep O— company while he eats in the kitchen, compelling us to blow on the soup to cool it.

We take it in turns. All day I have been conscious of the way he tries to be even-handed in his affection, equal in his requests to us. Andrew opens one yogurt, I open the other. Where has this sense of – what? empathy? – come from, and does the boy see it that way? Is it that conscious?

As the time comes for us to leave, he seems to trust that we will return. He transfers his affection back to T— for the evening. Healthy, I think, for how can he be certain that we will return? Do children his age have a sense of certainty? Do they understand what it means, or how uncertain certainty can suddenly become?

*

As we get into the car, I am knocked backwards by a quick and total fatigue.

How do you think that went? I ask Andrew.

I think it went well, he says. What about you?

There were moments when I wondered what we're getting ourselves into, but on the whole, I guess it went well.

It occurs to me that I felt no sense of disgust today. I was not disgusted by the runny nose that needed wiping, or O—'s sudden need to urinate out on the walk, or by the sandwichy hands wiping bread and butter on my jeans, or the chocolatey hands wiping chocolate on my sweater.

And yet there are elements of behaviour, a tendency towards gruffness and roughhousing, which I had not anticipated. Is it too late to redirect these energies or refashion them into a playfulness less hard-edged and aggressive, even less boyish? I want to give him a world where he does not need to be hard, where he does not have to turn away from pink things and soft things, where he can hold the bear and cuddle it when sad or anxious, as I suppose he must have been in that moment, instead of hitting it in the face, or deciding that the bear was not enough and hitting me instead.

Over the years, I have only been a very intermittent diary keeper. I start off determined to write every day, even just a record of minor events, and laboriously record whatever feels like a 'major' event in more detail, but then inevitably abandon the habit. At my mother's prompting, I start again. She says that when I was born she began writing about me every day, recording what I did and how she felt. I think this will be important, too, to look back on the days when we are getting to know O—. I sit down and most of what I write is full of excitement and surprise at the way he smells, how very differently he smells compared to Andrew or me. There is nothing bad about it, but the scent is present, distinct from the pervasive perfume of K—'s fabric softener. I write that I am surprised by my ability to incorporate O—'s scent into my sense of myself, and of Andrew and me as a unit. It is just another facet of the child, something to accept along with other invisible qualities.


## TUESDAY


Today, we are going to the nursery school. It's O—'s last day in attendance. There is a small room for younger children that adjoins a much larger one where the older children play, and where the whole nursery comes together for song time and snacks. Although strictly one of the older children, O— leads us to the smaller room which has a play kitchen with wooden food and plates and pots and pans and utensils. He cooks some wooden eggs on the plastic stove and serves them to us on a plate. We mime eating, making sounds of pleasure and appreciation.

When we have finished, I suggest we could go in the other room and look at the books, but no, O— wants to stay here and play with a boy who is disabled, who cannot speak, who sits in a tiny wheelchair at a table, continuously monitored by one of the teaching assistants and helped to play with clay, although this 'play' is little more than smacking his palms on the table. The boy blinks, he looks happy, he makes indistinct noises.

O—, I can see, is content in the boy's presence.

When we finally come together for song time in the large room, O— wants to sit at my feet. After turning on me yesterday and telling me I was horrible, he seems to be bonding more quickly to me than to Andrew, or perhaps this is only my desperately selfish misimpression.

One of the teachers leads the children through a repetitive song that allows one child to stand up and sing a brief solo and then choose another child to do so in the next verse and so on. The first children who sing solos know the words even if they cannot carry a tune, but when it comes to O—'s turn, he gets out only the first few words, so that the other children have to finish the solo for him.

Perhaps on another day, when his new parents were not there to help him say goodbye to his classmates, he would be able to sing the verse without error. Because the other children – some younger than he is – *are* able to do it, and because it is not a difficult song, this small failure, which I try not to blow out of proportion in my mind, settles in my heart as a piercing bright pain.

As parents arrive to collect their children and O— says goodbye to each of his friends, the head teacher, who was so reassuring back in August, takes us aside to speak privately.

He always wants to be in the room with the younger children, she says to us now, staring at the floor, as if there is more that she wishes to say. And then she does say other things. In London… she says, trailing off, as if 'London' signifies a space in which we might achieve a kind of clarity about the situation that we did not suspect we would need. The difference in the way she is now characterizing O— seems to come out of nowhere, but I understand that she is trying to help, to say what perhaps she could not say when we first met. Our anxieties begin to acquire a different sense of scale.

I look at Andrew and wonder what this means.

Marla has suggested we take a drive to show O— the airport as preparation for his trip to London. It takes us more than an hour to get there, and while T— sits in front with me, the man now chattering on as if we've known each other for years and are good friends, O— is in the back with Andrew, who points out things that we pass on the road.

Look at that tower, Andrew says.

Why?

227

Because it's interesting.

Why?

It just is.

Why?

A pause.

Oh, Andrew says, see those horses in the field? They look warm under their blankets, don't they?

Why?

Because the blankets keep them warm.

Why?

Because they're thick and it's cold and damp today.

Why?

Because it's almost winter.

Why?

Because it's nearly the end of autumn.

Why?

It's just that time of year.

Why?

Because we go through different seasons every year. Spring, summer, autumn, winter. It's almost winter now.

Why?

Because of what I just said.

Why?

At the airport, I find a parking place in the lot near the terminal. As we walk towards the entrance, a world of threat opens around me. Either Andrew or I has to hold tight to O—'s hand at all times or he starts running away, but he is also increasingly frustrated with having his hand held, wants to let go, and then, if he squirms out of my grip, he's off, running, a little gingerbread man, and I have to catch up to him, pausing and crouching down and telling him as calmly as I can that there are cars and he has to stay with me and hold my hand.

It's not safe to run off.

He nods, sort of, and sticks out his tongue.

You're horrible, he says.

Why does he only ever say this to me when the two of us are alone?

Inside the terminal, we visit the check-in desks before going to look at the security checkpoint.

We'll come get you and then the three of us will drive to the airport and fly back to London, I tell O—.

And K— and T—? he says.

No, just us.

No K— and T—? he says, shaking his head, chin wobbling.

K— and T— are staying here, I say, wondering how he could still think that getting two daddies does not mean losing his foster parents.

It's just going to be us, I say again, and give him a hug.

But what if we are not enough?

We spend a quarter of an hour, half an hour, an hour watching planes take off and land. O— has never been on a plane, cannot fathom what it means. I try to explain what it will feel like, that it will be like sitting in a room, in a chair, and we'll be able to look down at the clouds and the airport and the people from above, but he is not interested. He shushes me and turns to watch a 747 lift into the air.

T—, I discover, has also never been on a plane. Nor has K—. Their entire lives they have never been out of Britain, never been to London, have not even left their corner of the Southwest.

Even if Andrew and I were British ourselves, we would be nearly as foreign to them as we are in any case.

On the drive back to the village, the seating arrangement is the same: me driving, T— in the front, Andrew and O— in the back.

Good teacher that he is, Andrew points out some of the same things he pointed out earlier, as if to reinforce the lesson.

Look, there's the tower we saw on the way here, he says.

Why?

Because we passed it earlier.

Why?

Because it's on the same road. But this time it's on the other side of the road.

Why?

Because we're going in the other direction.

Why?

Because we're going back to K—'s and T—'s.

Why?

Because it's almost time for you to have your dinner and bath.

Why?

And at that moment, or perhaps later, after a similar exchange, Andrew simply stops answering and the boy falls silent. Any time Andrew or I point out anything, say anything at all, O— replies with the same 'Why', a 'Why' without curiosity, a 'Why' that is only sound to fill silence, a 'Why' that is not jokey or teasing or ironic.

If any of the information from earlier in the day has been retained, there is no indication that this is the case.

Today we are meant to stay for O—'s dinner, help give him his bath and put him to bed.

Once O— has had his bath, K— takes him into the kitchen. Ten minutes pass. Twenty. Andrew and I go to investigate and find K— giving O— his dinner alone. We stand and watch as O— finishes eating his sausages and mash. Then he gets to have an ice cream. A treat, I think, for his last dinner with the woman who has looked after him more than three times as long as the woman who gave birth to him.

In K—'s place, I would be beside myself with grief, and I suspect that she is.

Andrew and I sit with O— on his bed looking at the scrapbook we made for him. As I turn the pages, every photo, every aspect of our lives seems new to him. I ask him what he thinks of the photo of his bedroom in London.

It looks amazing, he says, and he sounds genuinely amazed, breathless. His use of the word surprises me, though. It seems too much, too sophisticated.

And then, as we try to make our way further in the scrapbook, O— loses patience, until finally we give up and say goodnight.

Driving back to the B&B, I say to Andrew what I said last night. There were moments today when I wondered what we're getting ourselves into.

The 'whys', Andrew says.

Yes. The whys.

The lack of focus.

That and other things as well. What the teacher told us, for instance. We ask ourselves what it means, all of it together. We don't know, and it doesn't seem as though anyone can tell us, but the uncertainty begins to weigh more heavily with each passing hour. We spend the evening making dinner for ourselves, but whatever sense of joy and excitement we might have had seems to have evaporated, leaving a crackling residue of anxiety and fatigue.

Tonight is the US presidential election. Though I have kept relatively calm about the race for the past few weeks, feeling as though it must go Clinton's way, I find myself so worried I can hardly eat. We agree not to check on the news during the night, to wait and see what the morning brings. Tomorrow we will be spending the day alone with

O—, picking him up after breakfast to go on an outing to a city more than an hour's drive away. We will take him to a museum and give him dinner before bringing him home for his bath and bedtime.

I can hardly sleep. Sometime around midnight, I move to the couch. I resist looking at my phone, but I have a sense of dread. I do not write in the diary I started yesterday.

Tomorrow, I think. I'll make up for it tomorrow.

## WEDNESDAY

Andrew wakes me before six. He whispers the news I have been fearing. I am exhausted, and now I am devastated. I cannot believe it is true. I cannot fathom that Clinton has lost. I struggle to get up, stumble to the shower, feel as if I have been dipped in acid, drunk it by the gallon, burned myself inside and out. My eyes sting, my stomach aches, all of my nerves are frayed and fried, scorched by an electrical fire. But today we have to be bright and happy. Today we have to see what it feels like to be alone with the boy who will be our son, to whom we are already his daddies.

Outside, there is a strong wind, gusts up to forty miles an hour, driving the sheep towards the building so that they stand grazing right up against the sliding glass doors.

It feels like the end of the world.

Our drive to the city takes in part of the same stretch of road we travelled back and forth to the airport yesterday. Andrew is sitting in front this time, O— in the back. It is our nature to comment on things that we see as we travel, and again Andrew points out the horses with their blankets, the tower, the same landmarks we noticed yesterday. Today, again, O— greets every statement we make in the car, every act of noticing, with a 'why' that holds neither curiosity nor memory. Equally, these do not sound like 'whys' as game. There is no sense of teasing or play. Each 'why' reverberates like a mechanical reflex.

We have planned to spend the day at a family-friendly museum with a menagerie of taxidermized animals and other natural history displays that look promising online. When we arrive, I am surprised by the size of the building and wonder if somewhere smaller might have been a better choice. O— has never been to this city. He has never visited a museum. Again, perhaps not the best choice, but Marla thought it sounded great, and we have blindly trusted the guidance of all the boy's social workers at every stage.

While Andrew checks our coats, I start taking O— through the exhibitions. We know that he likes animals, so we start there, but he spends two seconds at most looking at each display, whether skeleton or stuffed giraffe or diorama, whatever I try to point out to him. He dashes through gallery after gallery, upstairs and downstairs. When he starts running I jump to catch up to him. I crouch down, I talk in a low voice, telling him calmly that we don't run in museums and he needs to stay with me.

He shoots me his puckish grin. Sticks out his tongue. Wriggles away.

Andrew catches up to us. We see every room of the vast museum in less than an hour. The only things that keep O—'s focus for more than five seconds are objects that light up and make noise. Anything immobile, anything requiring a moment to understand or think about or appreciate, fails to capture his interest.

And in the space of that hour the future I have imagined as a family begins to disappear.

We will not be taking him to galleries in London, none of the museums I have been dreaming of visiting as a family. It may sound like a trivial concern, but visits to art museums were among the most important activities of my childhood, and now faced with a child who has no interest even in a museum designed for children and families, I start to despair. Is this a child who will change our lives beyond all recognition, and not in the ways we might wish?

O—'s behaviour shifts from distracted to resistant. He will not take my hand. He will not walk with me. He is finished.

We go to the café to have lunch. We order sandwiches. He wants a soft drink or juice. No, I think, no sugar. Water. We'll have water.

He wriggles in his chair while families with children the same age sit politely around us, eating sandwiches with devastating composure. It is horrible to feel embarrassed by the child in my charge, ashamed that people will think I am an inadequate parent. Already, he calls me 'Daddy' without hesitation, and Andrew is 'Papa', as we have suggested, as if we are turning ourselves into the characters from my story.

He eats the ham from the middle of his sandwich but refuses the bread.

He wants cake and sugary drinks.

No, we're not having those things.

Nuts and raisins, Andrew suggests, going back to the counter to buy several packets.

There are other things we begin to notice, such as a problem with pronouns. Men are often she or her. Women are often he or him. Andrew is she more than he. What am I? Do I have a gender in his mind? Should it matter?

More worrying, he has no sense of what the social work system has taught us to call 'stranger danger'. He walks up to a man in the museum and starts talking to him, takes his hand and embraces him. Even when he sees that this other man is not Andrew or me, he does not react. It's a more extreme version of running up to the child in the playground and kissing him. The city we're in right now is a fraction the size of London, many orders of magnitude less threatening, less rich with risk and danger. How quickly this boy might, when my back is turned, take the hand of a stranger who means him harm.

We return to the taxidermy displays, to other rooms we hope might be of interest, but again, he runs from object to object. When we crouch down and try to slow his pace, to talk about a display, he becomes impatient, looks away, refuses to make eye contact with us or listen, and then he is off again.

Is this what life will be like from now on?

I find myself losing patience.

I think, aghast at my own response, *run away then*.

Go on.

Run away as fast as you can.

If that's what you want.

I don't know what else to do, what to feel. This is a child who needs things I cannot give him, I begin to think. And even if I somehow manage to provide him with everything he does need, I suspect the effort will destroy me.

Having exhausted the museum, we go outside. The wind has died down, although there is still a strong breeze. I look on my phone to find a park with play equipment. We walk past a homeless encampment and some teenage alcoholics getting smashed, before arriving at the deserted playground.

O— attacks the slides and climbing equipment as if he has bottomless reserves of energy, while Andrew and I are both exhausted, in a state of despair. This is not what we imagined. There is no pleasure, no sense of connection, no feeling that this little boy enjoys being with us any more than he might enjoy being with the stranger in the museum.

Although we have been watching him closely, keeping him from doing anything dangerous on the play equipment, he suddenly dashes across the playground and climbs onto the stump of a tree. I run to steady him, but he's already falling, slipping forward and landing with a thud on his chest, luckily not hitting his head. How quickly it could have gone disastrously wrong, how easily he might have fallen backwards instead. I help him up, we look him over, and he starts to cry. I lift him in my arms, or perhaps Andrew does this time, I can't remember any more, and he cries for less than a minute. Then, miraculously, he stops.

He smiles, he's bubbly, everything's okay.

It seems too easy, this immediate consolation. In the evening, we'll wonder why he didn't ask for his foster parents. In fact, throughout the entire day, he does not ask about them even once. Why is he so quick to attach to us, these strange new daddies? Would he just as rapidly latch on to the stranger in the museum, allow himself to be consoled by that man, zigzagging along any path he might be led? This pliancy in combination with his bursts of aggression totally unnerves me. Each moment feels unpredictable and fraught with one sort of risk or another. Over the course of the day I begin to realize that taking care of him is unlike any experience I have had of looking after children in the past. Whatever skills I possess seem inadequate, or the wrong skills entirely. I start to doubt every decision I make, have no sense that what I do or suggest in any given moment is what this boy actually needs.

On the drive back to the village, O— responds to the horses under their blankets, the tower in the distance, the change of seasons, everything we have noticed before with the same litany of 'whys' until we simply stop answering him, stop speaking at all. Everything we say, even if not an attempt to inspire a sense of curiosity about the world around him, is met with a shattering 'Why?' And because this is not a child we have known since birth, a child to whom we feel bonded, it is even more difficult to muster a sense of patience.

When we stop speaking, it is as if something inside him has been turned off. Without aural stimuli he shuts down and goes to sleep.

It is mid-afternoon by the time we arrive back at the B&B where we're meant to spend an hour doing an activity and having a snack before making dinner. We have thought of drawing – perhaps drawing what we saw in the museum, or even just scribbling.

O— is still asleep when we arrive so we sit in the car, engine off, listening to his breathing. We look at each other and what I see in Andrew's face reflects what I feel: not joy or contentment at the sound of the child who is meant to be our son sleeping peacefully, but relief that he is unconscious, that for a brief stretch of time we do not have to engage with him.

We sit there for twenty minutes as the car gets colder and colder. I think about the US election, about my family and friends in America, my sense of utter devastation and fear about what this means for my country and for the world. I think about how this may affect our future, about the uncertainty of the years and decades ahead. I listen to the child's breathing, the steadiness of it, and think about starting the engine and driving off, driving around, just to keep him sleeping. Then, without prompting, he wakes.

It is the first time I have seen O— in a domestic space other than his foster parents' house. Other children I know might enter such an unfamiliar place cautiously, a little anxiously, but O— shoots in and surveys the territory, running from room to room. He starts opening all the drawers and cupboards in the kitchen. The latches I reinstalled in our flat before we left were not an unreasonable precaution.

We sit at the table and get out the pad of paper and crayons and markers we have bought. I suggest we draw dinosaurs or horses or the tower we passed, or he could even do a picture of himself. This does not seem too much to suggest to a child less than six months shy of his fifth birthday. I watch as he picks up a crayon and makes the least intentional of marks on the paper. When I show him how to change his grip, he produces a faint scribble of blue across the page.

And that's it. He's up, on his feet. He's had enough. The activity I hoped would fill at least ten minutes has taken less than one. Andrew tries to reengage him but he's not interested, and I notice the gesture I have seen but not wanted to see a thousand times today: when prompted to look or focus even for a moment, he shakes his head and makes a brushing off motion with his hand.

He's not interested.

He wants a tablet or a phone or an object that lights up and makes noise.

He wants the television turned on, but we say no, we're not putting it on.

In desperation, we ask if he's hungry. Yes, he's ready for dinner. We had intended cooking here, but he has no interest in the pasta we have on hand.

He wants a sandwich. Another ham sandwich. And we are too tired to argue.

We find a farm centre with a shop and a café where he orders a ham and cheese sandwich on white bread. This is also our chance to eat, so we both order sandwiches and sit in the children's play area, watching O— eating happily, occasionally sticking out his tongue at us, kicking his feet, squirming. And then he's done. He's had less than half of it.

When we arrive at K—'s and T—'s house, their daughter and grandchildren are there. O— calls the daughter 'auntie' and the grandchildren his 'cousins'. It occurs to me for the first time that this couple who have looked after so many foster children, who have their own adult child and grandchildren, are only a few years older than we are, no more than in their late forties.

We are meant to spend the evening alone with O— and his foster parents, give the boy his bath, read him a story, put him to bed, and come fetch him on Thursday morning before flying to London. I had imagined this last night as one of gentle and careful reassurance, us demonstrating that we would look after him just as well as K— and T—. But O— is suddenly caught in a game with the other children and Andrew and I recognize that we will never get him bathed and put to bed so long as the whole family is present. There is no indication when the auntie and cousins might be leaving.

How will we ever be able to extricate him – and ourselves – from this extended foster family who seems not to want him to go? Is it even right to take him from them? Are they not the family that he actually needs? There is no question that they love him, that he fits into their lives, has a place here, and has definitely made his mark.

Already, in some essential way, I know that we are giving up on this, without having spoken to each other about what we are feeling.

We say goodbye to O—, but he's not interested.

He seems not to care that we're leaving.

He does not hug us.

He does not ask us to stay.

He does not ask us to give him a bath or put him to bed. He seems totally unconcerned by our departure.

He is immersed in the family that has raised him since he was twelve months old. For more than three years they have been his family and loved him and treated him as their own.

His bond is with them, not with us.


By the time we get back to the B&B we are in crisis. We rehearse everything that seems to have gone wrong, everything that feels unmanageable. We have both been distressed by the fact that we could not speak to each other about anything of substance for the whole day, we who have done nothing but speak to each other for fourteen years, every day, sharing everything. We have both been upset by the feeling that this child has suddenly come between us and silenced us, on this most critical of days. We don't know how to understand what we have seen, but the boy we have met seems to bear little resemblance to the child who has been described to us over the course of the past six months. And on the basis of what we have observed, we begin to imagine a future in which we might have a permanent duty of care.

We have seen none of the boy's social workers since Monday, have not spoken with any of them since Tuesday.

We phone our friend R— who has been checking in with us regularly these past few days. We explain the situation, everything we have noticed, everything that has happened, how overwhelming it feels.

She listens, she asks gentle questions, she says there would be no judgement against us on her part if we decided we could not do this.

We cannot bring ourselves to phone either of our mothers.

We cannot bring ourselves to phone any other friends or family.

If there is *only one person* we can think to call, what happens when there is a much more serious crisis? The sense of loneliness and isolation is central to the complex terror of this moment. I feel torn apart by the urge to run away and an equally paralyzing determination to stay and see this through.

We phone Adriana, our senior social worker. We tell her what we told R—. She is alarmed that we have heard nothing from Marla, and astonished that we were allowed to take the boy for such a long trip on our own.

A museum like that, it was simply too much, she says, too overwhelming. It should have been something small, local.

Yes, we say, we can see that now, but it has given us a glimpse of problems not reflected in the files, problems that no one ever articulated to us over the last six months. I tell her what the head teacher told me, the concerns that she voiced for the first time, yesterday.

But it is clear that Adriana does not want us to change course. She tells us to stick with this. There will be difficult times, but it's impossible to know anything for certain. He may come through it all brilliantly.

But that note of uncertainty is ultimately what helps us make our decision. Perhaps there is nothing that could not have been healed by a secure family life, but in this present moment of crisis, one that is as much about the political as the personal, it is a hope in which we find ourselves unable to place our trust.


If we had both been British, if the families that are scattered across the United States and South Africa were instead concentrated here, could be called upon to come to our aid, to babysit, to give us a break when we needed –

If we had close friends living near us in London, the kinds of friends we could phone in the middle of the night if there were an emergency –

If we were an opposite-sex couple who did not also have to negotiate social acceptance or rejection or even ordinary tolerance of our union and the family we might become each day of our lives –

If we had grown up here and understood instinctively how this society works, how class and its constraints operate, how and why we signify in the ways that we do –

If Hillary Clinton had not lost and America did not in this moment seem a place in which we might never choose to live, as we had thought for some years we might –

If all of those things were true, then perhaps we might have been the right people to adopt this child.

But they are not. And we are not.

I don't remember whether the tears start that night or only the next morning, but we talk until very late, past midnight, and come to no resolution. I find myself arguing against giving up. We worry what our friends who have supported us will think, what our colleagues and families and mere acquaintances will think. We even worry what the foster parents will think.

We worry most of all about what this will do to O—.

But we also worry what it will do to him if we proceed as planned and everything goes to hell. Would that not be worse than disappointing him now?

We sleep separately, Andrew in the bed, me on the couch. Not because we are divided but because the mattress is terrible and every time one of us turns over the other wakes.

In the morning, we get up hours before dawn.

## THURSDAY

The tears start again quickly, but it's not me who's crying and that is what makes it so alarming. At this point, in the fourteen years we have been together, I have seen Andrew cry – really cry – only once. Now he is in floods of tears, burying his face in my neck, my chest. He says he is terrified of losing me and fears that this boy will occasion that loss. He is terrified of a life in which we go whole days without being able to speak to each other. He is terrified of struggling to form a bond and then finding, perhaps years later, that the claims of the birth family will always be stronger. He sobs uncontrollably. I hold him. I ask whether we might think of taking the child on a trial basis, for a week or two, and seeing whether he adjusts, whether we adjust.

But what if he doesn't? What if we don't? Wouldn't it be worse, Andrew says, to take him to London and then to say no, we can't do this, you're going back to foster care? Wouldn't it be kinder to end this now? I try once more, I suggest it again, but I also feel – and it's a feeling I do not share with Andrew in this moment, do not share with him for many months to come, not until he reads these words in a draft of this book – a sense of relief that we are not doing this, because nothing about it feels right.

It feels instead as if we entered into this, considering a child much older than we ever wanted, because we were desperate and grieving. Something about this situation, Andrew says, has triggered his grief for the loss of his father, precipitating a grieving process he did not manage at the beginning of this year, and now all of that grief, not just for his father but also for the idea of becoming a parent and having the kind of relationship with his own child that he had with his father, has coalesced around this boy who does not know any of this, who cannot understand it, who should never have been put in this situation, just as we should never have been.

I phone Marla. I tell her that we cannot do this. At first, she does not understand.

I say it again, more clearly this time.

What, not at all? she asks.

Not at all, I say. We cannot do this.

I try to explain to her why we have reached this decision.

But everything was going so well on Monday, she says.

Yes, but you have not seen us since Monday, I say. You haven't even been around.

She does not try to talk us out of it. In retrospect this seems strangest of all. As if she expected this was a possibility.

She comes to meet us at the B&B. We give her his car seat. We give her the pad of paper and markers and crayons. We want none of it.

Throughout all of this, Andrew is crying, sometimes sobbing. He cannot speak to her.

She asks that we follow her to the nearest town, thirty miles away, where the council offices are. She wants us to have a debriefing with her and Richard.

It is rural rush hour. A trip that should take half an hour takes twice that. Marla is on her phone, holding it to her ear, steering with one hand. At a traffic light, she takes out a brush, starts brushing her hair vigorously, almost violently. When the light turns green, she doesn't put down the brush, keeps drawing it through her long blonde hair as she drives.

When we reach the offices, Andrew says he can't manage this. I get out of the car and tell Marla that I will come in alone. No, she won't accept this, as if she could compel us to do what she asks. She knocks with her knuckle on the passenger window, badgers Andrew to come inside, pestering him until he relents.

We have to be buzzed into the building. There are teenagers lounging outside who look like they might recently have been released from prison. In the dingy room where we sit down with Richard and Marla there are toys scattered everywhere, as if a group of animals had been set loose to wreak havoc. Richard in particular seems barely able to contain his anger with us. They ask for an explanation. I rehearse again what I already said to Marla on the phone.

To his credit, Richard says that it's certainly better that we reached this conclusion now, better that we listened to our doubts and did not proceed than make things even harder for the boy.

We say how sorry we are, and we mean this. We feel the guilt of saying no to O— more acutely than any other feeling of grief or loss or disappointment or embarrassment at our failure to follow through on what we had planned.

On the drive to the airport, Andrew continues to cry, sobbing. He cries on the walk from the car rental return to the terminal. I take his arm, support him, have to stop when he suddenly stops, unable to proceed, and coax him forward. He cries at the check-in desk and through the security screening and at the gate and walking from the gate onto the plane and in the seat on the plane and then, at last, he stops crying ten minutes after we are in the air for the breathlessly short flight back to London.

I have held myself together all morning. I did not cry from the moment we woke up, through our hours of conversation and decision, through the debriefing with the social workers, through the drive to the airport, through the check-in and boarding and flight, through the trip from the airport back into central London and home on the Underground. I did not cry or even feel moved to cry until I walked in the door of our flat and then, reaching the top of the stairs, I walk almost blindly, without thought, with no more energy, over to the couch in the living room, collapse down upon it, and sob. I have never sobbed like this in my life. This is sobbing over which I have no control whatsoever. Andrew comes over and holds me, asks if I'm crying because I regret the decision we've made. No, I don't regret it. I'm just so sad that it didn't work out. And what I don't say, because I can't get the words out between sobs, is what Andrew said earlier this morning: that I fear, as he fears, that this might have been our only chance at having a family.

I am grieving for that.

We close the door of the bedroom full of books and toys and bright pillows and photographs of San Francisco and Cape Town. We do not open it for days. Perhaps weeks. We cannot open it. We cannot bear to look at it. It contains the child's toys and clothes. It contains the ruins of our hope.

At night, unable to sleep, I hear the ADM saying to her colleagues: You see, I was right, they weren't an appropriate match. They run away from trauma. They just can't face it.

# AFTER

We go to a two-day conference that Andrew and a colleague had organized a year earlier. She undertook to run it alone when we knew that Introductions were going ahead. It is a way of not being at home alone with each other and the room that was meant to be O—'s.

I tell a friend who will later become a colleague that I will write about it, that it will come quickly, I have to write about it to understand what has happened, but then I find that the pain of writing about it is so great it takes almost another year before I can begin in earnest, and even then, when the pain should not be so sharp, weeks pass during which I cannot bring myself to turn to this project, because every moment remembered is agony, every description of what happened scrapes off the scabs, rubs salt deep in exposed tissue, lights a match and holds it against my heart.

I cannot escape the sense of profound loss coupled with anger at a system I feel certain did us and O— a grave injustice. And containing it all is the feeling that we disappointed a child who did not deserve that to happen, who needed a different kind of family entirely.

As I write these words I have a pain in my chest and tears in my eyes. As I reread and revise them, the pain returns. I wish we had never tried. I wish we had not wasted four years of our lives struggling to achieve something at which it seems we were destined to fail.

One day, when I start scrolling through the photographs stored on my computer, I am shocked to find ones of us taken over the course of those three days. I had forgotten them, blocked them out entirely, and their sudden appearance on my screen creates a series of small explosions in my gut and my chest and I find myself doubling over, swiftly quitting the application so that I don't have to look any more at the child's face, at my face in his presence, at the joy I felt being a parent in those few captured moments.

A parent for not even three days.

Is that, I wonder, the only parenthood I will ever know?

In the weeks that follow, commuting to work on tubes and trains, I will suddenly find myself overwhelmed and trying to hold it together until I can stumble into a restroom or my office and cry. When a well-meaning colleague asks me questions I talk as long as I can, wait for her to leave, close the door, crawl under my desk, lie down on the floor, and cry for twenty minutes before I have to compose myself to teach a class.

Near the end of November, I ask Andrew whether he might want to get married at Christmas. We made plans back in September to go to the Hebridean island where his sister and brother-in-law live, to spend the holidays with his mother and nieces, and my mother and her partner, and of course with O— as well. It was going to be a big family Christmas. We rented a cottage for a week. Non-refundable. All the close family will be there.

Yes, he says, let's do it.

For a month we have been battling with Marla to arrange for the pick-up and shipping of O—'s toys and clothes. In desperation, I phone Adriana and ask her to intervene. If this isn't taken care of before the holidays, I say, I'm going to donate them. I can't have them in the flat any longer.

She suddenly sounds furious.

It would be incredibly wrong to get rid of them, she says angrily.

Wrong even though, back in September, when the ADM said no to the match, K— herself told me we could just donate everything? The boy wasn't attached to any of it, not to the toys or the clothes or the books, that's what she said. He has no sense of attachment to anything, not even to objects.

But okay, I say, then you make the effort to get Marla to arrange shipping.

At last the pick-up is arranged, and we say goodbye to all the belongings that stood briefly as the sign of the child's intended place in our lives. Before Andrew's mother arrives, we dismantle the bed and sell it. A family that lives nearby purchases it for their growing daughter. I give away the child-sized easel to neighbours who have a three-year-old. I want all of it gone, everything that speaks of a child. I unscrew all the cupboard latches and locks and throw them away. All the paraphernalia that remains I donate to a charity shop.

We don't usually take some of these things, the woman at the shop says, but I am already halfway out the door, cannot possibly be asked to take home what I can barely stand to contemplate.

The books from friends we keep, carefully packed away, waiting for a day when they might yet be put to use.

We try to throw ourselves into the festivity of the holidays but neither of us feels any joy. As we drive to Scotland with Andrew's mother in the back of the car, I think of how impossible a day-long drive to Glasgow from London would have been with O—, how the ferry crossing would have been fraught with anxieties about him running off and falling overboard.

Is it February? It might be January. In any case, time has passed. Adriana asks us to come for a meeting to discuss what happened

249

and how we might wish to proceed. Although she is sympathetic, the system needs someone to blame.

We, it quickly becomes clear, are those someones.

In order to continue as prospective adopters, she says, we would have to submit to an independent review in which we would need to give a full account of what happened and convince the reviewer that none of it was our fault.

Even still, she says, the reviewer might find against us, might decide that we are not suitable as prospective adopters. And even if the person found in our favour, we would have a 'black mark' on our record and it would be very unlikely that any social worker anywhere would risk matching us with a child for fear that we might, at the last second, decide that the match was not right for us.

At the time I feel almost relieved by this, because I know that I don't have it in me to go through a review, although Andrew has been holding open the possibility of trying again.

Now, with this new information, he no longer is.

Nonetheless, I also feel a sense of rage that the system should conclude, however implicitly, that we were the ones at fault, when it is clear to me that O— and we were all failed in countless ways by them.

When people ask us now whether we will try again, I say no, not adoption. My heart is too fragile, the world now too dangerous and too unpredictable. I cannot put myself through it. I cannot face the intrusiveness of new processes of approval. I would never consider trying to adopt in Britain, and to adopt abroad we would have to go through a private company, which might not even find us suitable, and even then our options as a same-sex couple are limited. Few countries want people like us. And who's to say, in this dark age through which we're now living, how long even those doors will remain open?

# ORDINARY

In *Blue Nights*, Joan Didion writes of her gradual process of realizing how much was wrong, how much went wrong, with her adopted daughter, Quintana, a child she brought home from the hospital two days after she was born. This confession undermines the narrative I have long clung to: if only we could adopt a child in the first days of its life, be certain of taking care of its every need as our mothers took care of ours, bonding with it from its first moments in this world, then everything would be okay, all of us happy and well adjusted and ordinary.

Whatever ordinary means for anyone.

Fucked up in a banal way rather than an unpredictable and volatile one.

Reading Didion, I realize that my idealization of raising children to independence may be deeply old-fashioned. Western society – American society at least, but British, too, and perhaps for much longer – has expanded the purview of parenting deep into the adulthood of the child, so that a duty of care seems practically if not actually a lifelong responsibility. This was not so for my own parents, who supported me financially until I was independent but only up to a point, as their parents supported them, but only up to a point. A net was there if something went catastrophically wrong, but at some juncture in all of our relationships the children became more independent, more stable, than the parents.

Ultimately, Andrew and I looked at O— and I feared we could

never be certain of having time enough to make sure O— would reach independence, make his own way in the world, because those first four and a half years of his life were lost to us, our knowledge of them able to fill a few pages at most, and even that built on the accounts of others, not even his own family, let alone himself. In the end, we did not trust that we were up to the task.

And although it is not the point of having children, at least not the only one, I could not trust that when I needed him at the end of my own life, he would be there to look after me.

# YOU

Although I have altered and obscured your name, many other details, the names of everyone around you, numerous details about them as well, perhaps you will still find yourself here, in these pages, some day in the future.

Nearly a year after the end of the process, I dream about you. These dreams come at least once a month, sometimes more frequently, and then there are days and weeks that I am free of those nightly conjurings. I know it is no longer my right to dream about you. We relinquished the right to dream of what life with you would be like when we decided we could not take you.

I only hope that in time you may understand how, in making the decision we did, we were doing the best for you because we were not equipped to look after you in the way we believed you needed. Your presence, your person, in all its richness and complexity, all its already existing personhood, was not the right match for two people wounded by our own childhoods and adolescences and adulthoods, by all the difficult experiences we each, in our particular ways, have experienced.

If we had been different people, we might have been able to give you what you needed, but the old saw that an experience of difficulty makes one able to empathize and respond to the difficult beginnings of another was not, in this case, the truth, or at least only partially the truth: we could empathize, but in the moment you reached us our reserves and capacity to respond were perilously low, and we knew that we could not summon the energies, collectively or individually, to make you a part of our lives, to give you what you needed.

At some point, I hope that if you remember what happened, if your brain has not erased or repressed the disappointment of our withdrawal, you will understand that we made the choice we did thinking of you, of what your experience might be, as much if not more than our own. The grief of disappointing you, and ourselves, is something from which we have not recovered, may never recover. We hope that you will recover, but we also know that you may not. We feel sorrow about our choice, as well as anger that the system allowed us to reach the point where it was the only choice we felt able to make.

# THE GINGER CHILD

A few weeks before Christmas, Andrew and I go to Amsterdam where a friend is being awarded a prize. The ceremony at the Royal Palace is followed by an intimate dinner at an historic house on a canal and it feels as though we have slipped out of nightmare and into a fairy tale. In a way that immediately strikes me as self-justifying, I realize that neither of us could have attended this event if we had adopted because one of us on our own would never have managed the boy, and he himself would not have managed the travel to Amsterdam, sitting still through a long ceremony, the flights, the waiting, the negotiation of public transport in a busy foreign city.

We would have missed seeing a friend honoured, and though I know how ridiculous it sounds, I would have missed my five minutes speaking with the King of the Netherlands, a once in a lifetime opportunity for the grandson of an Okie and a farmer's daughter, a madwoman who lost everything and an embezzling adulterous ne'er-do-well.

As I am all too painfully aware, it is an opportunity no rarer than the chance – for someone like me – of having a child.

The following morning, I wake up ill. Sicker than I have been in years. I shuffle to the bathroom and shower and slump against the tiles. However hard I have been trying to hold myself together, I am falling apart.

But we are in Amsterdam and this is a holiday, a restorative break from the hell of the last year, so we head off to the Stedelijk Museum where we happen upon 'MANIC/LOVE', a large exhibition of American artist Jordan Wolfson's work.

It seems to have been meant, horribly, for us.

Much of it I cannot take in. There is too much noise, too much chaos, too much colour and movement in the videos and not enough tenderness or beauty, not for the feverish state that I'm in. There are too many people shouting, Wolfson himself shouting. In a video titled *Raspberry poser* animated viruses plop and bounce around the streets of New York and Paris alternating with an animated red-haired kid, smiling frenziedly, who stabs himself, comes back to life, strangles himself to death, comes back to life, cuts his chest open so his organs and blood spill out, comes back to life, runs with an unnerving simian gait, is trapped in a cage, ranting, shaking the bars, always returning to life.

It has become routine to call Wolfson an *enfant terrible*, but while he is undoubtedly convincing in that role, he also lampoons and subverts both the category of bad-boy-artist and the art market that demands such figures. *Real violence*, a virtual reality film included in the Whitney Biennial in 2017, seemed to depict Wolfson beating a man to death with a baseball bat. His work is never less than dramatically provocative. It embraces an aesthetic of noise and ugliness, mining the possibilities of virtual media and digital technology in ways that are designed both to alienate viewers and to force them to reflect on that alienation. If the artist is interested in formal decisions that make him 'feel more', as he has said in interview, then he is just as committed to making his audiences feel more, too, and demanding that we ask ourselves what the excess of feeling produced by his works might mean.[39]

In Amsterdam, the piece with which I spend the most time is *Colored sculpture*, an animatronic polyurethane marionette of a seven-foot red-haired boy with glowing eyes. He is controlled by three heavy chains rigged to a system of gantries in turn controlled by software that takes him through a fifteen-minute cycle of movements. The chains drag and lift and toss him around this confined space, sometimes leaving him hanging in mid-air, watching the gallery visitors in silence, then moving him along and lowering him to the floor, head falling to the side, eyes blinking and flashing, the chains carrying him in an impossible position as if he were a doll being dragged by a child, or, worse, a child being dragged by an unseen adult, a child abused, as susceptible to careless handling as a shiny plastic toy.

Like the *Raspberry poser*, just when it seems he might be dead or dying he rises again, eyes bright and maniacal (eyes equipped with facial recognition software so that it often seems as if he is looking right at you), head turning then lowered again, chains dropping him in a terrible metallic rush, or, more ominously, slowly and deliberately, link by sonorous link, only for the one attached to his foot to drag him to the other end of the space before all three chains lift him in the air and lower him once more. Over and over, cycles of motion bleed into one another so the limits of each are difficult to discern.

Feverish, I stand through several cycles, making notes:

*Hand held aloft, raised, raising the body,*
*chain raising the head, whole body off the floor,*
*chains cascading to lower the whole body to the floor,*
*chain at the foot dragging him across the space,*
*other two chains lifting to suspend him in the centre,*
*lowered to the floor again,*
*chains unravelling in a y-shape across the floor,*
*shifting, leg pulled back and to the right,*
*suspending him upside down in mid-air,*
*lowered gently to the floor,*

*chain dragging him by the leg as his other foot, head, arms*
*are on the floor,*
*now lifted again by the foot,*
*suspended upside down,*
*pulled forward in space by the hand,*
*suspended in mid-air, holding still, no movement, silence,*
*silence,*
*head upside down, body suspended horizontally,*
*lowered again,*
*dragged forward by the arm, up,*
*turning, head lifted so face and eyes are facing front,*
*blinking bright eyes,*
*lowered to the floor,*
*head held just off the floor,*
*dragged by arm and head, slowly, back, lifted again,*
*feet on the floor, in mid-air, one arm raised to the side,*
*body suspended in mid-air, facing forward,*
*lowered again, bright staring eyes,*
*pulled backward by the foot, raised half off the ground,*
*then flat on the floor,*
*chains looping parabolas around him on the floor,*
*chains retracting, dragging him by head and hand*
*up, to the right,*
*then down, lowered to the floor,*
*face down,*
*eyes bright,*
*head chain slowly unspooling,*
*arm aloft, only thing off the ground,*
*and then, without warning,*
*Percy Sledge, song in medias res and the chains spill out,*
*cascading,*
*body drawn quickly back and to the left,*

*lifted by the foot, then*
*dropped on the head,*
*a slight bounce,*
*total collapse, then pulled forward, dragged aloft,*
*hanging mid-air as a man loves a woman,*
*mid-air dance,*
*dropped and dragged to the side,*
*fallen on the floor at the right,*
*lifted again by the head,*
*dropped,*
*lifted,*
*dropped.*
*Music stops as the lift,*
*the drop,*
*the lift,*
*the drop,*
*the lift,*
*the drop*
*the lift the drop the lift the drop the lift the drop*
*pulls him into the middle of the front of the space,*
*an abrupt dragging back and to the right, to the left,*
*dropped on the head over and*
*over and over and over and over,*
*dragged by the foot, dropped and*
*dropped and*
*dropped*
*on the head until*
*falling to a total collapse.*
*Silence. Stillness.*
*Chains start to move again,*
*dragging him forward by head and hand*
*across the floor,*

top chains twisted together then untwisting as he comes to the
    front,
bright-eyed, staring, looking forward, slowly rising,
demonic,
suspended just off the floor, moving to the right,
and the voiceover starts, a young man's voice,
voice of the artist,
and flashing animations in the eyes.
When the voiceover stops, he falls to the ground,
dropped again,
dropped on the head,
a burst of music,
dropped on the head,
dropped again
dropped
dropped,
pulled to the front,
pulled up in mid-air,
dangling, watching us watching,
abuse and recovery,
child as symptom of man loving woman,
child the abused monster of love.

It is a ghastly, visceral dance of manipulation and control. Much of
each fifteen-minute cycle occurs in a silence so pregnant with the
expectation of violence and noise that I find it excruciating to watch,
but also impossible to avert my gaze.

Wolfson has said the figure is derived from Huckleberry Finn,
mid-century American television marionette Howdy Doody, and
Alfred E. Neuman, the cartoon mascot of *MAD* magazine. To me
he also suggests the murderous doll Chucky from the *Child's Play*
movies. As I am writing this, Nikolas Cruz, a boy who looks like

a demonic mash-up of Finn and Doody and Neuman, but also like one of American-born, South Africa-resident photographer Roger Ballen's subjects, kills seventeen people at Marjory Stoneman Douglas High School in Broward County, Florida, on Valentine's Day, 2018. Like the *Colored sculpture*, Cruz's eyes seem to *register* an audience, a viewer, but without any indication he actually *sees* the people who might be watching, or being able to understand them as anything other than faces, an assortment of features that might themselves be as constructed, and artificial, as Wolfson's sculpture's own precursors.

What is Wolfson doing with all these citations of boyhood – and specifically of white, American boyhood? Might the answer lie in this particular work's implicit reference to earlier polychrome sculpture, from classical Greek and Roman to medieval Catholic traditions, works that were, in their own ways, puppets for various ideologies and belief systems? In this case, the ideology could perhaps be white nationalist American masculinity itself. Earlier versions of the *Colored sculpture* character have appeared elsewhere in Wolfson's work – as a two-dimensional cartoon boy aiming a gun into his abdomen, or poised over a bucket defecating while gazing at himself in a mirror under tabloid-style headlines that read, variously, 'AMERICANO SEX RED SEX... SLAVE... Racist... AMERICAN BLACK'. *White America*, the figure seems to be saying, *take a good long look at yourself and all the shit you're producing.*

If *Colored sculpture* is the puppet of an ugly, racist American ideology, then it seems also to insist we acknowledge the trauma inflicted by that culture on white boys, and the ways in which such trauma produces violence in its victims. It would not be outrageous to conclude that *Colored sculpture* stands for any number of young American men who resort to horrific acts of violence but who are also often survivors of abuse: boys who keep getting up off the floor in preparation for the next cycle of beatings, their actions programmed by the culture that has produced and continues to control them, boys for whom it is nonetheless difficult or impossible to feel sympathy even as we acknowledge the complexity and violence of the forces that have determined who they are and what they do.

*Colored sculpture*'s voiceover, read by Wolfson himself, conflates the energies of sex and death, as if the puppet were at once sex-worker, victim, and murderer for hire:

Two to kill you
Three to hold you
Four to bleed you
Five to touch you
Six to move you
Seven to ice you
Eight to put my teeth in you
Nine to put my hand on you
Ten to hand inside your hair [sic]
Eleven your leg over my shoulder...
Thirteen I killed you
Fourteen you're blind
Fifteen you're spoiled
Sixteen to lift you
Seventeen to show you
Eighteen to weigh you...

Do the numerical headings imply payment or digital programming or even a sequence of dance positions in a mechanical ballet? Or can they be read as a monstrous riff on a counting nursery rhyme, 'One for Sorrow' for a post-human age? It seems no accident that the sequence ends at eighteen, the age of legal adulthood. What is indisputable is that the voiceover text is all about the interplay of eroticism and sadism, particularly in the first few lines, oscillating between violence and tenderness, until the syntax breaks down in the ninth line: 'Ten to hand inside your hair'.

Roberta Smith, in her review of *Colored sculpture* in the *New York Times*, wrote that she believed this speech was 'clearly directed at a woman', that the puppet is 'a prisoner of love, tormented by his own emotions or perhaps an abusive woman'.[40] But surely the point is that whomever is being addressed might be anyone at all, man or woman or child. This is what makes the work so distressing. We should not assume, either, that the voice is necessarily meant to be that of the puppet itself, *him*self, although his eyes flash with an array of animations and found footage as the voiceover plays. We could even think of the puppet, or the child figure he stands for, as a screen onto which we project our own responses: our disgust and empathy, our revulsion and horror.

Wolfson has described the sculpture as 'a cartoony, life-size figure that's almost like a piece of sports equipment… Formally, it's extremely glossy, reflective.' Ajay Kurian, writing about the piece in *Artspace*, claims that it's 'stupid to feel for the puppet', but equally that 'it's impossible not to'.[41] As disturbing as I find *Colored sculpture*, I cannot agree that it's stupid to feel something for this strange mechanical creature. The violence might seem inconsequential *because* the figure is so toy-like, so stylized in its imitation of the human, but inconsequential it is not. Wolfson has created an object that insists we engage with the duelling forces of empathy and revulsion it engenders.

The question is, what do we do with those feelings?

As so often happens when we are faced – in public for instance – with an adult mistreating a child, do we choose to inhabit our disgust and discomfort and so look away, refusing our natural feelings of empathy for the vulnerable? Or do we watch and live the feelings concurrently, conscious of the fact that it is our own shame at our helplessness, our social inability or incapacity to intervene, that creates a sense of disgust when the subject himself – the abused puppet child – is doing nothing objectively disgusting? He is acted upon. He is without agency. He is pulled and dragged and held aloft by invisible hands.

Kurian argues that the figure is a symptom and sign of a moment in which white men in America feel themselves victimized by greater racial equality. This seems plausible enough. But to call Wolfson's puppet a 'petulant child', 'freckled, sneering, bucktoothed', who 'distills something deeply unsettling about our moment and potentially our foreseeable future', fails to see the figure as at once passive, victimized, resilient, and potentially still enraged by his mistreatment, and by the ways in which he has been rendered object rather than subject.

Kurian published his article a week after the 2016 presidential election, a week after those awful three days of our failed Introductions. While I cannot agree with all of his conclusions, it is nonetheless helpful to see him locate Wolfson's work in its larger context, and reading the article more than a year later, looking at the photograph of Donald Trump alongside the image of the red-haired *Colored sculpture*, I am struck by something else: Trump, too, was once a ginger child.

This is not to suggest that I feel sympathy for Trump. But I realize that I have come to see this period of our lives as the season of the ginger child, the child we realized we could not take, the mechanical child of art that suggests both victim and villain, the queer and sensitive child I was myself.

Even the Dutch king, at some point in his life, vaguely strawberry blonde as he is now, might once have been called a ginger child.

But then isn't every child ultimately a ginger child, even if not red-haired, even if not, as ginger suggests in Cockney rhyming slang, queer (*ginger beer*, *queer*)? At some point in childhood are we not all 'cautious, careful; gentle', as well as 'easily hurt or broken', 'sensitive' or 'fragile'?

And each of us – depending on our own particular experience, that series of events, triggers, situations, acts, opportunities, and constraints that constitutes a childhood – has the possibility of growing up to be a killer or a king, or any of the countless identities in between.

# ACKNOWLEDGEMENTS

'Interior: Monkeyboy' originally appeared in *Granta* 136: Legacies of Love, Summer 2016.

Portions of the chapter 'The Ginger Child' appeared in slightly different form on the *Times Literary Supplement* website in June 2018 under the title 'Punch and Injury'.

Thanks to Kate Gottgens, Zoë Wicomb, Sigrid Rausing, Gail Flanery, Nan van der Vlies, Clare Drysdale, Tamsin Shelton, Sarah Chalfant, Alba Ziegler-Bailey, Rebecca Nagel, and everyone at Atlantic Books and the Wylie Agency.

Thanks as always to Andrew, who survives it with me.

# BIBLIOGRAPHY

'Munby slates "sloppy practice" in adoption: President of Family Division concerned about recurrent inadequacy of analysis & reasoning put forward in support of the case of adoption', *New Law Journal*, 20 September 2013, online: www.newlawjournal. co.uk/content/munby-slates-sloppy-practice-adoption

*Alien: Covenant*, Dir. Ridley Scott, 2017, DVD, 20th Century Fox Home Entertainment, 2017

*American Horror Story: Hotel*, Dir. Ryan Murphy, 2015, 20th Century Fox Home Entertainment, 2016

*Annie*, Dir. John Huston, 1982, DVD, UCA, 2010

*Blade Runner 2049*, Dir. Denis Villeneuve, 2017, DVD, Sony Pictures, 2018

*Brothers and Sisters*, Dir. Blake Bedford, 2006–2011, DVD, Walt Disney Home Entertainment, 2011

Butler, Patrick, 'Adoption numbers drop steeply as government's flagship policy falters', *The Guardian*, 29 September 2016, online: www.theguardian.com/society/2016/sep/29/adoption-numbers-drop-steeply-as-governments-flagship-policy-falters

*Caché*, Dir. Michael Haneke, 2006, DVD, Artificial Eye, 2006

*Citizen Ruth*, Dir. Alexander Payne, 1996, DVD, Lionsgate, 2012

Colker, Ruth, *Pregnant Men: Practice, Theory, and the Law* (Bloomington and Indianapolis: Indiana University Press, 1994)

Davidson, Michael, 'Pregnant Men: Modernism, Disability, and Biofuturity in Djuna Barnes', *NOVEL: A Forum on Fiction* 43.2, Summer 2010: 207–26

Didion, Joan, *Blue Nights* (London: Fourth Estate, 2011)

Edelman, Lee, *No Future: Queer Theory and the Death Drive* (Durham, NC and London: Duke University Press, 2004)

Eribon, Didier, *Returning to Reims*, trans. Michael Lucey (Los Angeles: Semiotext(e), 2013)

Flanery, Patrick, 'Interior: Monkeyboy', *Granta* 136: Legacies of Love, July 2016: 69–93

—— 'Punch and Injury', *Times Literary Supplement*, 13 June 2018, online: https://www.the-tls.co.uk/articles/public/punch-and-injury

Fouzer, Monidipa, 'Commission begins work on "not fit for purpose" surrogacy laws', *The Law Gazette*, 4 May 2018, online: https://www.lawgazette.co.uk/law/commission-begins-work-on-not-fit-for-purpose-surrogacy-laws/5065988.article

Freud, Sigmund, 'On Narcissism: An Introduction', trans. James Strachey, in Joseph Sandler, Ethel Spector Person and Peter Fonagy, eds., *Freud's On Narcissism: An Introduction* (London: Routledge, 2018)

Gayle, Damien, and Press Association, 'High court orders surrogate mother to hand baby to gay couple', *The Guardian*, 6 May 2015, online:https://www.theguardian.com/law/2015/may/06/high-court-orders-surrogate-mother-baby-gay-couple

Joyrich, Lynne, 'Queer Television Studies: Currents, Flows, and (Main) streams', in *Cinema Journal* 53:2, Winter 2014: 133–9

July, Miranda, *No one belongs here more than you* (Edinburgh and London: Canongate, 2015; 2007)

Klein, Melanie, 'Envy and Gratitude' in *Envy and Gratitude and Other Works*, 1946–1963 (London: Virago Press, 1988)

Kurian, Ajay, 'The Ballet of White Victimhood: On Jordan Wolfson, Petroushka, and Donald Trump', *Artspace*, 15 November 2016, online: https://www.artspace.com/magazine/contributors/jottings/ajay-kurian-on-jordan-wolfson-colored-sculpture-54364

Mead, Margaret, *Male and Female* (New York: HarperCollins, 2001; 1949)

Minsky, Rosalind, '"Too Much of a Good Thing": control of

containment in coping with change?', *Psychoanalytic Studies* 1.4, 1999: 391–405

Money, John, and Geoffrey Hosta, 'Negro Folklore of Male Pregnancy', *The Journal of Sex Research* 4.1, Feb. 1968: 34–50

Ngai, Sianne, *Ugly Feelings* (Cambridge, MA: Harvard University Press, 2005)

Nussbaum, Emily, 'How Ryan Murphy Became the Most Powerful Man in TV', *The New Yorker*, 14 May 2018, online: https://www.newyorker.com/magazine/2018/05/14/how-ryan-murphy-became-the-most-powerful-man-in-tv

*Orange is the New Black*, Created by Jenji Kohan, 2013–2018, DVD, Lionsgate, 2018

*Prometheus*, Dir. Ridley Scott, 2012, DVD, 20th Century Fox Home Entertainment, 2012

Reynolds, Emma, 'Sickest artwork of all time allows viewers to watch man beaten to death', news.com.au, 8 August 2017, online: https://www.news.com.au/lifestyle/real-life/news-life/sickest-artwork-of-all-time-allows-viewers-to-watch-man-beaten-to-death/news-story/9492c9f143535d7aa69694f9c95ff736

Rudgard, Olivia, 'Tell children created through surrogacy how they were born, says first-ever Government guidance', *The Daily Telegraph*, 28 February 2018, online: https://www.telegraph.co.uk/news/2018/02/28/tell-children-created-surrogacy-born-says-first-ever-government

—— 'Surrogate mother who changed her mind must hand baby to gay couple, court rules', *The Daily Telegraph*, 17 November 2017, online: https://www.telegraph.co.uk/news/2017/11/17/surrogate-mother-changed-mind-giving-baby-must-hand-child-gay

Sedgwick, Eve Kosofsky, 'Anality', in *The Weather in Proust* (Durham, NC and London: Duke University Press, 2011)

Semmelhack, Diana, et al., 'Womb envy and Western society: On the devaluation of nurturing in psychotherapy and society', *Europe's Journal of Psychology* 7.1. February 2011: 164–86

Smith, Roberta, 'Jordan Wolfson's Herky-Jerky Puppet at David Zwirner', *The New York Times*, 10 June 2016, 23

Stockton, Kathryn Bond, *The Queer Child: Or Growing Sideways in the Twentieth Century* (Durham, NC and London: Duke University Press, 2009)

Thomas, June, 'The Thing That Made Me Monstrous to Some People Is Also the Thing That Empowered Me', *Slate*, 9 May 2014, online: http://www.slate.com/blogs/outward/2014/05/09/penny_dreadful_s_john_logan_why_a_gay_writer_feels_a_kinship_with_frankenstein.html

Trumbore, Dave, 'WonderCon 2012: *Prometheus* Panel Recap Featuring Sir Ridley Scott and Damon Lindelof', 17 March 2012, Collider.com, online: collider.com/prometheus-wondercon

Van Niekerk, Marlene, *Agaat*, trans. Michiel Heyns (Johannesburg: Jonathan Ball, 2006)

Wolfson, Jordan, *Colored sculpture*, 2016

# NOTES

1   See, for instance: Olivia Rudgard, 'Surrogate mother who changed her mind must hand baby to gay couple, court rules', *The Daily Telegraph*, 17 November 2017, online: https://www.telegraph. co.uk/news/2017/11/17/surrogate-mother-changed-mind-giving-baby-must-hand-child-gay/. See also: Damien Gayle and Press Association, 'High court orders surrogate mother to hand baby to gay couple', *The Guardian*, 6 May 2015, online: https://www. theguardian.com/law/2015/may/06/high-court-orders-surrogate-mother-baby-gay-couple. As of 2018, there is a movement to reform British surrogacy law and the Law Commission is undertaking a three-year review. For further information, see: Monidipa Fouzer, 'Commission begins work on "not fit for purpose" surrogacy laws', *The Law Gazette*, 4 May 2018, online: https://www.lawgazette. co.uk/law/commission-begins-work-on-not-fit-for-purpose-surrogacy-laws/5065988.article. The government has also issued advice on surrogacy for the first time; see: Olivia Rudgard, 'Tell children created through surrogacy how they were born, says first-ever Government guidance', *The Daily Telegraph*, 28 February 2018, online: https://www.telegraph.co.uk/news/2018/02/28/tell-children-created-surrogacy-born-says-first-ever-government/

2   Elsewhere, Edelman makes such polemical assertions (though these are part of a more nuanced argument) as 'Fuck the social order and the Child in whose name we're collectively terrorized; fuck Annie; fuck the waif from *Les Mis*'. Lee Edelman, *No Future: Queer Theory*

*and the Death Drive* (Durham, NC and London: Duke University Press, 2004), 75, 29.

3  Ibid., 17, 31.

4  The in-joke is that the character played by Lady Gaga, whose fans in real life are known as 'Little Monsters', gives birth to a little monster.

5  For a suggestive exploration of the ghostly gay child, whom The Countess's vampire children in some ways recall, see Kathryn Bond Stockton, *The Queer Child: Or Growing Sideways in the Twentieth Century* (Durham, NC and London: Duke University Press, 2009). I am grateful to Theresa Geller for this suggestion.

6  Sigmund Freud, 'On Narcissism: An Introduction', trans. James Strachey, in Joseph Sandler, Ethel Spector Person and Peter Fonagy, eds., *Freud's On Narcissism: An Introduction* (London: Routledge, 2018), 21. This passage is also cited by Edelman in *No Future*.

7  Let us not forget, however, that Alex's husband (Bentley's character, John Lowe) is the biological father from hell: a serial killer so normatively retrogressive that he murders those who violate the Ten Commandments – surely every queer adoptive parent's worst nightmare. It is he who ultimately kills Elizabeth.

8  Later in the season, Alex will lure them back to the hotel and sacrifice them to bisexual vampire Ramona Royale (Angela Bassett).

9  See Emily Nussbaum's article 'How Ryan Murphy Became the Most Powerful Man in TV', *The New Yorker*, 14 May 2018, online: https://www.newyorker.com/magazine/2018/05/14/how-ryan-murphy-became-the-most-powerful-man-in-tv. For an illuminating analysis of *The New Normal*, see Lynne Joyrich, 'Queer Television Studies: Currents, Flows, and (Main)streams', in *Cinema Journal* 53:2, Winter 2014: 133–9.

10  Didier Eribon, *Returning to Reims*, trans. Michael Lucey (Los Angeles: Semiotext(e), 2013): 72–73; my emphasis.

11  In a discussion that reveals the connections between pro-choice and LGBTQ rights movements in the United States, American lawyer

and legal scholar Ruth Colker describes clients in Louisiana who were active in the struggle for access to abortion services, noting that 'many... were committed to working with gay and lesbian people to defend abortion clinics' as they regarded 'pro-choice efforts as closely linked to the political rights of lesbian and gay people'. She notes that in their work as clinic defenders, such clients and 'their supporters wore nontraditional clothing, with many of the women wearing combat boots and many of the men wearing earrings and other "effeminate" items of clothing' that marked them in the 'conservative Baton Rouge community' where the protests were taking place, as 'quite radical and... visibly lesbian or gay'. Ruth Colker, *Pregnant Men: Practice, Theory, and the Law* (Bloomington and Indianapolis: Indiana University Press, 1994), 33.

12 See 'Munby slates "sloppy practice" in adoption: President of Family Division concerned about recurrent inadequacy of analysis & reasoning put forward in support of the case of adoption', *New Law Journal*, 20 September 2013, online: www.newlawjournal. co.uk/content/munby-slates-sloppy-practice-adoption. See also Patrick Butler, 'Adoption numbers drop steeply as government's flagship policy falters', *The Guardian*, 29 September 2016, online: www.theguardian.com/society/2016/sep/29/adoption-numbers-drop-steeply-as-governments-flagship-policy-falters.

13 All quotations from Sianne Ngai's *Ugly Feelings* (Cambridge, MA: Harvard University Press, 2005) are from the Introduction (21) or from the chapter 'Envy', 126–43.

14 Ngai does not elaborate on her marshalling of 'effete' (nor, when she uses 'effete' elsewhere in the book to describe other feelings and subjects, does she unpack its freighted etymology). This seems a strange lacuna in the argument, which is founded on thinking through envy's calibration in contemporary discourse as an affect that is inherently gendered, although she does discuss the 'feminization' of envy historically and the way that the 'envious subject is so frequently suspected of being hysterical' alongside, in the twentieth

century, 'intensified social prohibition against [the] expression' of envy. Ibid., 129.

15 "effete, adj." *OED Online*. Oxford University Press, July 2018. Web. 18 September 2018.

16 In Miranda July's story 'The Shared Patio', there is a wry commentary on the 'New Men' who 'want to have children' and 'long to give birth' to such an extent that 'sometimes when they cry, it is because they can't do this; there is just nowhere for a baby to come out'. Miranda July, 'The Shared Patio', in *No one belongs here more than you* (Edinburgh and London: Canongate: 2015; 2007), 3–4. For an anthropoligical consideration of womb envy, see Margaret Mead, *Male and Female* (New York: HarperCollins, 2001; 1949), 72–02/.

17 John Money and Geoffrey Hosta, 'Negro Folklore of Male Pregnancy', *The Journal of Sex Research* 4.1, February 1968: 34–50.

18 Diana Semmelhack, Larry Ende, Karen Farrell, Julieanne Pojas, 'Womb envy and Western society: On the devaluation of nurturing in psychotherapy and society', *Europe's Journal of Psychology* 7.1, February 2011: 164–86.

19 Rosalind Minsky, '"Too Much of a Good Thing": control of containment in coping with change?', *Psychoanalytic Studies* 1.4, 1999: 391–405, 403.

20 In his excellent analysis of modernist tropes of male pregnancy, poet and critic Michael Davidson notes that in many cases 'male pregnancy is linked to the conflation of material wealth and biological dystopia'. Michael Davidson, 'Pregnant Men: Modernism, Disability, and Biofuturity in Djuna Barnes', *NOVEL: A Forum on Fiction* 43.2, Summer 2010: 207–26, 214. Davidson also reminds us of the Nighttown chapter in Joyce's *Ulysses* in which Leopold Bloom cries, 'O, I so want to be a mother' and gives birth to 'eight male yellow and white children', while Buck Mulligan describes Bloom in this nightmare as 'a finished example of the new womanly man'.

21 Dave Trumbore, 'WonderCon 2012: *Prometheus* Panel Recap

Featuring Sir Ridley Scott and Damon Lindelof', 17 March 2012, Collider.com, online: collider.com/prometheus-wondercon.

22 When Elizabeth asks David what he will do when Weyland is no longer around to program him, David responds, 'Doesn't everyone want their parents dead?'

23 One might protest that Weyland has a flesh-and-blood daughter, and therefore the argument does not hold, but we have no sense from the film that they are biologically related. Weyland privileges David in his holographic welcome to the crew on their arrival at the moon, but says nothing of Vickers.

24 Meredith Vickers could even be read as an analogously 'adopted' sister like Elizabeth Lavenza in Shelley's novel.

25 Eve Kosofsky Sedgwick, 'Anality: News from the Front', in *The Weather in Proust* (Durham, NC and London: Duke University Press, 2011), 176–7.

26 Melanie Klein, 'Envy and Gratitude' in *Envy and Gratitude and Other Works*, 1946–1963 (London: Virago Press, 1988), 201, 193, 181.

27 Ibid, 201.

28 Klein states: 'The envied person is felt to possess what is at bottom most prized and desired – and this is a good object, which also implies a good character and sanity. Moreover, the person who can ungrudgingly enjoy other people's creative work and happiness is spared the torments of envy, grievance, and persecution' (ibid., 203).

29 Klein describes a male patient who 'desires to possess all the feminine attributes of his mother', 'to be a woman, to have babies, and deprive his mother of them. The effect of this step in integration was a strong onset of depression due to his having to face the aggressive components of his personality' which were 'experienced… as a shock and as horror of himself'. She continues, 'Even when the depression had lifted after having been worked through, the patient was convinced that he would never see himself again in the way he had done before, though this no longer implied a feeling of dejection

but a greater knowledge of himself as well as greater tolerance of other people. What the analysis had achieved was an important step in integration, bound up with the patient being capable of facing his psychic reality. In the course of his analysis, however, there were times when this attitude could not be maintained. That is to say, as in every case, the working-through was a gradual process' (ibid., 211–12).

30 "envy, n." *OED Online*. Oxford University Press, July 2018.

31 "envie, n.f." *Dictionnaire de l'Académie Française* (9e edition), 2005. Online.

32 Klein, 202.

33 It is also a neat inversion of the Engineer's ingestion scene at the beginning of *Prometheus*.

34 In describing his rendering of a scene of Victor Frankenstein creating his monster in the series *Penny Dreadful*, Logan says: 'when I was sitting down to write that scene, I thought… [i]t's giving birth to a child, with all the complexity and heartbreaking emotion of that, with all the poignancy of promise and all the realization that things have irrevocably changed.' June Thomas, 'The Thing That Made Me Monstrous to Some People Is Also the Thing That Empowered Me', *Slate*, 9 May 2014, online: http://www.slate.com/blogs/outward/2014/05/09/penny_dreadful_s_john_logan_why_a_gay_writer_feels_a_kinship_with_frankenstein.html.

35 The *OED* definitions include: '[m]alignant or hostile feeling; ill-will, malice, enmity', '[a]ctive evil, harm, mischief', '[t]he feeling of mortification and ill-will occasioned by the contemplation of superior advantages possessed by another', '[d]esire to equal another in achievement or excellence', 'longing for the advantages enjoyed by another person', or simply '[w]ish, desire, longing; enthusiasm'. See: "envy, n." *OED Online*. Oxford University Press, July 2018.

36 "effete, adj." Ibid.

37 In South African English this is a term inherited from apartheid racial categories and is distinct from 'colored' in American English.

It designates a diverse group that includes people of mixed race, autochthonous South Africans (the San and Khoi peoples who were not regarded as black African), and descendants of the slaves who were brought to the Cape from the Indian Ocean littoral during the late seventeenth and eighteenth centuries. Although contested during the apartheid period and since, it continues to be widely used both within and outside of the community it describes.

38  The suggestion is that they were pushed by the police into the Seine in what has come to be known as the *Massacre du 17 octobre 1961*.

39  Emma Reynolds, 'Sickest artwork of all time allows viewers to watch man beaten to death', news.com.au, 8 August 2017, online: https://www.news.com.au/lifestyle/real-life/news-life/sickest-artwork-of-all-time-allows-viewers-to-watch-man-beaten-to-death/news-story/9492c9f143535d7aa69694f9c95ff736.

40  Roberta Smith, 'Jordan Wolfson's Herky-Jerky Puppet at David Zwirner', *The New York Times*, 10 June 2016, 23.

41  Ajay Kurian, 'The Ballet of White Victimhood: On Jordan Wolfson, Petroushka, and Donald Trump', *Artspace*, 15 November 2016, online: https://www.artspace.com/magazine/contributors/jottings/ajay-kurian-on-jordan-wolfson-colored-sculpture-54364.

PATRICK FLANERY is the author of the critically acclaimed novels *Night for Day*, *I Am No One*, *Fallen Land* and *Absolution*, which was shortlisted for the 2014 International IMPAC Dublin Literary Award and Royal Society of Literature Ondaatje Prize. Born and raised in the US, he has lived in Britain since 2001. His work has appeared in *Granta*, *Zoetrope: All-Story*, the *Guardian*, the *Spectator*, *Newsweek*, the *Washington Post* and the *Los Angeles Times*. He is Professor of Creative Writing at Queen Mary University of London and Professor Extraordinary at the University of Stellenbosch.